DIEGO SIMEONE ATTACKING TACTICS

Tactical Analysis and Sessions from Atlético Madrid's 4-4-2

Written by
ATHANASIOS TERZIS

Published by

DIEGO SIMEONE ATTACKING TACTICS

Tactical Analysis and Sessions from Atlético Madrid's 4-4-2

First Published July 2020 by SoccerTutor.com
info@soccertutor.com | www.SoccerTutor.com

UK: 0208 1234 007 | **US:** (305) 767 4443 | **ROTW:** +44 208 1234 007
ISBN: 978-1-910491-40-9

Copyright: SoccerTutor.com Limited © 2020. All Rights Reserved.

All rights reserved. No part of this publication may be reproduced, stored in a retrieval system, or transmitted in any form or by any means, electronic, mechanical, photocopy, recording or otherwise, without prior written permission of the copyright owner. Nor can it be circulated in any form of binding or cover other than that in which it is published and without similar condition including this condition being imposed on a subsequent purchaser.

Author
Athanasios Terzis © 2020

Edited by
Alex Fitzgerald - SoccerTutor.com

Cover Design by
Alex Macrides, Think Out Of The Box Ltd.
Email: design@thinkootb.com Tel: +44 (0) 208 144 3550

Diagrams
Diagram designs by SoccerTutor.com. All the diagrams in this book have been created using SoccerTutor.com Tactics Manager Software available from www.SoccerTutor.com

Note: While every effort has been made to ensure the technical accuracy of the content of this book, neither the author nor publishers can accept any responsibility for any injury or loss sustained as a result of the use of this material.

CONTENTS

Meet The Author: Athanasios Terzis 8
Diego Simeone's Achievements 9
Simeone's Incredible Success with Atlético Against the Odds 10
Atlético Madrid's 4-4-2 Formation (2017-18 Season) 12
Atlético Madrid's 4-4-2 Formation (2018-19 Season) 13
Atlético Madrid Players 14
Coaching Format 15
Key 15

THE ATTACKING PHASE 16

The Attacking Phase 17
Benefits of Atlético Madrid's Attacking Shape Against a 4-Man Defence 18
Benefits of Atlético Madrid's Attacking Shape Against a 3-Man Defence 19

TACTICAL SITUATION 1: Build-up Play from the Back 20

Build-Up Play Against the 4-4-2 21
Build-Up Play Against the 4-2-3-1 26
Build-Up Play Against the 4-3-3 28
Build-Up Play Against the 3-5-2 30

Session (2 Practices) for "Build-up Play from the Back" 33

1. Build-up Play from the Back in a 6v6 Dynamic Small Sided Game with Mini Goals ... 34
2. Build-up Play from the Back in a 10v9 Game 35

TACTICAL SITUATION 2: Dragging the Centre Back Out of Position to Create and Exploit Space 36

Creating Space for the Full Back to Receive Unmarked High Up the Flank 37

Session (4 Practices) for "Dragging the Centre Back Out of Position to Create and Exploit Space" 41

1. Dragging the Centre Back Out of Position to Create and Exploit Space in a Technical Passing Practice 42
2. Dragging the Centre Back Out of Position to Create and Exploit Space in a Functional Practice ... 44
3. Dragging the Centre Back Out of Position to Create and Exploit Space in a Functional Small Sided Game 46
4. Dragging the Centre Back Out of Position to Create and Exploit Space in a Conditioned Game 48

TACTICAL SITUATION 3: Options for the Full Back After Receiving High Up the Pitch 49
Advanced Full Back Receives Up Against the Opposing Full Back. 50

Session (4 Practices) for "Options for the Full Back After Receiving High Up the Pitch" 54
1. Options for the Full Back After Receiving High Up the Pitch in a Technical Passing Practice with Finish 55
2. Options for the Full Back After Receiving High Up the Pitch in a Functional Practice 57
3. Options for the Full Back After Receiving High Up the Pitch in a Functional Small Sided Game 60
4. Options for the Full Back After Receiving High Up the Pitch in a Conditioned Game 62

TACTICAL SITUATION 4: Synchronised Movements of the Full Back and Wide Midfielder 63
Creating and Exploiting an Overload Out Wide with Synchronised Movements 64

Session (4 Practices) for "Synchronised Movements of the Full Back and Wide Midfielder" 67
1. Synchronised Movements of the Full Back and Wide Midfielder in a Technical Practice 68
2. Synchronised Movements of the Full Back and Wide Midfielder in a Functional Practice with Finish 69
3. Synchronised Movements of the Full Back and Wide Midfielder in a 10v4 (+GK) Functional Practice 70
4. Synchronised Movements of the Full Back and Wide Midfielder in a Conditioned Game 72

TACTICAL SITUATION 5: Forward Exploits Space Behind the Opposing Full Back 73
Forward Exploits Space Behind the Opposing Full Back with Wide Midfielders Central 74
Variation: Forward Creates Space for the Wide Midfielder in the Centre 79
Forward Exploits Space Behind the Full Back with Width Created by Wide Midfielder 80

Session (4 Practices) for "Forward Exploits Space Behind the Opposing Full Back" 83
1. Forward Exploits Space Behind the Opposing Full Back in a Technical Practice with Finish 84
2. Forward Exploits Space Behind the Opposing Full Back in a Functional Practice with Finish 86
3. Forward Exploits Space Behind the Opposing Full Back in a Functional Game 89
4. Forward Exploits Space Behind the Opposing Full Back in a Conditioned Game 90

TACTICAL SITUATION 6: Forward Drops Back to Receive or Create Space in Behind 91
Forward Drops Back to Receive or Create Space in Behind 92

Session (4 Practices) for "Forward Drops Back to Receive or Create Space in Behind" 96
1. Forward Drops Back to Receive or Create Space in Behind in a Technical Practice with Finish 97
2. Forward Drops Back to Receive or Create Space in Behind in a Functional Practice 101
3. Forward Drops Back to Receive or Create Space in Behind in a Small Sided Game 103
4. Forward Drops Back to Receive or Create Space in Behind in a Conditioned Game 104

TACTICAL SITUATION 7: Weak Side Forward Drops Back to Create Space in Behind 105
Weak Side Forward Drops Back to Create Space in Behind for Wide Midfielder..................... 106

Session (3 Practices) for "Weak Side Forward Drops Back to Create Space in Behind" 108
1. Weak Side Forward Drops Back to Create Space for Wide Midfielder in a Functional Practice (1) .. 109
2. Weak Side Forward Drops Back to Create Space for Wide Midfielder in a Functional Practice (2) .. 111
3. Weak Side Forward Drops Back to Create Space for Wide Midfielder in a Conditioned Game 113

TACTICAL SITUATION 8: Creating an Overload and Attacking Through the Centre 114
Creating an Overload and Attacking Through the Centre 115

Session (3 Practices) for "Creating an Overload and Attacking Through the Centre" 118
1. Creating an Overload and Attacking Through the Centre in a Technical Practice................. 119
2. Creating an Overload and Attacking Through the Centre in a Dynamic Zonal Practice 121
3. Creating an Overload and Attacking Through the Centre in a Conditioned Game 122

TACTICAL SITUATION 9: Making a Run on Blind Side of Defender to Receive a Long Pass in Behind 123
Making a Run on the Blind Side of the Defender to Receive a Long Pass in Behind................. 124

Session (3 Practices) for "Making a Run on Blind Side of Defender to Receive a Long Pass in Behind" 125
1. Making a Run on Blind Side of Defender to Receive a Long Pass in Behind in a Technical Practice 126
2. Making a Run on Blind Side of Defender to Receive a Long Pass in Behind in a Dynamic Zonal Practice 127
3. Making a Run on Blind Side of Defender to Receive a Long Pass in Behind in a Conditioned Game 128

TACTICAL SITUATION 10: Forward Creates and Exploits Space to Receive in Behind 129
Forward Creates and Exploits Space to Receive in Behind 130
Getting Onside to Exploit the Space Between the Opposing Defenders 132

THE TRANSITION FROM DEFENCE TO ATTACK 134
The Transition from Defence to Attack (Positive Transition) 135
Factors that Affect the Positive Transition 136

TACTICAL SITUATION 1: Counter Attack After Winning the Ball in a Wide Position 137
Counter Attack After Winning the Ball in a Wide Position 138

Session (3 Practices) for "Counter Attack After Winning the Ball in a Wide Position" 141
1. Counter Attack After Winning the Ball Wide in a Functional Practice (Passive Centre Backs) 142
2. Counter Attack After Winning the Ball Wide in a Functional Practice (Active Centre Backs) 144
3. Counter Attack After Winning the Ball Wide in a Conditioned Game 145

TACTICAL SITUATION 2: Counter Attack After Winning the Ball in the Centre (Direct Threat) 146
Counter Attack After Winning the Ball in the Centre (Direct Threat) 147

2 Practices for "Counter Attack After Winning the Ball in the Centre (Direct Threat)" 150
1. Counter Attack After Winning the Ball in the Centre in a Functional Practice 151
2. Counter Attack After Winning the Ball in the Centre in a Functional Game 152

TACTICAL SITUATION 3: Defensive and Counter Attack-Minded Positioning of the Forwards 153
Defensive-Minded Positioning of the Forwards 154
Counter Attack-Minded Positioning of the Forwards 157

Session (4 Practices) for "Defensive and Counter Attack-Minded Positioning of the Forwards" 165
1. Positioning of the Forwards and Counter Attack After Winning the Ball Out Wide in a Functional Practice 166
2. Positioning of the Forwards and Counter Attack After Winning the Ball in the Centre in a Functional Practice 167
3. Positioning of the Forwards and Counter Attack After Winning the Ball Out Wide in a Functional Game 168

4. Positioning of the Forwards and Counter Attack After Winning the Ball in the Centre in a Functional Game... 169

TACTICAL SITUATION 4: Counter Attack with an Open Ball Situation............ 170
Possession is Won in the Central Area and an Open Ball Situation is Created..................... 171
Role of the Midfielders During a Counter Attack with an Open Ball Situation 174

2 Practices for "Counter Attack with an Open Ball Situation" 176
1. Counter Attack with an Open Ball Situation in a 6v6 (+GK) Functional Practice................... 177
2. Counter Attack with an Open Ball Situation in a 6v8 (+GK) Functional Practice................... 178

TACTICAL SITUATION 5: Counter Attack with a Closed Ball Situation............ 179
Counter Attack with a Closed Ball Situation 180
Tactical Solutions After Winning the Ball in a Closed Ball Situation 181

2 Practices for "Counter Attack with a Closed Ball Situation"...................... 185
1. Forwards Read the Situation (Open or Closed Ball) & Apply Correct Decision Making in a Functional Practice.. 186
2. Counter Attack with a Closed Ball Situation in a Dynamic Conditioned Game 188

TACTICAL SITUATION 6: Exploiting Width During a Counter Attack 189
Exploiting Width During a Counter Attack.. 190

Practice for "Exploiting Width During a Counter Attack"........................... 193
Exploiting Width During a Counter Attack in a Dynamic Conditioned Game...................... 194

MEET THE AUTHOR: ATHANASIOS TERZIS

- **UEFA 'A' Coaching Licence**
- **M.S.C. in Coaching and Conditioning**
- **Greek Football Federation Instructor (HFF)**
- **Former Coach of Professional Teams in Greece**
- **Former Coach of Semi-Pro Teams in Greece**
- **Former Technical Director of DOXA Dramas Academy** (Greek 2nd division)
- **Former Professional Football Player**

Athanasios Terzis is a football tactics expert and is regularly invited as an instructor to many coaching seminars and workshops around the world.

Athanasios has written many successful football coaching books published by **SoccerTutor.com**, which have sold thousands of copies worldwide in multiple languages (English, Spanish, German, Italian, Greek, Japanese, Korean, and Chinese):

- **Pep Guardiola Attacking Tactics - Tactical Analysis and Sessions from Manchester City's 4-3-3** (2019)
- **Creative Attacking Play - From the Tactics of Conte, Allegri, Simeone, Mourinho, Wenger & Klopp** (2017)
- **Marcelo Bielsa - Coaching Build Up Play Against High Pressing Teams** (2017)
- **Coaching the Juventus 3-5-2 - Tactical Analysis and Sessions: Attacking and Defending** (2016)
- **Jürgen Klopp's Attacking and Defending Tactics: Tactical Analysis and Sessions from Borussia Dortmund's 4-2-3-1** (2015)
- **FC Barcelona Training Sessions: 160 Practices from 34 Tactical Situations** (2014)
  * Winner of the Italian FA Award for "Best Coaching Book" 2014
- **Jose Mourinho's Real Madrid - A Tactical Analysis: Attacking and Defending in the 4-2-3-1** (2012)
- **FC Barcelona - A Tactical Analysis: Attacking and Defending** (2012)

DIEGO SIMEONE'S ACHIEVEMENTS

Coaching Roles

- Atlético Madrid (2011 - Present)
- Racing Club (2011)
- Catalania (2011)
- San Lorenzo (2009 - 2010)
- River Plate (2007 - 2008)
- Estudiantes La Plata (2006 - 2007)
- Racing Club (2006)

Honours

- Spanish La Liga Primera División (2014)
- UEFA Champions League Runner-up (2014 & 2016)
- UEFA Europa League (2012 & 2018)
- UEFA Super Cup (2012 & 2018)
- Argentine Primera División (2006 & 2008)
- Copa Del Rey (2013)
- Supercopa de España (2014)

Individual Awards

- European Coach of the Season (2012)
- La Liga Coach of the Year (2013, 2014 & 2016)
- IFFHS World's Best Club Coach (2016)
- Miguel Muñoz Trophy (2014 & 2016)
- Globe Soccer Master Coach Special Award (2017)

SIMEONE'S INCREDIBLE SUCCESS WITH ATLÉTICO AGAINST THE ODDS

LA LIGA

2014 CHAMPION

UEFA CHAMPIONS LEAGUE

 +

2014 RUNNER-UP   **2016 RUNNER-UP**

UEFA EUROPA LEAGUE

 +

2012 CHAMPION   **2018 CHAMPION**

UEFA SUPER CUP

 +

2012 CHAMPION   **2018 CHAMPION**

COPA DEL REY

2013 CHAMPION

* Trophy images from **PIXSECTOR.com**

©SOCCERTUTOR.COM   DIEGO SIMEONE'S ATTACKING TACTICS

The Winning Culture at Atlético Madrid Under Diego Simeone

During his years at Atlético Madrid, Diego Simeone has managed to build an extraordinarily strong team which has won or been the runners-up of the most significant titles against all odds.

The Argentine coach brought with him a culture of commitment, passion, aggressiveness, and determination. From the first moment of his arrival at Atlético Madrid, he made it clear that nobody and nothing is above the team and in order to achieve greatness, the players have to give everything and work all together within a strong team spirit.

This culture was, from the first day, transferred to the players and since the beginning of Diego Simeone's era, it is more than obvious that they fight in every match like warriors and are willing to support each other until the very end.

Teamwork is paramount as Atlético Madrid lack superstars like Messi and Ronaldo, who they have consistently competed against.

Even though they are forced to sell every big player like Falcao, Diego Costa and Griezmann and their budget is relatively low compared to other top clubs, they still remain the same ultra-competitive side that refuses to surrender.

Diego Simeone's Atlético Madrid era may not have produced a team which plays attractive and free-flowing football, but nobody can deny that they are often the toughest team to play against in the whole of Europe.

Diego Simeone's Atlético Madrid Tactics

The tactical organisation has had a lot to do with the culture that Diego Simeone has created at Atlético Madrid. Simeone built a game plan which relied on good defensive organisation.

The players must carry out their basic defensive tasks with commitment, passion, aggressiveness, and determination (elements of the culture brought by the Argentine).

This has made them extremely difficult to break down, even by the very top attacking sides.

Atlético have also been very efficient in their **attacking play** (analysed in this second part of a two book set) **and have great success in scoring goals with a counter attacking style, and by exploiting set pieces.**

ATLÉTICO MADRID'S 4-4-2 FORMATION
(2017-18 SEASON)

Atlético Madrid's First XI

Diego Simeone's Atlético Madrid team mainly use the 4-4-2 formation.

There were some matches where Simeone adapted and used the 4-1-4-1, 4-4-1-1 and 4-3-3 formations. However, this book will focus solely on how Atlético implemented the 4-4-2.

This was the first XI for Atlético during the 2017-18 season, with **Thomas (5)** the most regular change, making 50 appearances in central midfield.

Squad Players

Thomas (5) often played with **Saúl (8)** or in place of him if he moved into the right midfield position.

Lucas (19) made 44 appearances as cover at left back and centre back. **Savić (15)** and **Vrsaljko (16)** played many games at centre back and right back respectively.

D. Costa (18) was bought in January 2018 and became a starter, while **Gameiro (21)** made 36 appearances as cover and often as a substitute.

ATLÉTICO MADRID'S 4-4-2 FORMATION
(2018-19 SEASON)

Atlético Madrid's First XI

This was the first XI for Atlético during the 2018-19 season.

However, the wide midfielders were changed often:

- **Lemar (11)** made 43 appearances mainly as a left midfielder.
- **Correa (10)** made 49 appearances mainly as a right midfielder.

Squad Players

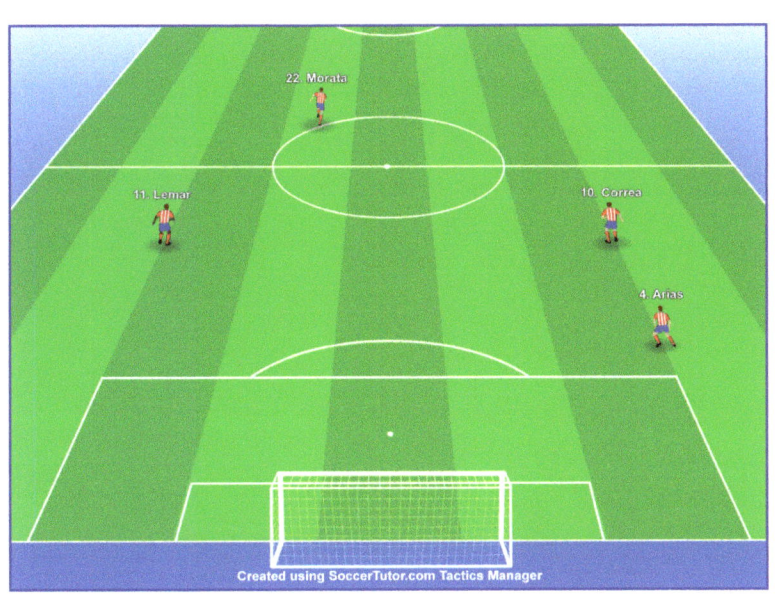

As explained above, **Lemar (11)** and **Correa (10)** often played as wide midfielders. They would play in place of **Koke (6)** or **Saúl (8)** if either of them was playing in central midfield and sometimes purely just because it was Diego Simeone's preference for a particular game.

Arias (4) made 33 appearances as cover at right back and **Morata (22)** made 17 appearances as a forward.

DIEGO SIMEONE'S ATTACKING TACTICS

ATLÉTICO MADRID PLAYERS

GOALKEEPER

Jan Oblak (13) has been one of Europe's most outstanding goalkeepers in the last few years, providing a high level of consistency and security for Atlético's goal.

CENTRE BACKS

Diego Godín (2) was a top class defender for Atlético, together with **Stefan Savić (15)** or the younger **Jose Giménez (24)**. Either would form a strong duo with **Godín (2)** in the centre of defence. All 3 centre backs are highly effective in aerial duels, as well as in duels on the ground.

FULL BACKS

Juanfran (20) and **Simo Vrsaljko (16)** at right back, together with **Filipe Luis (3)** and **Lucas Hernandez (19)** on the left, are very quick, good in 1v1 situations and are all capable of contributing well in the attacking phase too.

CENTRAL MIDFIELDERS

Gabi (14) was the player who could always play at a high tempo and with full energy for the entirety of the 90 minutes. His contribution was outstanding as he could fill every possible gap in midfield, as well as in the defensive line. **Gabi (14)** could also block through passes and apply heavy pressure in every single attempt. His tactical awareness was fantastic as well, as he read the game perfectly and applied the appropriate tactical response in each moment.

Gabi's (14) partner was the versatile **Saúl Niguez (8)** who is exceptionally good tactically and technically, as well as extremely hard-working, perfectly matching the demands of Simeone. **Thomas (5)** was often used in central midfield as well, playing a mainly defensive role.

During the 2018-19 season, **Rodri (14)** took over **Gabi's (14)** role and was partnered with **Saúl (8)** or **Thomas (5)** if **Saúl (8)** played as a right midfielder.

WIDE MIDFIELDERS

Angel Correa (11) and especially **Koke (6)** are not "winger-type" wide midfielders, and mainly play as inside midfielders. They are Atlético Madrid's most creative players. They can dribble, make key passes, and shoot well from long distance. In addition, during the defensive phase they are very hard-working players who provide a great contribution. **Saúl (8)** also played as a wide midfielder, mostly during the 2018-19 season.

FORWARDS

Antoine Griezmann (7), **Diego Costa (18/19)**, **Fernando Torres (9)** and **Kevin Gameiro (21)** are all quick and capable of playing on the counter attack. They are highly effective in dribbling and finishing. During the defensive phase, they played a crucial role as they controlled their zone of responsibility effectively using well-coordinated movements.

COACHING FORMAT

1. TACTICAL SITUATION AND ANALYSIS

- The analysis is based on recurring patterns of play observed within **Diego Simeone's Atlético Madrid** team. Once the same phase of play occurred several times (at least 10), the tactics would be seen as a pattern.
- Each action, pass, individual movement (with or without the ball) and the positioning of each player on the pitch including their body shape, are presented with a full description.

2. FULL TRAINING SESSION FROM THE TACTICAL SITUATION

- Technical and Functional Practices, Tactical Practices and Games
- Objective and Full Description
- Restrictions, Progressions, Variations & Coaching Points (if applicable)

KEY

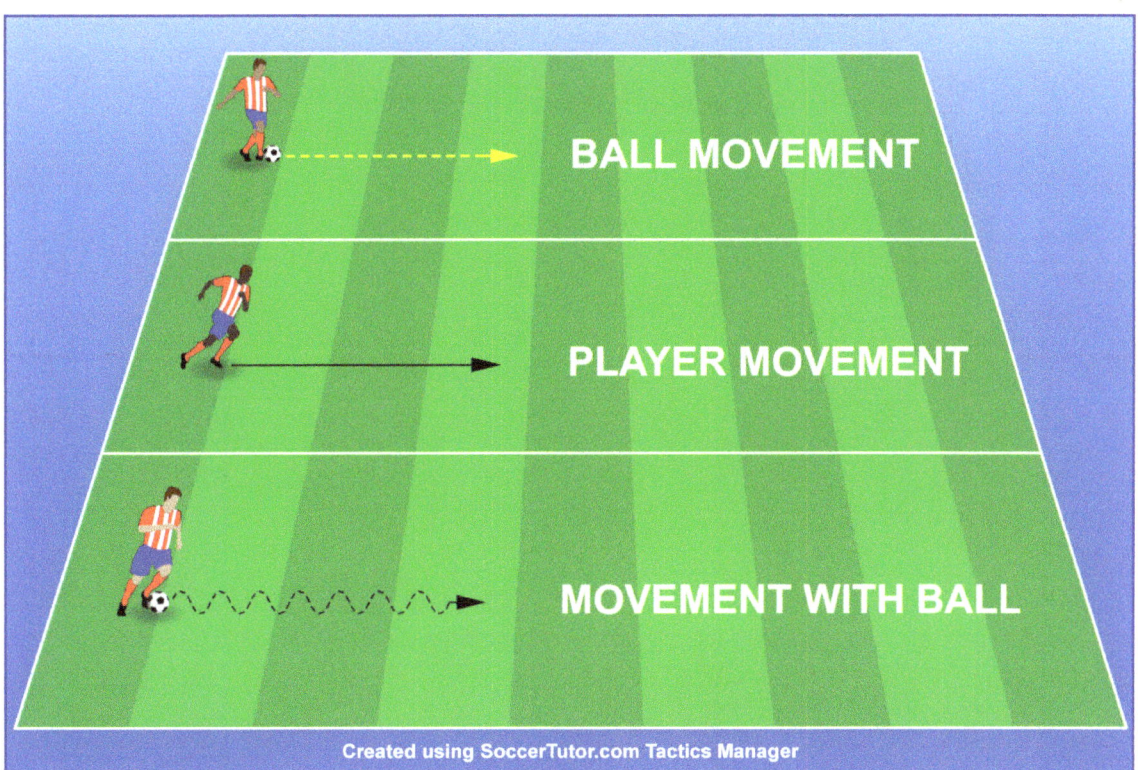

THE ATTACKING PHASE

DIEGO SIMEONE'S ATTACKING TACTICS

THE ATTACKING PHASE

DEFINITION: When a team has possession of the ball and the opponents have managed to get well-organised defensively, then the attacking team is in the attacking phase.

Atlético Madrid are not often thought of as an exciting team during the attacking phase. However, despite what many think, Diego Simeone's team have been very effective during the attacking phase for many years. For a team to be as successful as Atlético have, they need to be highly effective in all of 4 phases of the game.

THE STAGES OF THE ATTACKING PHASE

The attacking phase includes different stages. These stages are:

1. Building up play from the GK and moving the ball to a player in the defensive line (usually to a defender or a midfielder who drops deep).

2. Moving the ball to a player between the opposition's forward and midfield lines (usually to a midfielder).

3. Moving the ball to a player between the opposition's midfield and defensive lines (usually to a midfielder or forward).

4. Playing a final pass in behind the defensive line (or shooting at goal).

5. Receiving the final pass and finishing on goal.

In order not to skip any of these stages, the attacking phase should start from the GK and gradually build from there. However, this is not always possible as Atlético often win the ball in more advanced areas before the ball ever reaches the GK **Oblak (13)**.

In some situations, the attacking phase starts from the GK but some of the stages can be skipped if the GK **Oblak (13)** is forced to play a long pass straight to the forwards (due to the opposition's high pressing).

When building up play from the GK, Diego Simeone's philosophy is very specific. No risky options are allowed. If the opposition apply a high press and the Atlético players feel that a short pass might be risky, they prefer to make a long pass and play with safety.

If there are good possibilities to use short passing in order to move the ball from the GK to a player in a more advanced position, then the team can build up from the GK using short passing combinations.

In conclusion, Atlético use a mix of different tactics, depending on the tactics of the opposition.

In this book, we focus on how Diego Simeone's Atlético Madrid team attack against middle or low block teams.

The Attacking Phase

BENEFITS OF ATLÉTICO MADRID'S ATTACKING SHAPE AGAINST A 4-MAN DEFENCE

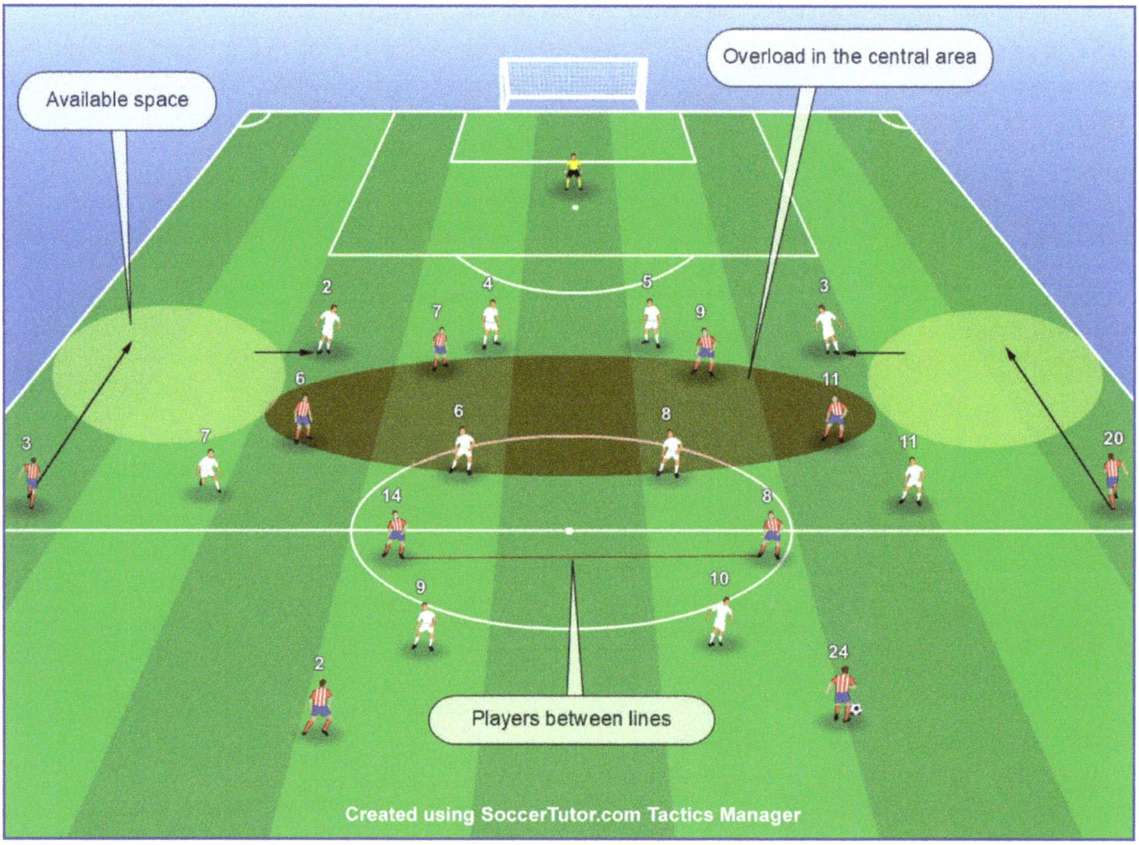

Atlético's attacking shape has both full backs in wide and advanced positions.

The 2 wide midfielders are positioned inside between the lines. This creates a dilemma for the opposing full backs, who must decide whether to follow them or not. Additionally, the 2 wide midfielders overload the central area. So, if the ball is moved to one of them, it can be crucial for the outcome of the attacking move, as most key passes or shots are made within this area. Furthermore, their central positioning can also create overloads in specific zones of responsibility of opposing players.

For example, there can be an overload within the zone of responsibility of the opposing full back or centre back. These overloads create dilemmas and Atlético's aim is to take advantage of them to create scoring opportunities.

Finally, the central positioning of the wide midfielders usually forces the opposing full backs to move towards the inside. This reaction creates available space out wide, which can be exploited by Atlético full backs. If the opposing full backs do not converge (move centrally), then it is easier for the Atlético forwards to find available gaps between the defenders and take advantage.

DIEGO SIMEONE'S ATTACKING TACTICS

The Attacking Phase

BENEFITS OF ATLÉTICO MADRID'S ATTACKING SHAPE AGAINST A 3-MAN DEFENCE

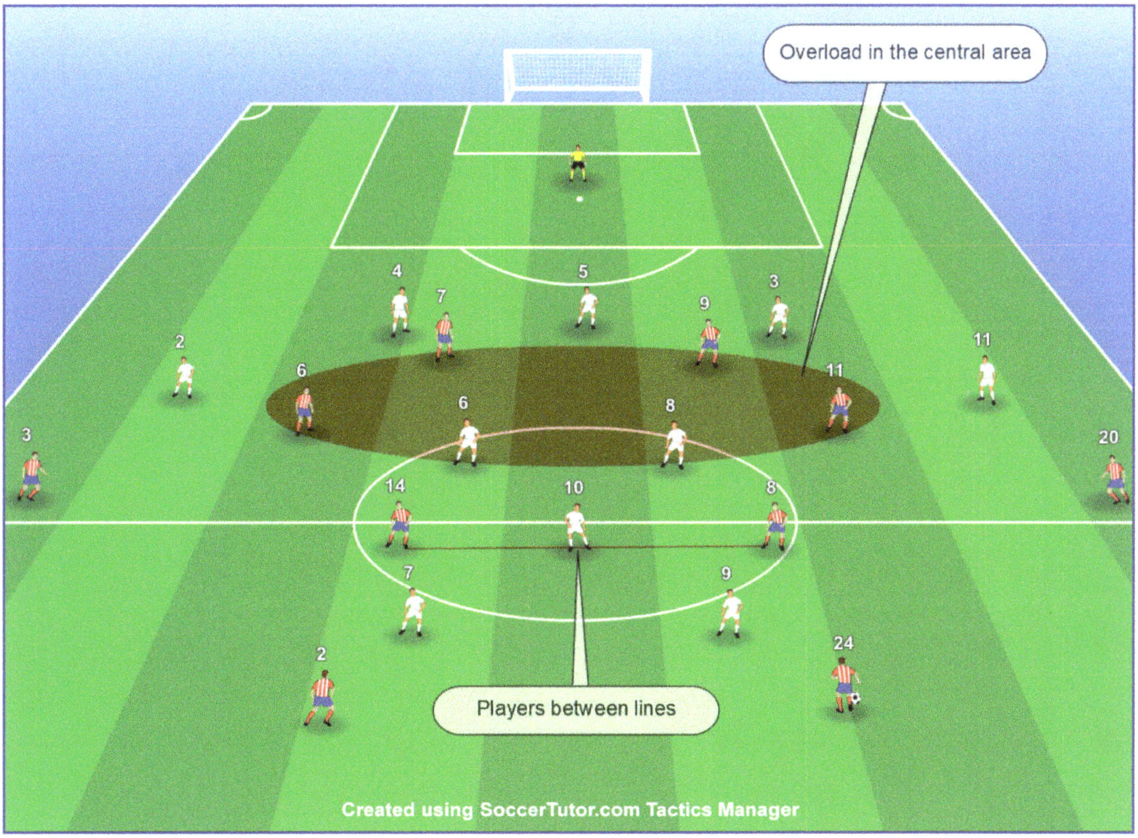

If the opposition are using a formation with 3 centre backs e.g. 3-5-2, Atlético are no longer able to exploit wide areas with their advanced full backs like they can against a 4-man defence.

The potential space out wide is usually restricted by the opposing wing backs.

Against teams with a 3-man defence, the Atlético full backs receive in the space available in deeper positions.

They are still able to create the same overload in the central area between the opposition's midfield and defensive lines, with the wide midfielders **Koke (6)** and **Correa (11)** taking up the central positions shown.

DIEGO SIMEONE'S ATTACKING TACTICS

TACTICAL SITUATION 1

Build-up Play from the Back

The content in this section is from analysis of Diego Simeone's Atlético Madrid teams during the 2017/2018 and 2018/2019 seasons.

The analysis is based on recurring patterns of play observed within the Atlético Madrid team. Once the same phase of play occurred several times (at least 10), the tactics would be seen as a pattern. The analysis on the following pages are examples of the team's tactics being used effectively.

Each action, pass, individual movement with or without the ball, and the positioning of each player on the pitch including their body shape, are presented.

The analysis is then used to create a session to coach this specific tactical situation.

Tactical Situation 1 - Build-up Play from the Back

BUILD-UP PLAY AGAINST THE 4-4-2

1. Available Space for the Centre Backs and Central Midfielders when Building Up Play

When playing against the 4-4-2 formation and against 2 forwards, the 2 Atlético centre backs had available space to exploit by moving the ball forward.

This space could be exploited by the central midfielders, who moved back into wide positions to receive (**see next page**).

©SOCCERTUTOR.COM

DIEGO SIMEONE'S ATTACKING TACTICS

Tactical Situation 1 - Build-up Play from the Back

2. Central Midfielder Moves into the Available Space to Receive and Turn Between the Opposition's Forward and Midfield Lines

When the Atlético centre backs had to play against 2 forwards who were not very active defensively, no real adjustments had to be made.

Godín (2) and **Giménez (24)** try to move the ball to the central midfielders **Gabi (14)** and **Saúl (8)**, who use good positioning to find space to receive in.

In this tactical example, the central midfielder **Gabi (14)** drops back and towards the side-line into the available space (red highlighted area).

This positioning creates an overload because the opposing right midfielder No.7 now has 2 players within his zone of responsibility.

In this situation, it is most likely that white No.7 will not move forward, so **Gabi (14)** can receive, turn free of marking, and then make a forward pass to progress Atlético's attack.

DIEGO SIMEONE'S ATTACKING TACTICS

Tactical Situation 1 - Build-up Play from the Back

3. Opposing Wide Midfielder Moves Forward and the Full Back Receives Unmarked via an Aerial Pass from the Centre Back

In this variation of the previous example, the opposing right midfielder No.7 tries to restrict the available space for **Gabi (14)** by moving forward to mark him.

Atlético's new solution is for the centre back in possession **Godín (2)** to play an aerial pass into the available space which has been created for left back **F. Luis (3)** to receive.

4. Opposing Wide Midfielder Moves Forward and the Full Back Receives Unmarked via an Aerial Pass After Combination Play

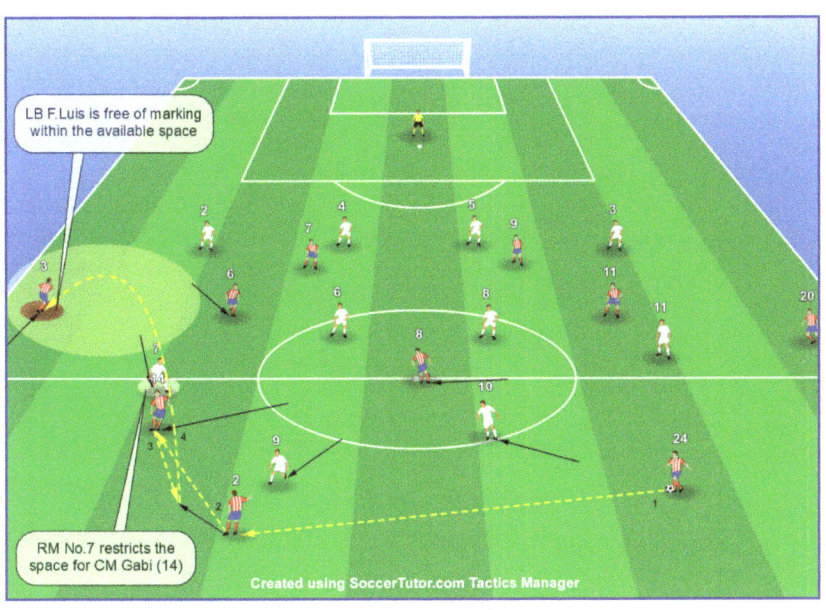

If white No.7 moves forward only after the pass from **Godín (2)** to **Gabi (14)** is played (to prevent turn), a passing combination can be used to move the ball to **F. Luis (3)**.

Godín (2) passes to **Gabi (14)**, who lays the ball back. **Godín (2)** then plays an aerial pass into the available space near the side-line for the forward run of **F. Luis (3)**. The same can be achieved with an inside pass to **Saúl (8)** and then a pass to **F. Luis (3)**.

DIEGO SIMEONE'S ATTACKING TACTICS

Tactical Situation 1 - Build-up Play from the Back

5. Central Midfielder Drops into the Defensive Line to Create a Numerical Advantage and Move the Ball to the Free Player

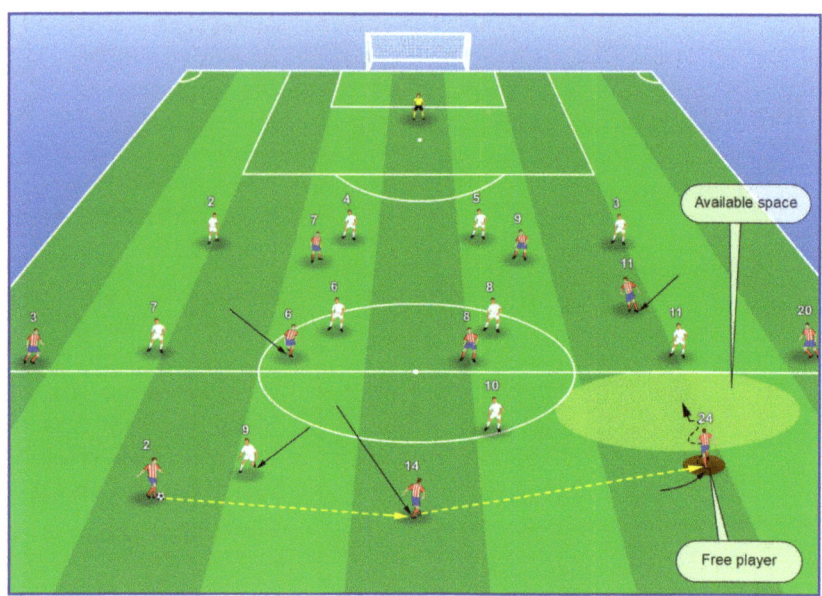

When the 2 opposing forwards were more active in their pressing and limited the Atlético centre backs' time on the ball, one of the central midfielders would drop back to create a back 3.

This created a numerical advantage at the back and the next step was to move the ball to the free player to exploit the space and then make a forward pass. In this example, **Gabi (14)** passes to **Giménez (24)**.

6. Central Midfielder Finds Space to Receive Behind the Forwards from the Full Back

In this example, we show how Atlético created space behind the opposing forwards after a pass from a centre back to a full back.

Giménez (24) passes to the right back **Juanfran (20)**.

If the white forward No.10 doesn't drop back to restrict the available space, central midfielder **Saúl (8)** is highly likely to receive free of marking and be able to turn.

DIEGO SIMEONE'S ATTACKING TACTICS

Tactical Situation 1 - Build-up Play from the Back

7. Moving the Ball to the Wide Midfielder in Between the Lines when the Opposing Central Midfielder Moves Forward

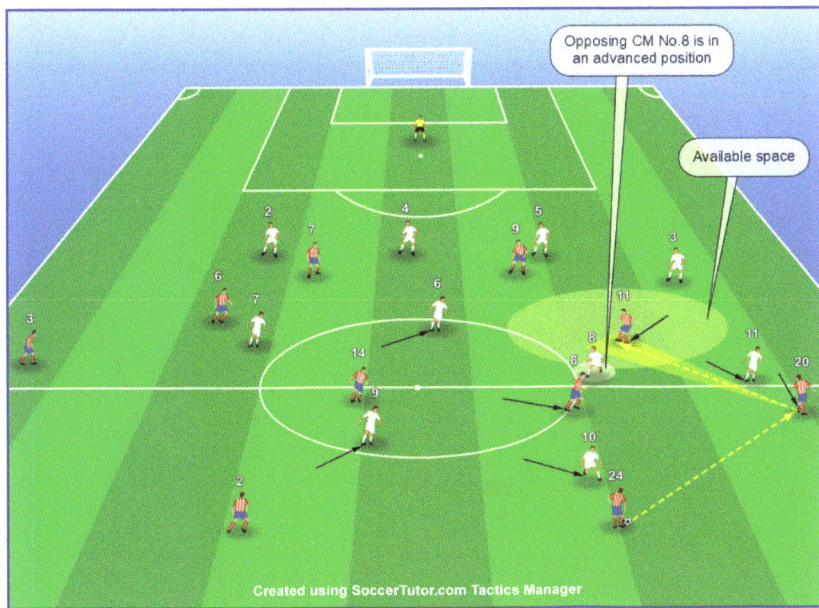

If the opposing central midfielder (white No.8) is in a high position to restrict the available space for central midfielder **Saúl (8)**, it is highly likely that the inside passing lane is left relatively wide, as well as available space being created behind him.

In a situation like this, Atlético try to move the ball directly towards the wide midfielder in a central position. This is right midfielder **Correa (11)** in this example.

8. Central Midfielder Finds Space to Receive in the Centre of the Pitch when the Opposing Forwards Have Flat Positioning

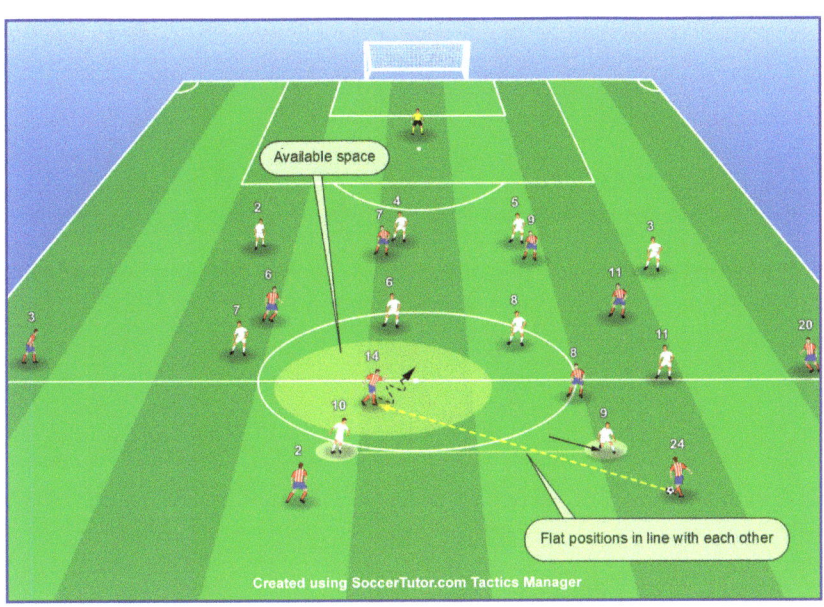

The Atlético central midfielders are always aware of the available spaces.

If the opposing forwards did not work in collaboration (e.g. Flat positions in line with each other) and space was created, they tried to exploit this by receiving from their centre backs unmarked, turning, and progressing the attack.

Tactical Situation 1 - Build-up Play from the Back

BUILD-UP PLAY AGAINST THE 4-2-3-1

1. Available Space for the Centre Backs and Central Midfielders when Building Up Play

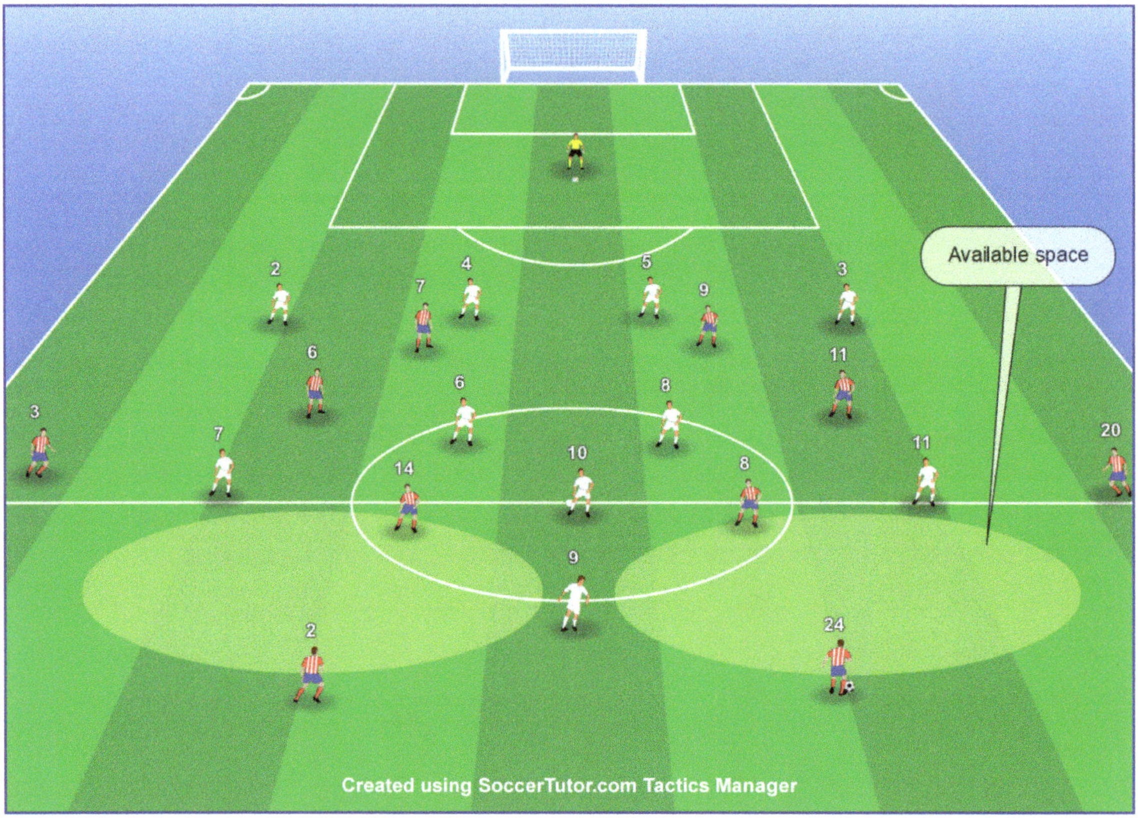

When playing against the 4-2-3-1 formation and against 1 forward, there are larger areas of available space compared to when playing against 2 forwards.

There is available space to the right and left of the 1 opposing forward.

DIEGO SIMEONE'S ATTACKING TACTICS

Tactical Situation 1 - Build-up Play from the Back

2. Centre Back Exploits the Available Space Easily to Receive and Move Forward with the Ball

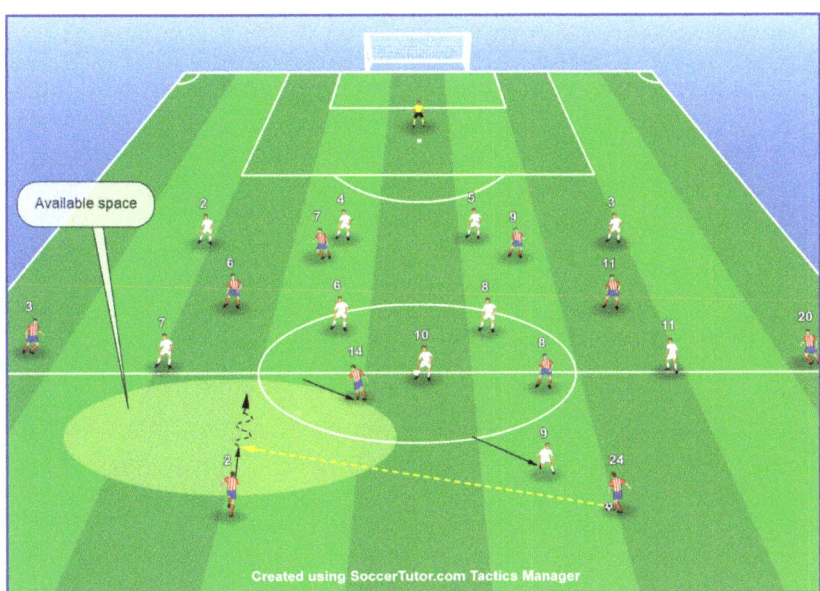

When there is a large amount of available space either side of 1 forward, one of the Atlético centre backs usually exploits it by receiving and moving forward with the ball.

In this example, the white forward No.9 moves to press **Giménez (24)** and he passes in front of **Godín (2)**, who moves forward to receive in plenty of space, dribbles the ball forward and looks for a forward pass.

3. Central Midfielder Opens Up to Receive and Turn Easily within the Available Space

In this variation, the central midfielder **Gabi (14)** can receive easily in the available space and doesn't have to open up very wide to receive a pass from a centre back.

In this example, the white forward No.9 moves to press **Giménez (24)** and he passes across to **Godín (2)**, who then passes to central midfielder **Gabi (14)**.

Gabi (14) receives on the half-turn and looks for a forward pass.

DIEGO SIMEONE'S ATTACKING TACTICS

Tactical Situation 1 - Build-up Play from the Back

BUILD-UP PLAY AGAINST THE 4-3-3

1. Available Space for the Centre Backs and Central Midfielders when Building Up Play

When playing against 1 forward and 2 attacking midfielders (4-3-3 formation), there is still available space to the right and left of the opposing forward No.9.

However, the available space is more limited due to the advanced positioning of the opposing attacking midfielders No.8 and No.10.

DIEGO SIMEONE'S ATTACKING TACTICS

Tactical Situation 1 - Build-up Play from the Back

2. Opposing Attacking Midfielder Restricts the Available Space for the Centre Back Attempting to Move Forward

Compared to playing against the 4-2-3-1, there is less available space to exploit against the 4-3-3.

One of the Atlético centre backs is still free to receive and move forward, but he is put under pressure much quicker.

In this example, **Godín (2)** receives and moves forward. He is quickly closed down by the white attacking midfielder No.10.

3. Opposing Attacking Midfielder Restricts the Available Space for the Central Midfielder Attempting to Receive and Turn

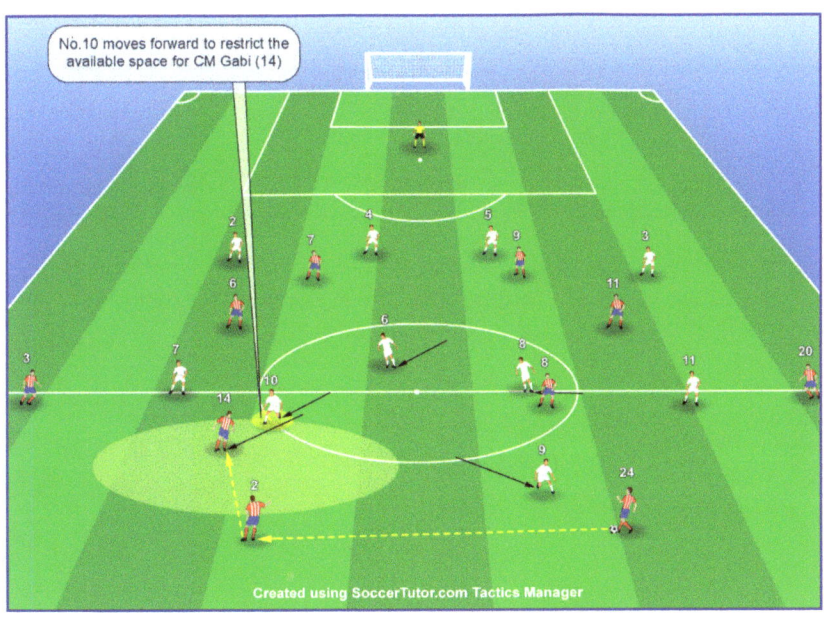

In this variation, the central midfielder **Gabi (14)** moves across to receive in the available space.

Gabi (14) can still receive from **Godín (2)** as shown, but he doesn't have much time on the ball before he is pressed by the white attacking midfielder No.10.

Tactical Situation 1 - Build-up Play from the Back

BUILD-UP PLAY AGAINST THE 3-5-2

1. Available Space for the Centre Backs and Central Midfielders when Building Up Play

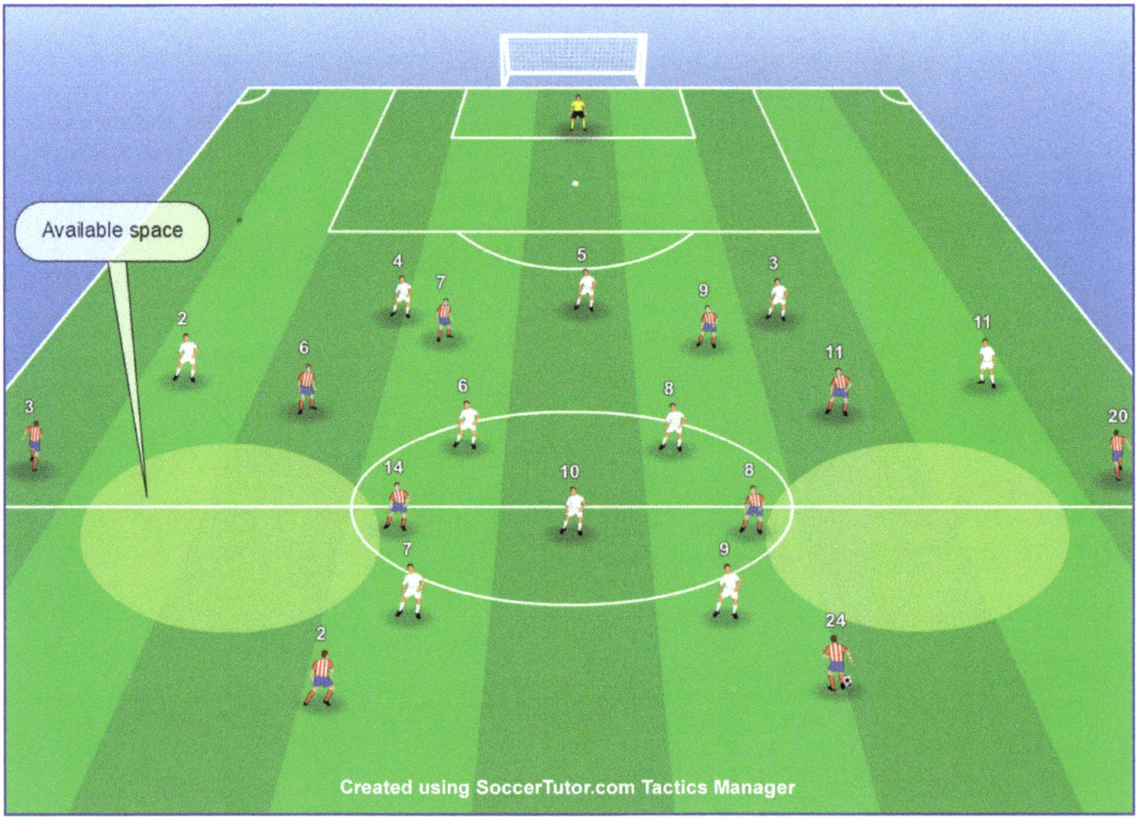

When playing against the 3-5-2 formation, which has 2 forwards and 1 attacking midfielder, there is available space to the right and left of the 2 opposing forwards.

There is a numerical disadvantage in the centre, so the available space for Atlético is towards the side, as shown.

As there are no wingers or wide midfielders to contest with, the available space includes an area inside the opposition's half.

Tactical Situation 1 - Build-up Play from the Back

2. Centre Back Exploits the Available Space Towards the Side to Receive and Move Forward with the Ball

If the opposing forwards aren't active enough, the available space can be exploited after a quick switch of play from one centre back to the other.

In this example, the centre back **Giménez (24)** passes to the other centre back **Godín (2)**, who moves forward to receive in the available space and dribble forward into the opposition's half.

3. Central Midfielder Opens Up to Receive and Turn within the Available Space Towards the Side

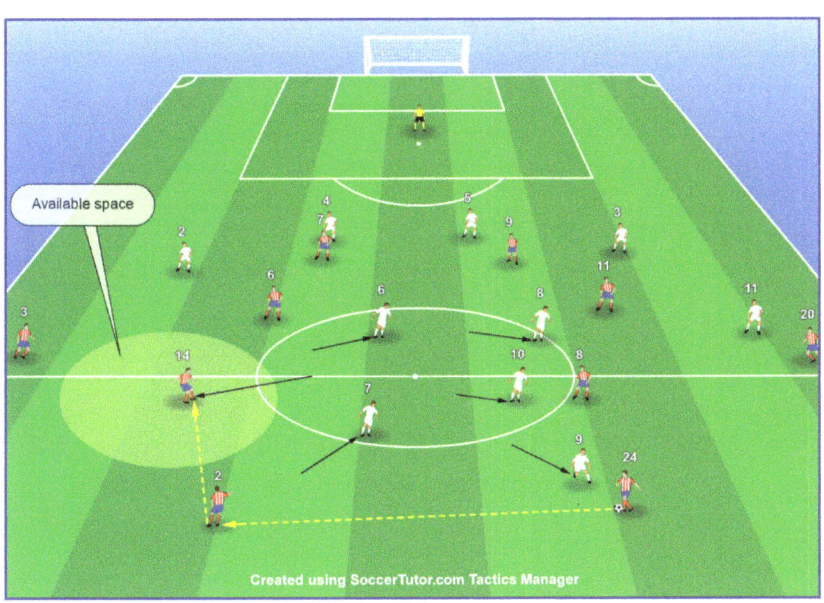

In this variation, the central midfielder **Gabi (14)** moves wide to receive in the available space.

Giménez (24) passes across to **Godín (2)**, who then passes to central midfielder **Gabi (14)**.

Gabi (14) receives on the half-turn free of marking and can easily move into the opposition's half.

©SOCCERTUTOR.COM   DIEGO SIMEONE'S ATTACKING TACTICS

Tactical Situation 1 - Build-up Play from the Back

4. Central Midfielder Drops into the Defensive Line to Create a Numerical Advantage and Exploits the Space Towards the Side

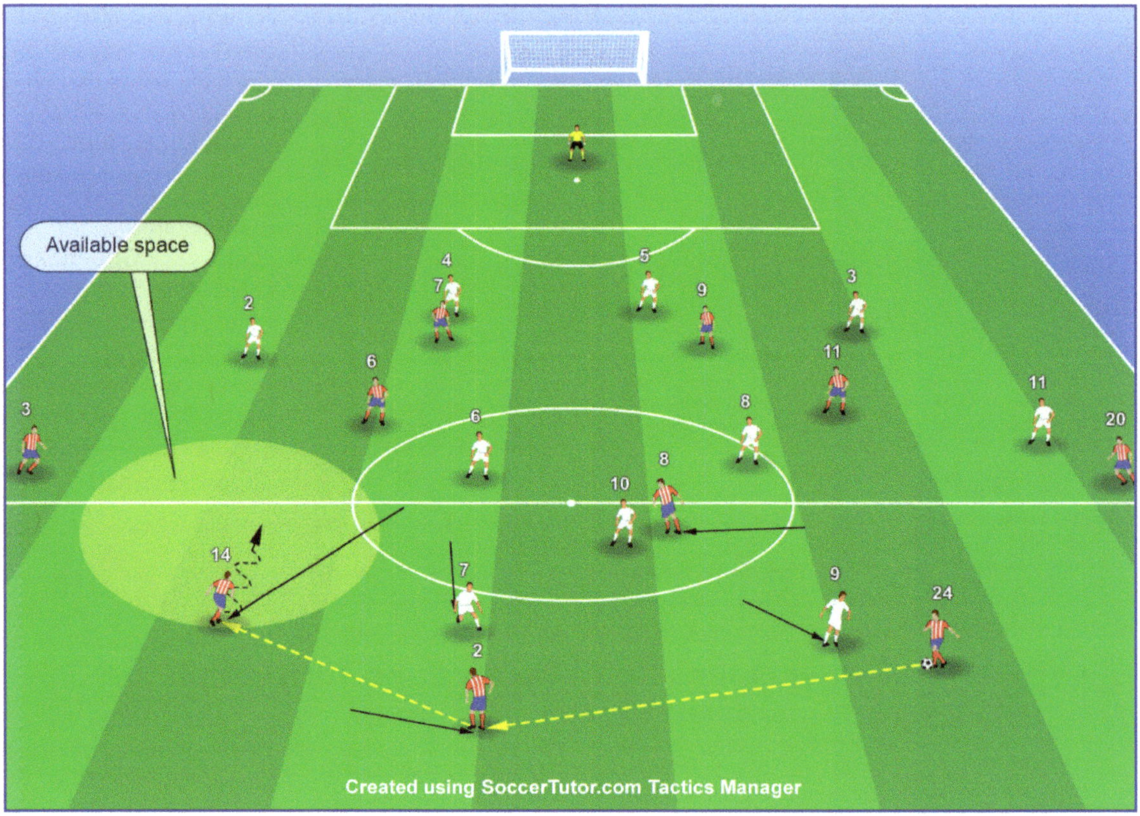

When the 2 opposing forwards actively press the 2 Atlético Madrid centre backs rather than defending the space, Diego Simeone's players make some needed adjustments.

One of the central midfielders drops back towards the side to create a 3 man defence. In the diagram example, this is **Gabi (14)** moving into the available space on the left side.

Atlético now have a 3v2 numerical advantage at the back, so their aim is to move the ball to the free player. The free player could either be the right centre back **Giménez (24)** or the central midfielder **Gabi (14)**, depending on the positioning and movements of the 2 opposing forwards.

In this example, the 2 opposing forwards are focussed on the 2 Atlético centre backs **Giménez (24)** and **Godín (2)**.

Giménez (24) passes to **Godín (2)**, who passes to the central midfielder **Gabi (14)** in the available space towards the side (highlighted area).

DIEGO SIMEONE'S ATTACKING TACTICS

SESSION (2 PRACTICES) FOR "BUILD-UP PLAY FROM THE BACK"

Tactical Situation 1 - Build-up Play from the Back

SESSION FOR THIS TACTICAL SITUATION (2 PRACTICES)
1. Build-up Play from the Back in a 6v6 Dynamic Small Sided Game with Mini Goals

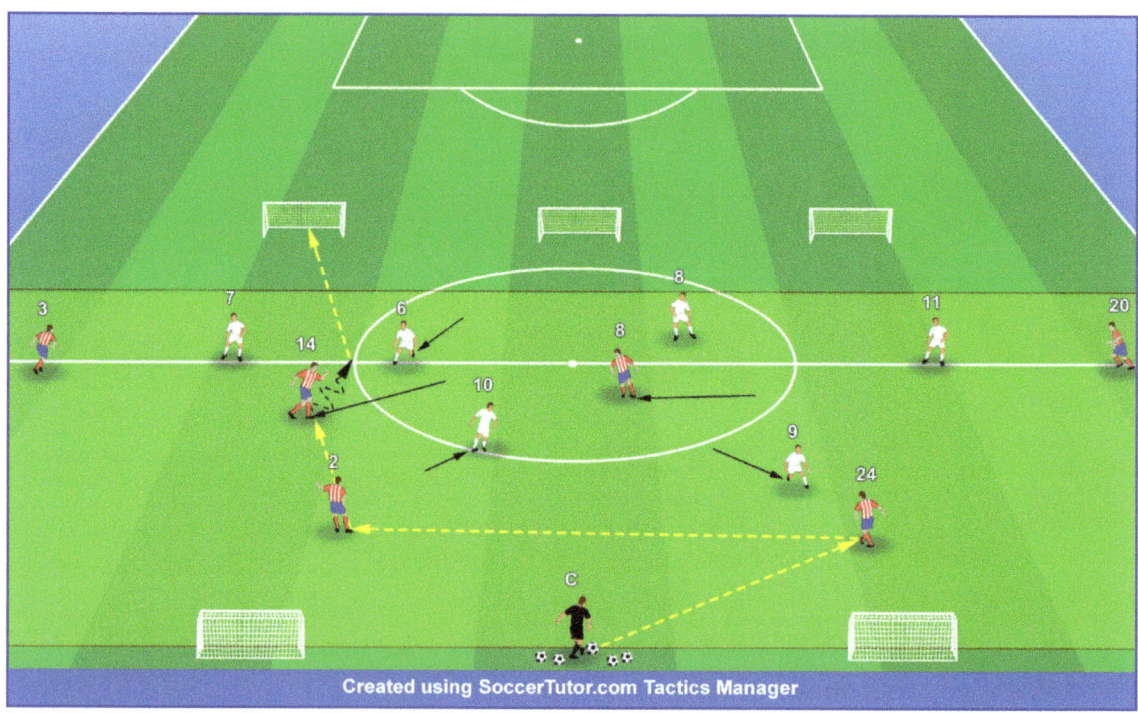

Description
- The two teams play 6v6 within the marked-out area. There are 2 mini goals at one end and 3 mini goals outside the area at the other end. In this example, the whites are in a 4-2 formation from the 4-4-2.
- The practice starts with the Coach's pass and the reds aim to move the ball to the central midfielders with available time and space to then score in any of the 3 mini goals.
- Another option is for one of the centre backs to receive, move forward into available space and score in any of the 3 mini goals.
- Finally, the full backs can also score when the white team blocks the central area. They stay free of marking, receive and score.

- Please **see the analysis pages** for a full explanation of how the red players should build-up play from the back.
- The whites defend the mini goals, try to win the ball, and then counter to score in either of the 2 mini goals at the other end.

Variation
Adjust the white team's formation to practice playing against the 4-2-3-1, 4-3-3 and 3-5-2 (<u>see analysis pages in this section</u>).

Coaching Points
1. Quick 1 or 2 touch passing and moving.
2. The focus is on finding the available space to receive.

©SOCCERTUTOR.COM   DIEGO SIMEONE'S ATTACKING TACTICS

Tactical Situation 1 - Build-up Play from the Back

PROGRESSION
2. Build-up Play from the Back in a 10 v 9 Game

Description

- In this progression, we add 2 red wide midfielders, 1 red forward and 2 white centre backs. The size of the area is increased and there are now 2 large goals with GKs. The 2 teams play a 10 v 9 game within the marked-out area.

- The game starts from the GK and the red team aim to build-up play by exploiting the available spaces, and then try to score.

- Please **see the analysis pages** for how the players should build-up play.

Variation

Adjust the white team's formation to practice playing against the 4-2-3-1, 4-3-3 and 3-5-2 (**see analysis pages in this section**).

Coaching Points

1. Quick 1 or 2 touch passing and moving.
2. The focus is on finding the available space to receive.

DIEGO SIMEONE'S ATTACKING TACTICS

TACTICAL SITUATION 2

Dragging the Centre Back Out of Position to Create and Exploit Space

The content in this section is from analysis of Diego Simeone's Atlético Madrid teams during the 2017/2018 and 2018/2019 seasons.

The analysis is based on recurring patterns of play observed within the Atlético Madrid team. Once the same phase of play occurred several times (at least 10), the tactics would be seen as a pattern. The analysis on the following pages are examples of the team's tactics being used effectively.

Each action, pass, individual movement with or without the ball, and the positioning of each player on the pitch including their body shape, are presented.

The analysis is then used to create a session to coach this specific tactical situation.

Tactical Situation 2 - Dragging the Centre Back Out of Position to Create and Exploit Space

CREATING SPACE FOR THE FULL BACK TO RECEIVE UNMARKED HIGH UP THE FLANK

Attacking on the flanks depended on Atlético's attacking shape. The width is created by the advanced positioning of the full backs.

The role of the full backs is to exploit space on the flanks and receive in advanced positions which are favourable to deliver a cross. This was only possible when full backs received in very advanced positions close to the box.

If a full back receives in an advanced position but is then closed down, combination play with the forwards or the wide midfielders is used to move the ball into a favourable position with time and space to deliver a cross.

The first option (**see next page**) is simple but highly effective. It demands good synchronisation between the players involved (well-timed runs), as well as accurate passing. It was usually carried out close to the box and Atlético's aim was first to move the ball to one of the forwards, who dropped between lines. From there, they moved the ball into the available space on the flank.

Tactical Situation 2 - Dragging the Centre Back Out of Position to Create and Exploit Space

1. The Ball is Moved to the Full Back High Up the Flank After Dragging the Opposing Centre Back Out of Position

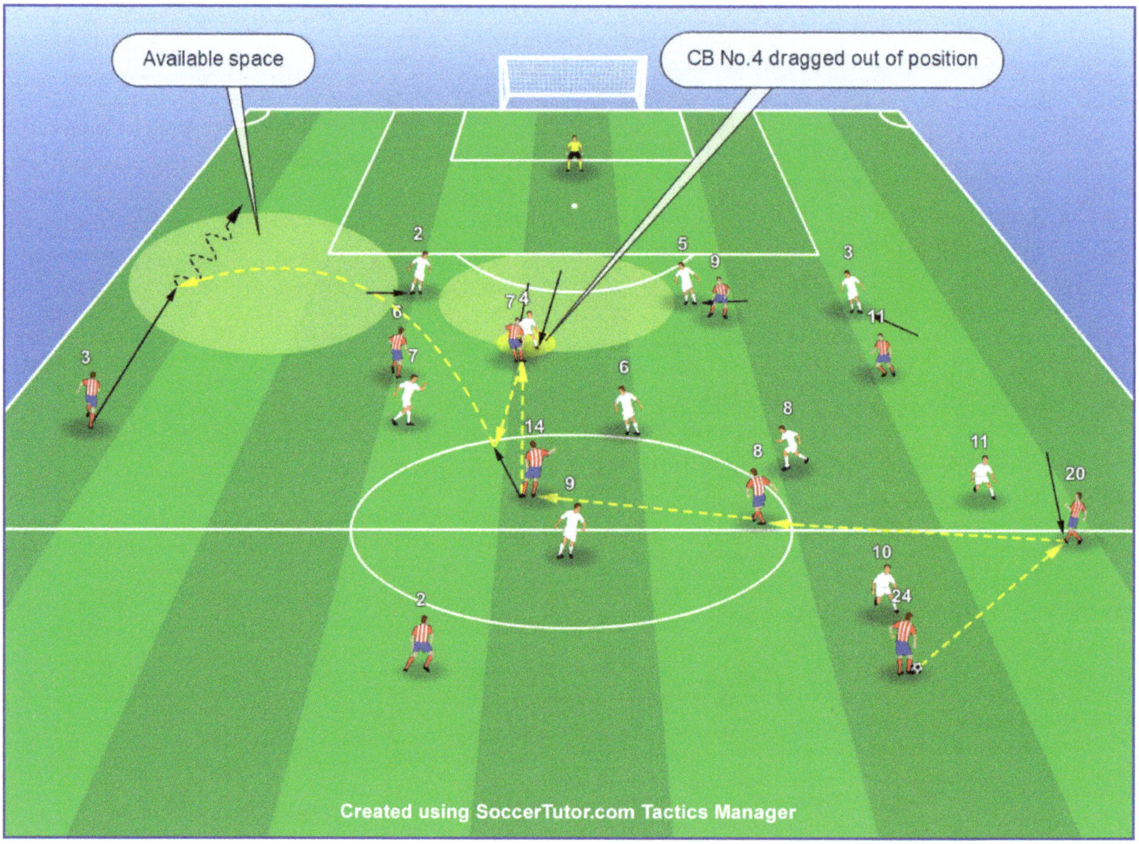

Gabi (14) passes to **Griezmann (7)**, who drops between the lines. The white centre back No.4 follows him to prevent the turn. No.4's movement means the other white defenders have to converge to provide cover.

The white right back No.2 moving inside creates space for **F. Luis (3)** out wide.

Griezmann (7) lays the ball back for **Gabi (14)** to pass out wide.

F. Luis (3) receives with white No.2 unable to close him down (neutralised) and No.4 out of position.

DIEGO SIMEONE'S ATTACKING TACTICS

Tactical Situation 2 - Dragging the Centre Back Out of Position to Create and Exploit Space

2a. The Ball is Moved to the Full Back into the Available Space High Up the Flank via a Direct Pass from the Forward

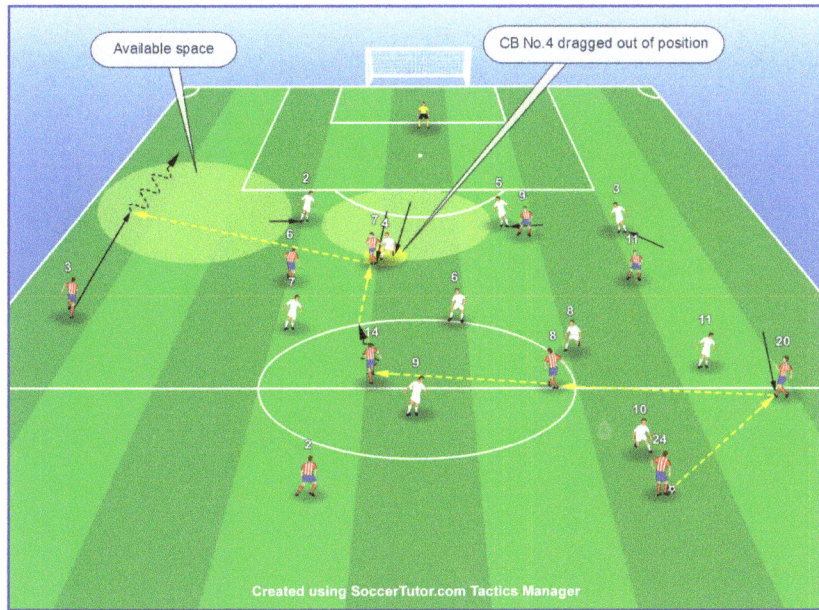

This is a variation of the previous diagram.

The forward **Griezmann (7)** spots that the white right back No.2 has moved inside, so he passes directly to the left back **F. Luis (3)** in the available space out wide, instead of laying the ball back for **Gabi (14)**.

This is an even better option for Atlético if it is possible, as the ball is moved into a dangerous area more quickly.

2b. The Full Back Delivers a Cross and the Wide Midfielder Exploits the Space in the Centre Vacated by the Opposing Centre Back

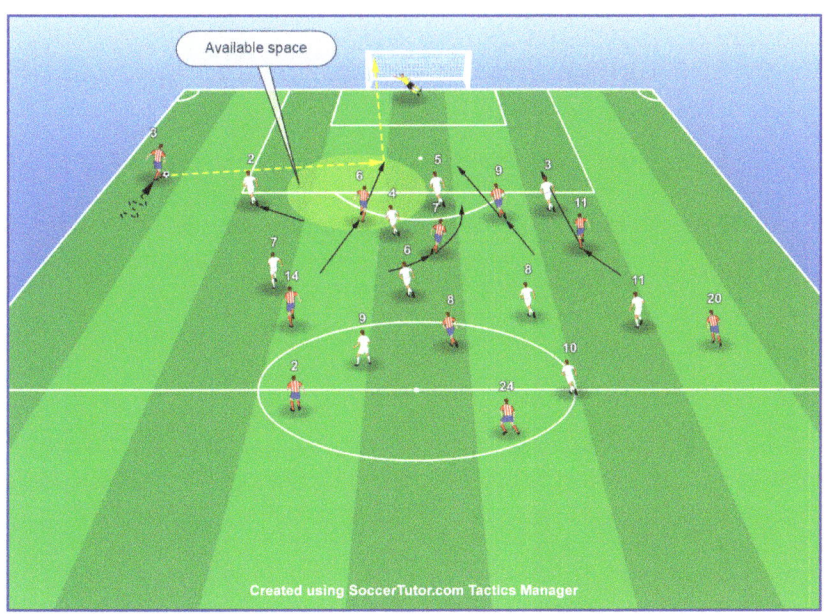

F. Luis (3) receives on the run, takes no more than 2 touches and delivers a cross for his team-mates in the box. The left midfielder **Koke (6)** exploits the space created by white No.4 leaving his position, receives the cross and shoots at goal.

It is highly likely that Atlético create a numerical advantage in the box if the wide midfielders **Koke (6)** and **Correa (11)** use well-timed runs.

DIEGO SIMEONE'S ATTACKING TACTICS

Tactical Situation 2 - Dragging the Centre Back Out of Position to Create and Exploit Space

3. Alternate Option to Attack Through the Centre if the Opposing Full Back Retains Position to Restrict the Space Out Wide

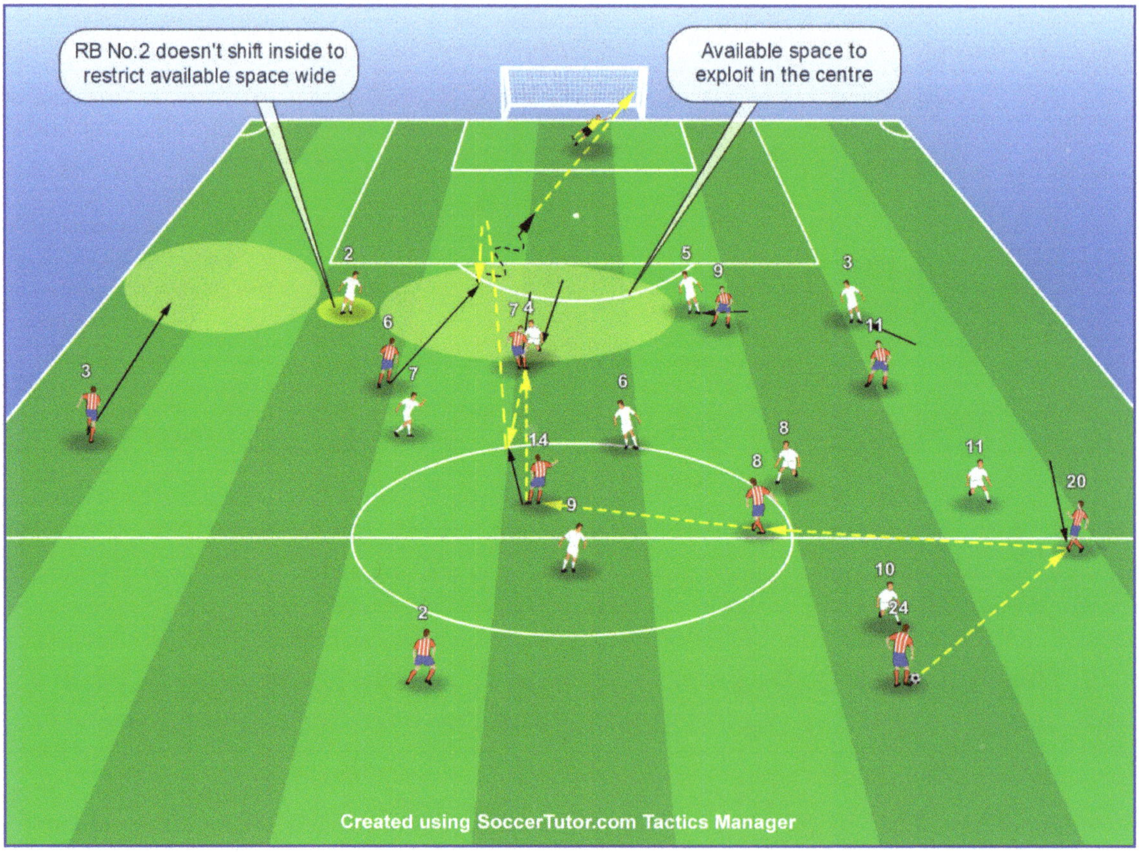

If the opposing full back No.2 doesn't move inside to provide cover behind the white centre back No.4, there is limited space for the Atlético full back to exploit out wide.

In this situation, Atlético instead exploit the space in the centre.

After **Griezmann's (7)** lay-off, the central Midfielder **Gabi (14)** plays a straight aerial pass for left midfielder **Koke (6)**, who makes a run into the space created by white No.4's forward movement.

ASSESSMENT

In this situation, Diego Simeone's Atlético Madrid have a double aim. The first aim is to create space on the flank for the full back to receive in an advanced position and overcome the pressure from the opposing full back. The second aim is to drag the opposing centre back out of position and be ready to exploit the gap in the defensive line and the potential numerical advantage inside the box.

©SOCCERTUTOR.COM DIEGO SIMEONE'S ATTACKING TACTICS

SESSION (4 PRACTICES) FOR "DRAGGING THE CENTRE BACK OUT OF POSITION TO CREATE SPACE FOR THE FULL BACK"

Tactical Situation 2 - Dragging the Centre Back Out of Position to Create and Exploit Space

SESSION FOR THIS TACTICAL SITUATION (4 PRACTICES)

1. Dragging the Centre Back Out of Position to Create and Exploit Space in a Technical Passing Practice

Scenario A: Exploiting Space Created in the Centre

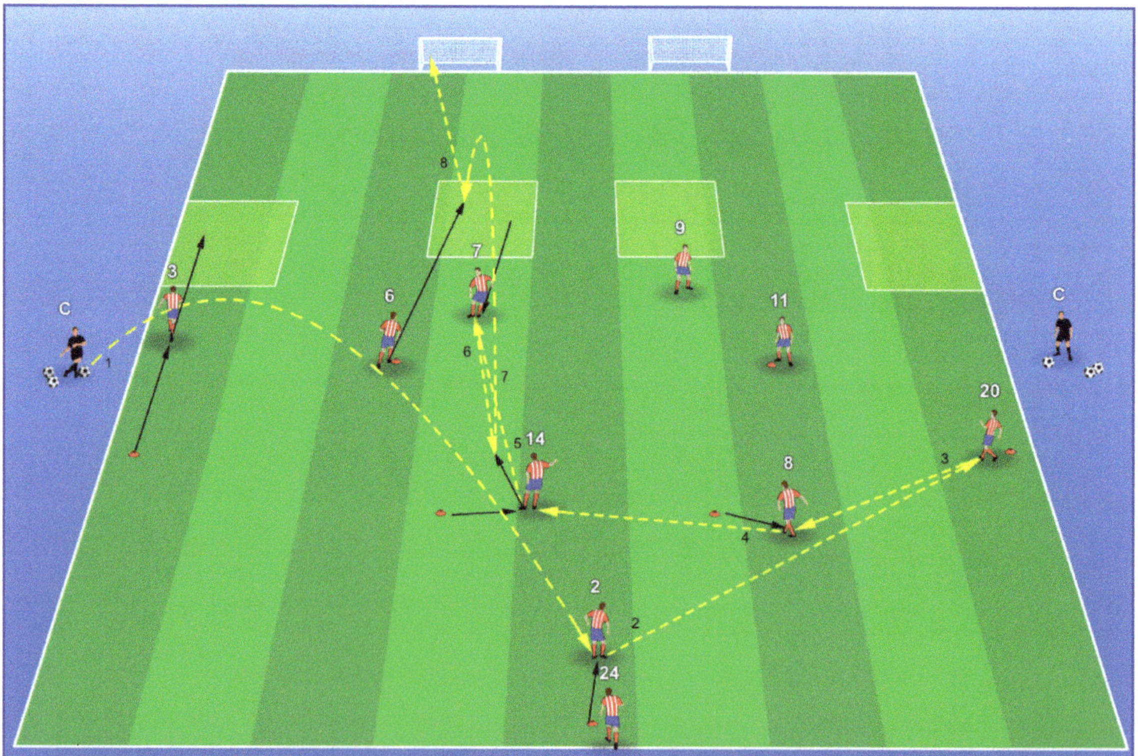

Description (Scenario A)

- The Coach starts the practice with a long pass to the centre back (**2**), who moves forward to receive and pass to the full back (**20**).

- As soon as the switch of play is achieved by passing from the one central midfielder (**8**) to the other (**14**), the forward (**7**) drops back to receive and lays the ball back for **No.14**.

- The central midfielder (**14**) then either directs the ball to the wide or central area on the left side of the pitch.

- Both the left midfielder (**6**) and the left back (**3**) make well-timed forward runs.

- In this first example, we imagine the opposing centre back has followed **No.7** and the right back has retained his position to limit the available space out wide for **No.3** - see analysis page 40.

- Therefore, the pass is played towards the central area for the left midfielder (**6**) to receive and score in the mini goal.

©SOCCERTUTOR.COM DIEGO SIMEONE'S ATTACKING TACTICS

Tactical Situation 2 - Dragging the Centre Back Out of Position to Create and Exploit Space

Scenario B: Exploiting Space Created Out Wide

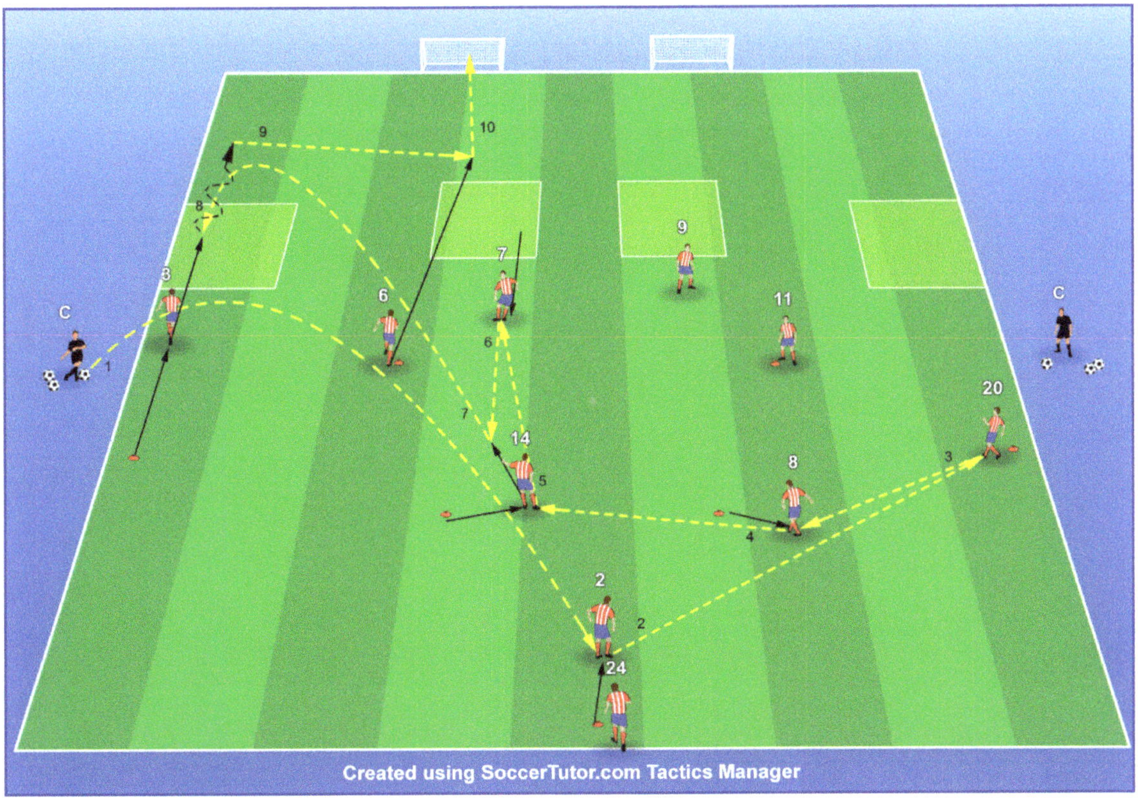

[Diagram of soccer field showing tactical movement]

Description (Scenario B)

- In this second example, we imagine the opposing centre back has followed **No.7** and the right back has moved inside to provide cover, thus creating space out wide for the full back **No.3** to exploit - **see analysis pages 38 and 39**.

- Therefore, the pass is played towards the wide area for the left back **(3)** to receive and score in the mini goal.

- The practice is then repeated on the other side and the centre backs rotate.

- There can be 2 players in each full back and wide midfielder position to keep the practice running at a high tempo.

Variations

1. Swap the mini goals for a large goal and GK.
2. The pass to the wide area is played directly by the forward that drops back (**see Page 39**).

Coaching Points

1. There needs to be well-timed runs and synchronisation in players movements (especially the forward, wide midfielder, and full back).
2. Accurate passing is required throughout.

DIEGO SIMEONE'S ATTACKING TACTICS

Tactical Situation 2 - Dragging the Centre Back Out of Position to Create and Exploit Space

PROGRESSION
2. Dragging the Centre Back Out of Position to Create and Exploit Space in a Functional Practice

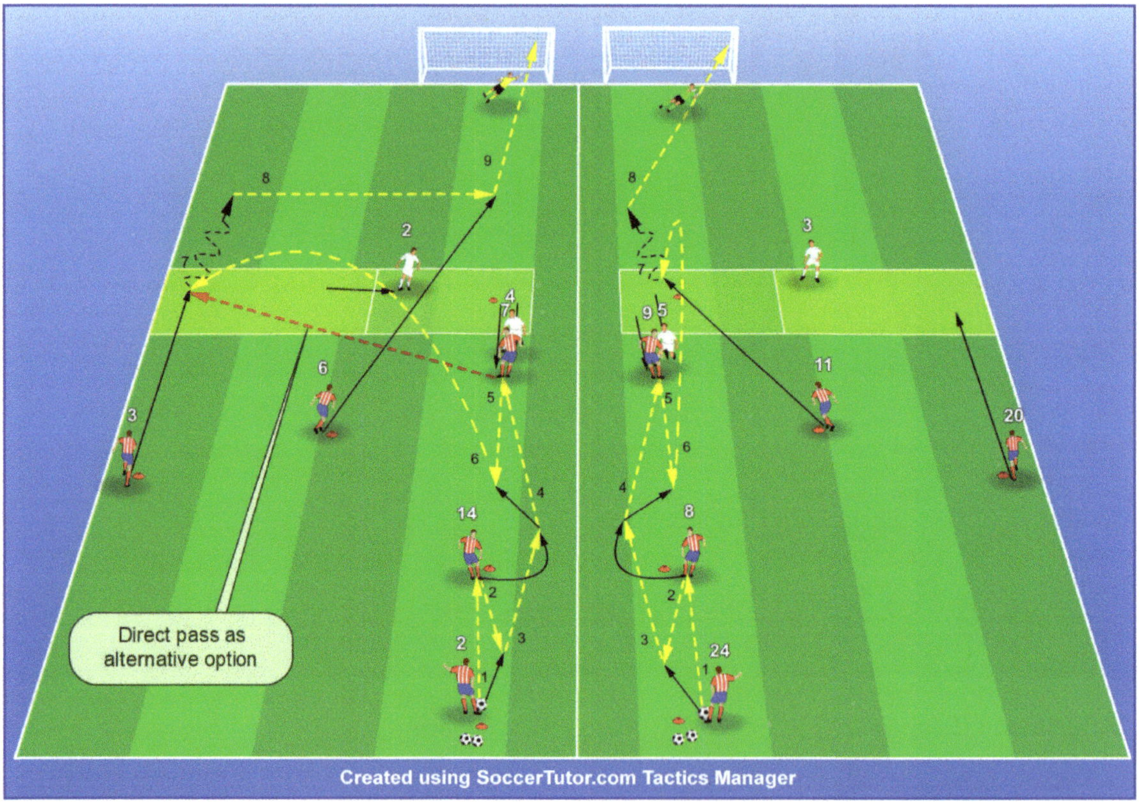

Description

- In a total area of 40 x 50 yards, mark out 2 wide yellow areas (10 x 5 yards) and 2 central white areas (7 x 5 yards).

- The players are trained on decision making and work on both sides at the same time.

- The centre back (**2/24**) starts by passing to the central midfielder (**14/8**), who lays the ball back and then opens up to receive the next pass.

- As soon as the central midfielder (**14/8**) receives the third pass, the forward (**7/9**) drops back and receives to feet.

- At the same time, the wide midfielder (**6/11**) make forward runs. The white centre back (No.4 or No.5) follows the forward's run and the forward (**7/9**) lays the ball back to the central midfielder (**14/8**).

- After receiving the lay-off, the direction of the central midfielder's (**14/8**) next pass depends on the reaction of the opposing full back.

- If the white full back leaves the wide yellow area and enters the central white area to provide cover, then the pass is directed to the red full back (**3/20**) within the wide yellow area (**Option 1 - see left side of diagram**).

DIEGO SIMEONE'S ATTACKING TACTICS

Tactical Situation 2 - Dragging the Centre Back Out of Position to Create and Exploit Space

- If the white full back retains his position, there is limited space out wide for the red full back **(3/20)**, so the pass should be directed for the forward run of the wide midfielder **(6/11)** into the white central area (**Option 2 - see right side of diagram**).

- Whether it is the full back **(3/20)** or wide midfielder **(6/11)** who receives the aerial pass from the central midfielder **(14/8)**, they must receive the pass within the correct area.

- If the full back **(3/20)** receives out wide, he crosses for the wide midfielder **(6/11)** to finish.

- If the wide midfielder **(6/11)** receives in the centre, he moves towards goal and shoots.

- **NOTE:** The forwards can also use a direct pass towards the full back if they see that the opposing full back has already shifted inside (**see red arrow**).

- There can be 2 players in each full back and wide midfielder position to keep the practice running at a high tempo.

Restrictions: The white centre backs are coached to follow the forwards every time.

Coaching Points

1. There needs to be well-timed runs and synchronisation in the player movements (especially the forward, wide midfielder, and full back).

2. The players need to read the specific tactical situation and make the correct decision according to the positioning and reaction of the opposing full back (**see analysis pages in this section**).

3. Accurate passing is required throughout, as well as quick finishing.

Tactical Situation 2 - Dragging the Centre Back Out of Position to Create and Exploit Space

PROGRESSION

3. Dragging the Centre Back Out of Position to Create and Exploit Space in a Functional Small Sided Game

Scenario A: Exploiting Space Created in the Centre

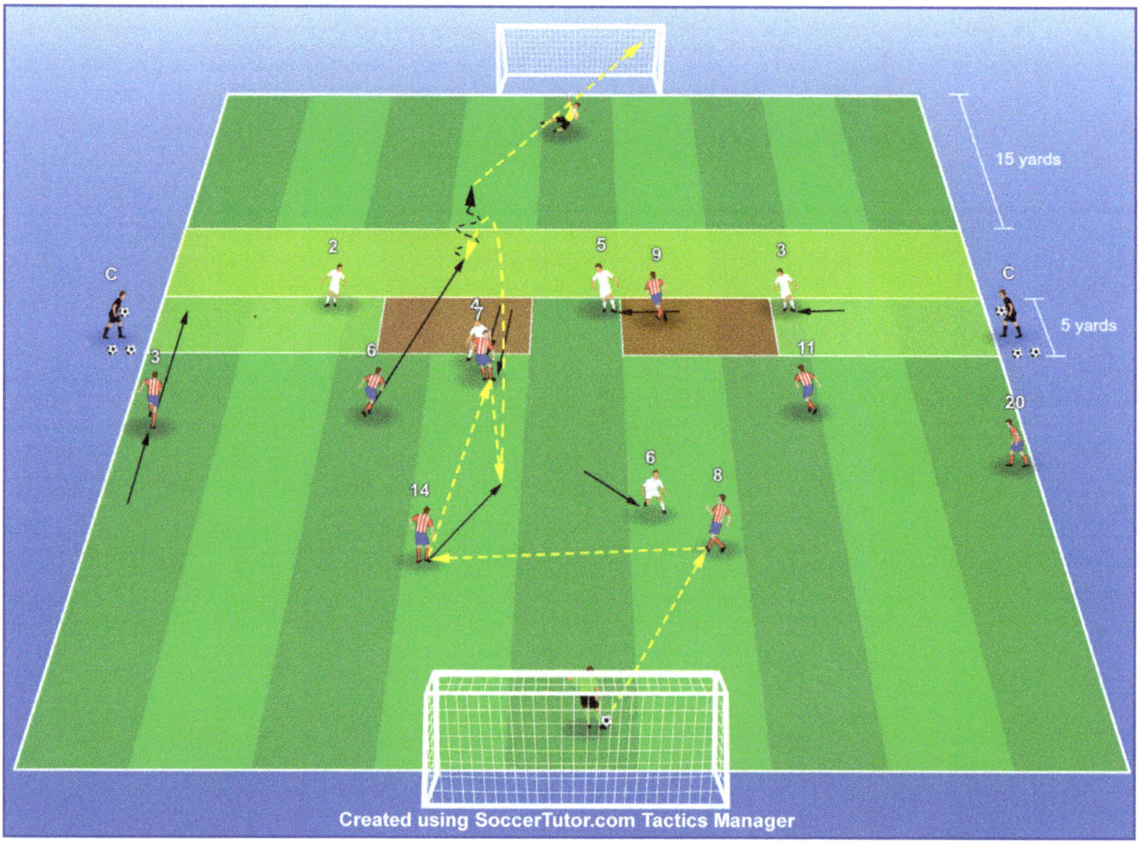

Description (Scenario A)

- In a 40 x 50 yard area, we play a game with 8 red outfield players and 5 white outfield players. Mark out 2 wide white areas (10 x 5 yards), 2 red central areas (8 x 5 yards) and a large yellow "Receiving Zone" (40 x 5 yards).

- The reds aim to drag a white centre back out of position by passing to a forward (**No.7** in diagram example), who drops back to receive. The forward lays the ball back to the central midfielder (**14**), who has to decide whether to play the ball wide or behind the white centre back No.4. After the pass is received, the reds try to score.

- In this first example, the white full back No.2 retains his position, so there is limited space out wide for the red full back (**3**) to exploit. Therefore, the central midfielder's (**14**) pass is directed centrally for the forward run of the wide midfielder (**6**) in behind the white centre back No.4. The wide midfielder (**6**) receives and shoots at goal.

©SOCCERTUTOR.COM

DIEGO SIMEONE'S ATTACKING TACTICS

Tactical Situation 2 - Dragging the Centre Back Out of Position to Create and Exploit Space

Scenario B: Exploiting Space Created Out Wide

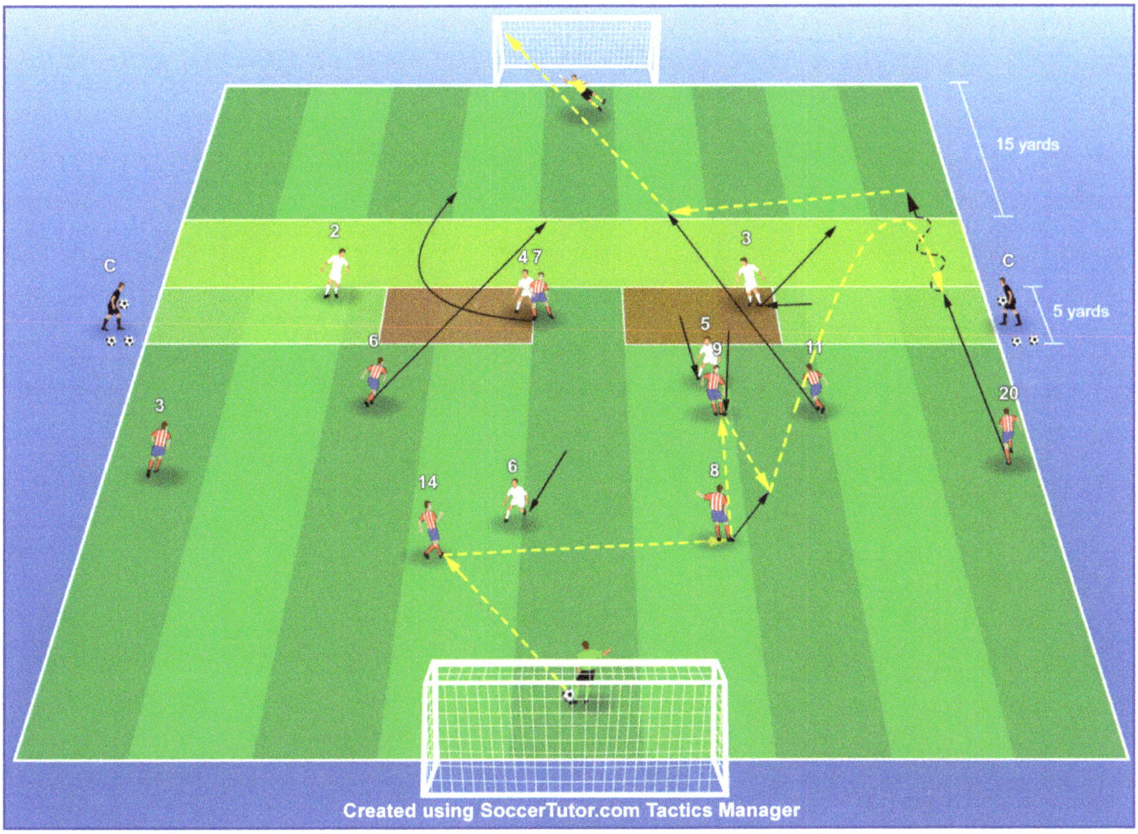

Description (Scenario B)
- In this second scenario, the play is on the right side of the pitch.
- The white full back No.3 leaves the wide white area and enters the central red area to provide cover for white No.5 and available space is created out wide.
- Therefore, the central midfielder's **(8)** pass is directed out wide for the forward run of the red full back **(20)**, who receives and crosses for the right midfielder **(11)** to finish.
- If the reds make a wrong decision, the Coach on the strong side throws a ball to the white team, who then attack and try to score within 12-15 seconds.

Restrictions: The white centre backs must follow the forwards every time and the centre backs and GK cannot enter the "Receiving Zone."

Progression: After a few minutes, add 2 more white midfielders. The reds can score freely but if they manage to do it by dragging the centre back out of position and make the right decision where to direct the next pass, they score 3 goals.

Coaching Points
1. There needs to be synchronisation in the player movements (especially the forward, wide midfielder, and full back).
2. The players need to read the specific tactical situation and make the correct decision according to the positioning and reaction of the opposing full back (**see analysis pages**).

DIEGO SIMEONE'S ATTACKING TACTICS

Tactical Situation 2 - Dragging the Centre Back Out of Position to Create and Exploit Space

PROGRESSION

4. Dragging the Centre Back Out of Position to Create and Exploit Space in a Conditioned Game

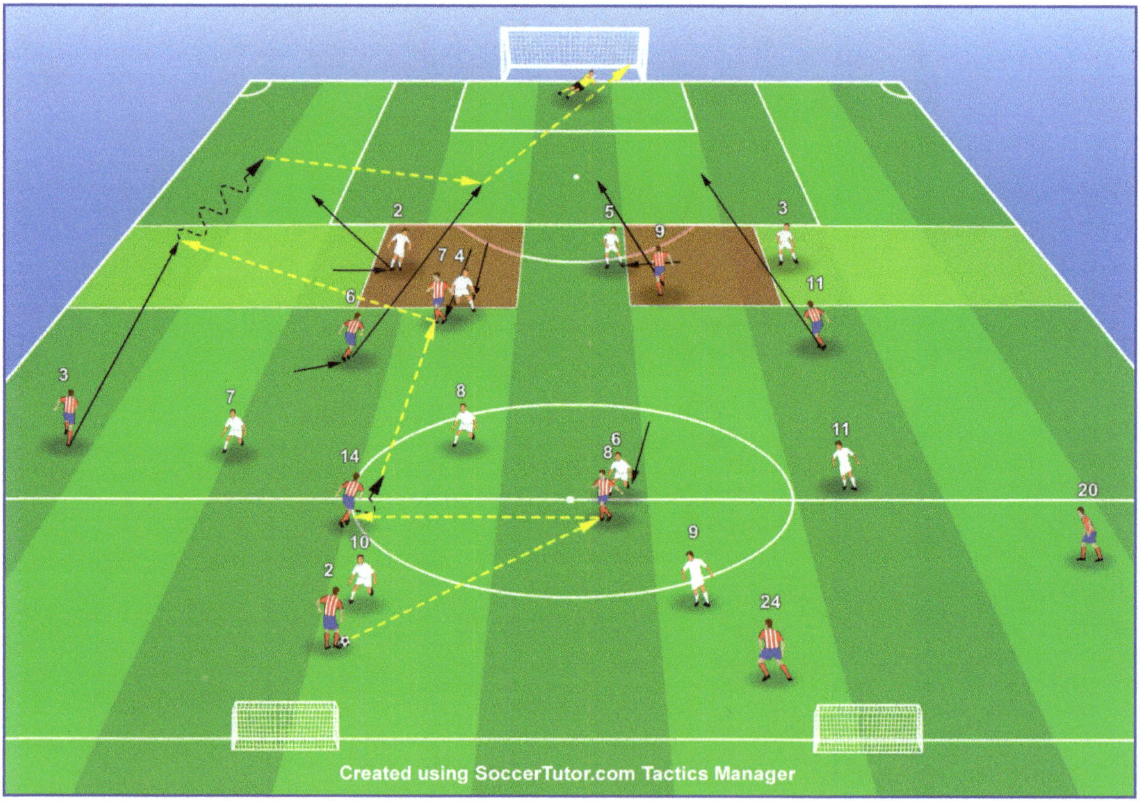

Description

- In the final practice of this session, the 2 teams play a 10 v 10 (+GK) game. Mark out 2 white wide areas (15 x 10 yards), and 2 red central areas (8 x 10 yards).

- The red team start, and the first aim is to drag one of the centre backs out of position by passing to a forward **(7)**. From there, they either exploit space out wide or in behind the white centre back No.4, depending on the positioning of the opposing full back.

- **See the previous practices in this session and analysis pages** for the correct decisions.

- **NOTE:** Forwards can use a direct pass out wide if they see that the opposing full back has already shifted inside (**see diagram example**).

Restrictions

- The white centre backs must follow the forwards every time.

- Reds can score in any way but if they do it by using these specific tactics, they score 3 goals.

Progression: 11 v 11 game using 2/3 of pitch. The reds can score in any way but if they do it after exploiting the space out wide or in behind the centre back, they score 3 goals.

DIEGO SIMEONE'S ATTACKING TACTICS

TACTICAL SITUATION 3

Options for the Full Back After Receiving High Up the Pitch

The content in this section is from analysis of Diego Simeone's Atlético Madrid teams during the 2017/2018 and 2018/2019 seasons.

The analysis is based on recurring patterns of play observed within the Atlético Madrid team. Once the same phase of play occurred several times (at least 10), the tactics would be seen as a pattern. The analysis on the following pages are examples of the team's tactics being used effectively.

Each action, pass, individual movement with or without the ball, and the positioning of each player on the pitch including their body shape, are presented.

The analysis is then used to create a session to coach this specific tactical situation.

Tactical Situation 3 - Options for the Full Back After Receiving High Up the Pitch

ADVANCED FULL BACK RECEIVES UP AGAINST THE OPPOSING FULL BACK

Full Back Receives from the Central Midfielder in an Advanced Position on the Flank with the Opposing Full Back Able to Contest

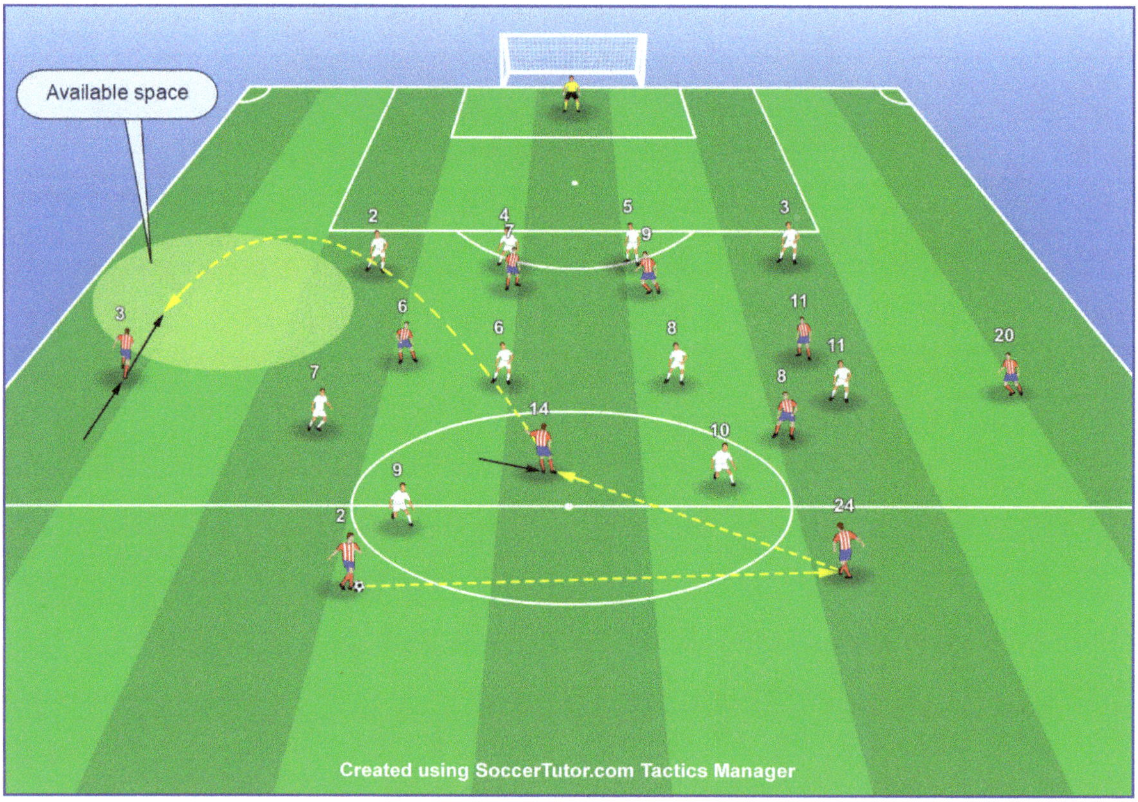

If in a similar situation to the one in the previous section, the full back receives in an advanced position from the central midfielder's pass, but this time the opposing full back is in position to contest him.

In this situation, the Atlético full back uses combination play to break through the opposing full back's pressure and get in behind the opposition's defensive line.

In this specific tactical example, the Atlético left back **F. Luis (3)** receives in an advanced position from central midfielder **Gabi (14)**.

DIEGO SIMEONE'S ATTACKING TACTICS

Tactical Situation 3 - Options for the Full Back After Receiving High Up the Pitch

Option 1: Full Back Plays a 1-2 with the Forward to Receive in Behind and Deliver a Cross

As white No.2 moves to press **F. Luis (3)**, the forward **Griezmann (7)** moves into a supporting position and offers an option for a 1-2.

F. Luis (3) receives the return pass in behind and delivers a cross for his team-mates.

A 1-2 combination can also be played with the left midfielder **Koke (6)** if he is in a more advanced position.

Option 2: Full Back Passes in Behind for the Forward Run of the Wide Midfielder

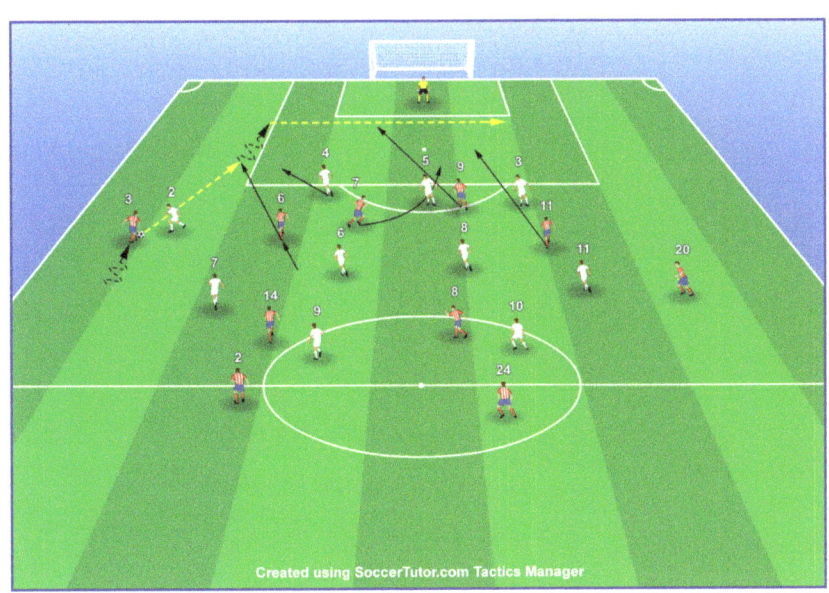

In this variation, the left midfielder **Koke (6)** makes a run in behind the white full back No.2.

With this movement, it is possible to pass to **Koke (6)** free of marking in a position to deliver a cross.

The opposition will only have 2 players defending the cross.

©SOCCERTUTOR.COM　　　　DIEGO SIMEONE'S ATTACKING TACTICS

Tactical Situation 3 - Options for the Full Back After Receiving High Up the Pitch

Option 3: Forward Drops Back to Receive in the Space Created by the Wide Midfielder's Forward Run in Behind

In this variation of the previous example, the white centre back tracks **Koke's (6)** run very well, so the pass to him is not on.

Therefore, the forward **Griezmann (7)** moves into the available space created (highlighted area) and receives unmarked in a dangerous area for playing a final pass or shooting at goal.

As soon as **Griezmann (7)** receives, the other players in advanced positions make movements to receive a final pass in behind the defensive line to score.

Griezmann (7) has 3 options:

1. The left midfielder **Koke (6)**.
2. The forward **Torres (9)**.
3. The right midfielder **Correa (11)**.

Tactical Situation 3 - Options for the Full Back After Receiving High Up the Pitch

Option 4. Wide Midfielder Receives in the Space Created in the Centre by the Forward's Movement Out Wide

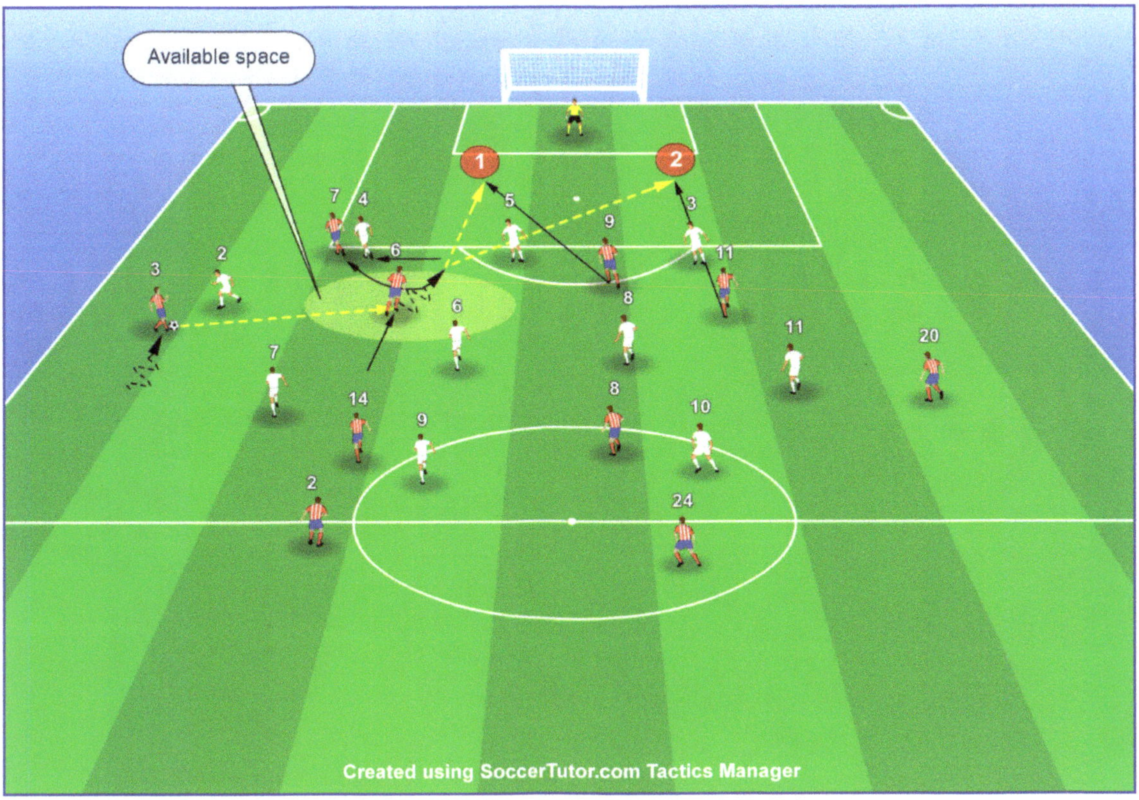

In this variation of the previous option, a similar situation can be created with the synchronised movements of the same players.

In this example, the forward **Griezmann (7)** moves into the space behind the white full back No.2 and forces the centre back No.4 to follow him.

This reaction creates space for the left midfielder **Koke (6)** in the centre, who is able to receive unmarked in a dangerous area for playing a final pass or shooting at goal.

As soon as **Koke (6)** receives, the other players in advanced positions make runs into the box.

Koke (6) has 2 options:

1. The forward **Torres (9)**.
2. The right midfielder **Correa (11)**.

DIEGO SIMEONE'S ATTACKING TACTICS

SESSION (4 PRACTICES) FOR "OPTIONS FOR THE FULL BACK AFTER RECEIVING HIGH UP THE PITCH"

Tactical Situation 3 - Options for the Full Back After Receiving High Up the Pitch

SESSION FOR THIS TACTICAL SITUATION (4 PRACTICES)

1. Options for the Full Back After Receiving High Up the Pitch in a Technical Passing Practice with Finish

Options 1 & 2: Pass in Behind to W. Midfielder + Pass Inside to Forward

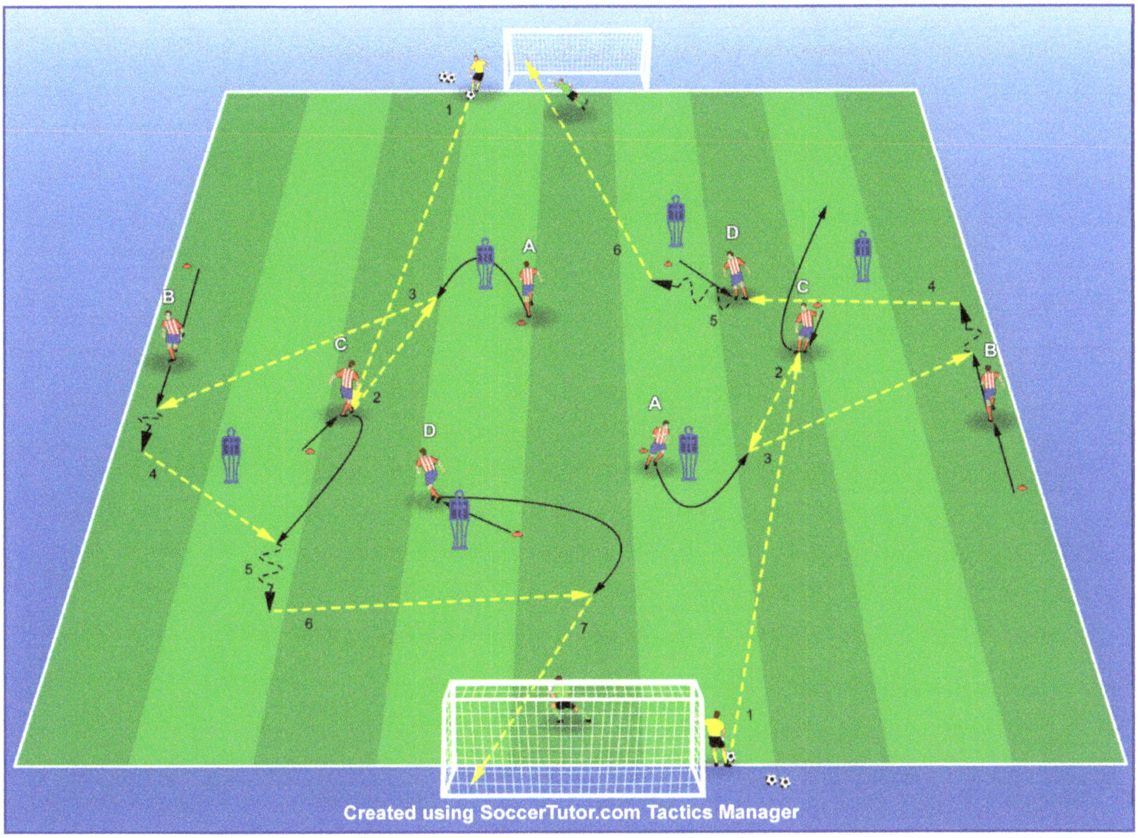

A = Central midfielder, **B** = Full back,
C = Wide midfielder, **D** = Forward.

Description (Options 1 & 2)

- Using an area approximately the size of half a full pitch, the practice starts at both ends simultaneously with both GKs.
- As soon as A drops back in front of the mannequin, the GK passes to C, who lays the ball back for A to run onto. Player A passes in front of B to receive on the run. Player C turns and moves forward.
- As soon as B receives, C should be close to the mannequin but not beyond it (offside rule). D provides an inside passing option.

Player B then decides where to direct the ball. In this first diagram, options 1 and 2 are shown:

1. On the left side of the diagram, B passes beyond the mannequin for the run of C, who receives and crosses for D to score.
2. On the right side of the diagram, B passes inside to D, who receives, turns, and shoots.

©SOCCERTUTOR.COM　　DIEGO SIMEONE'S ATTACKING TACTICS

Tactical Situation 3 - Options for the Full Back After Receiving High Up the Pitch

Options 3 & 4: Pass Inside to W. Midfielder + 1-2 Combo with Forward

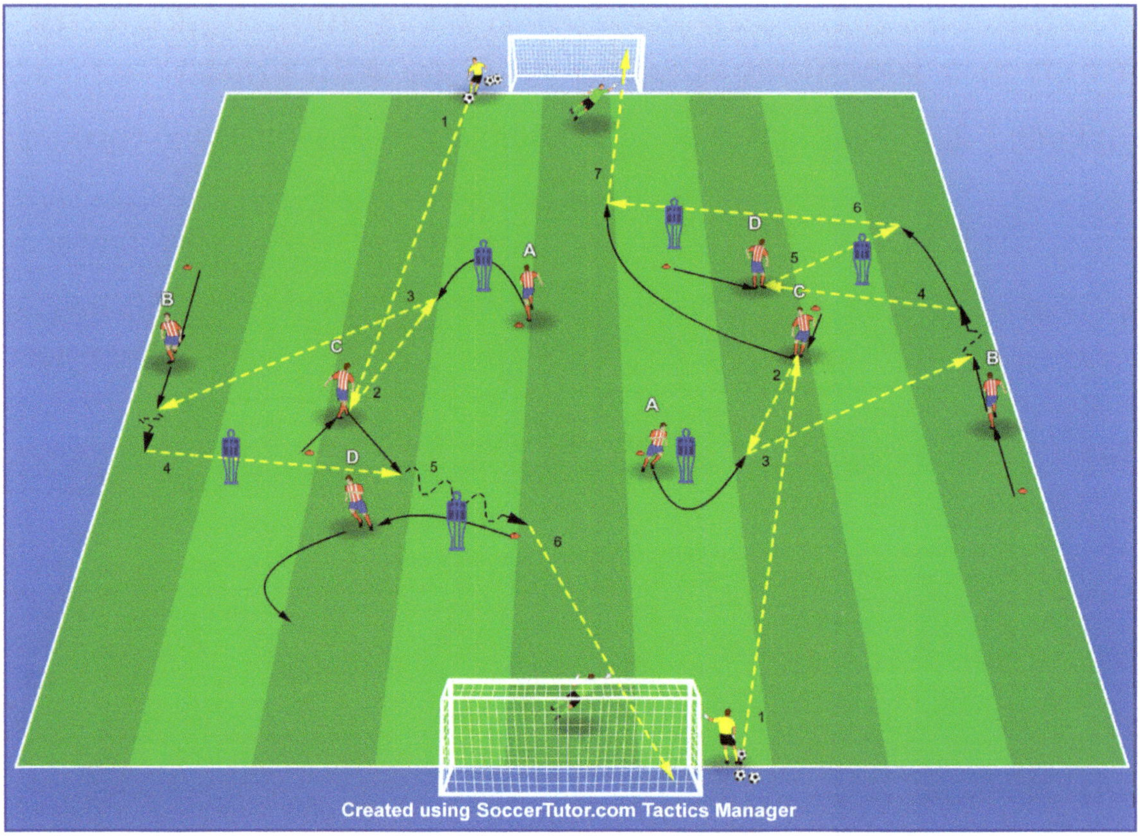

Description (Options 3 & 4)

In this second diagram, options 3 and 4 are shown:

3. On the left side of this second diagram, as soon as B receives, D makes a curved run around the mannequin and towards the side. C moves into the space created by D. B passes into C's path, who receives, dribbles the ball and shoots at goal.

4. On the right side of the diagram, D moves across to play a 1-2 combination with B, who receives the return pass in behind the mannequins. C makes a curved run to meet the cross and score.

- Each player moves to the next position (A -> B -> C -> D -> A).

- The 2 GKs at each end switch positions after a few repetitions.

- After practicing these different options on one side of the pitch (right), change the set-up to practice on the left side.

Coaching Points

1. There needs to be synchronisation in the players' movements (especially the forward and the wide midfielder).
2. Quick and accurate passing (1 or 2 touches).
3. Accurate finishing.

Tactical Situation 3 - Options for the Full Back After Receiving High Up the Pitch

PROGRESSION

2. Options for the Full Back After Receiving High Up the Pitch in a Functional Practice

Scenario A: Full Back Passes in Behind for Run of the Wide Midfielder

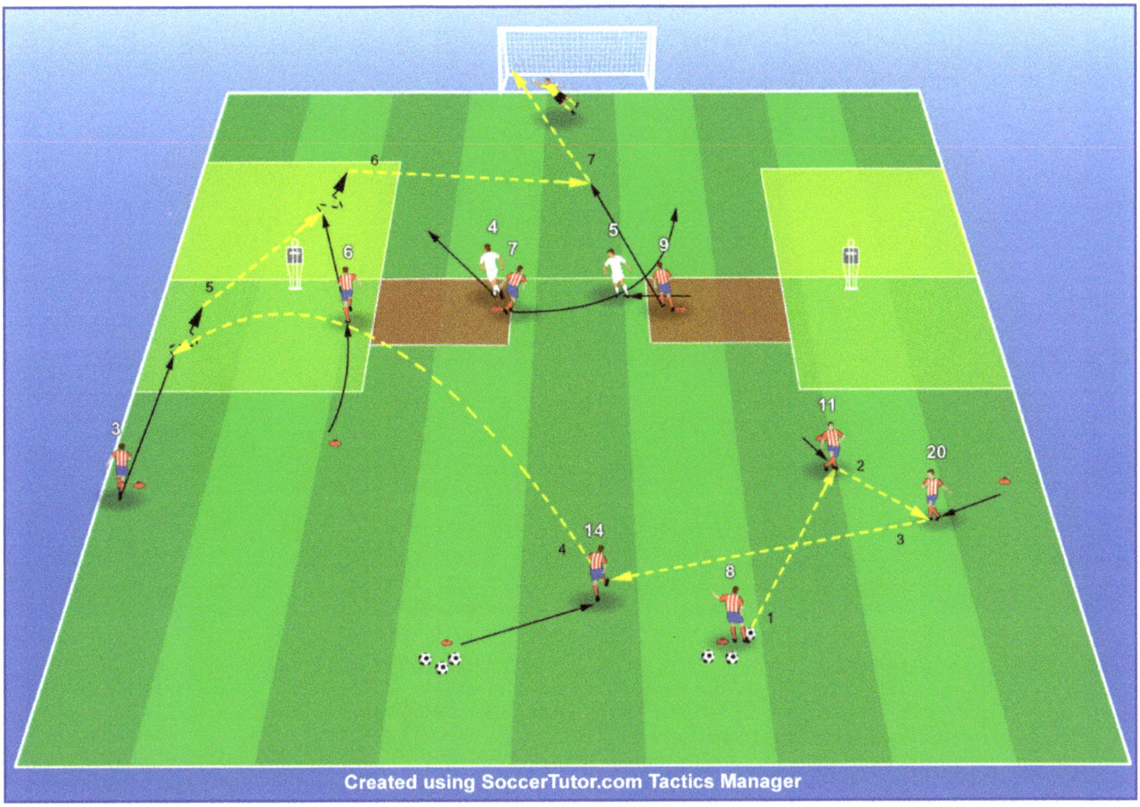

The reds play against 2 white centre backs. Their aim is to read the tactical situation and make the best decision to break through the defence.

Description (Scenario A)

- In a 40 x 50 yard area, the white areas are 10 x 10 yards, the yellow areas are 10 x 12 yards and the small red areas are 6 x 6 yards.

- The practice starts with the central midfielder (8) and after 3 passes it ends up with the other central midfielder (14), who passes out wide to the left back (3) in the white wide area.

- As soon as the long pass is played, the left midfielder (6) starts his forward run. When the left back (3) receives, there are 4 options (**see previous practice and analysis**). The full back (3) should read the situation and decide where is best to direct the ball.

- In this first example, the white centre back No.4 is too far away to track the red wide midfielder's (6) run, so the full back (3) passes in behind for him to receive and cross.

DIEGO SIMEONE'S ATTACKING TACTICS

Tactical Situation 3 - Options for the Full Back After Receiving High Up the Pitch

Scenario B: Forward Receives in Space Created by Wide Midfielder's Run

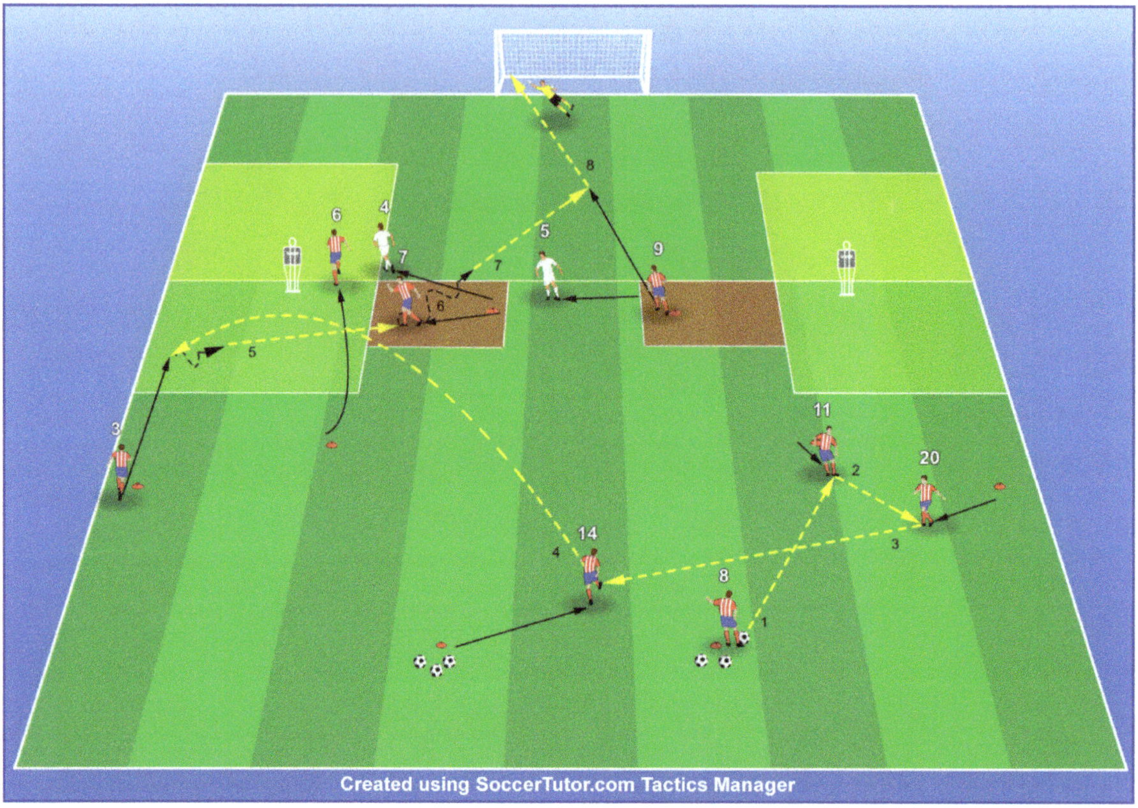

Description (Scenario B)

- In this second scenario, the white centre back No.4 has shifted across in time to track the forward run of the red left midfielder (6).

- However, white No.4's movement away from his position creates space in the centre.

- The red forward (7) moves towards the left back (3), receives within the small red area and turns to face the goal.

The forward (7) has 2 options:

1. Shoot at goal.
2. Pass in behind for the run of the other forward (9), who tries to score.

NOTE: If the wide midfielder doesn't make a forward run, there is an option for the full back to play a 1-2 combination with the forward, receive in behind and deliver a cross.

DIEGO SIMEONE'S ATTACKING TACTICS

Tactical Situation 3 - Options for the Full Back After Receiving High Up the Pitch

Scenario C: Wide Midfielder Receives in Space Created by Forward's Run

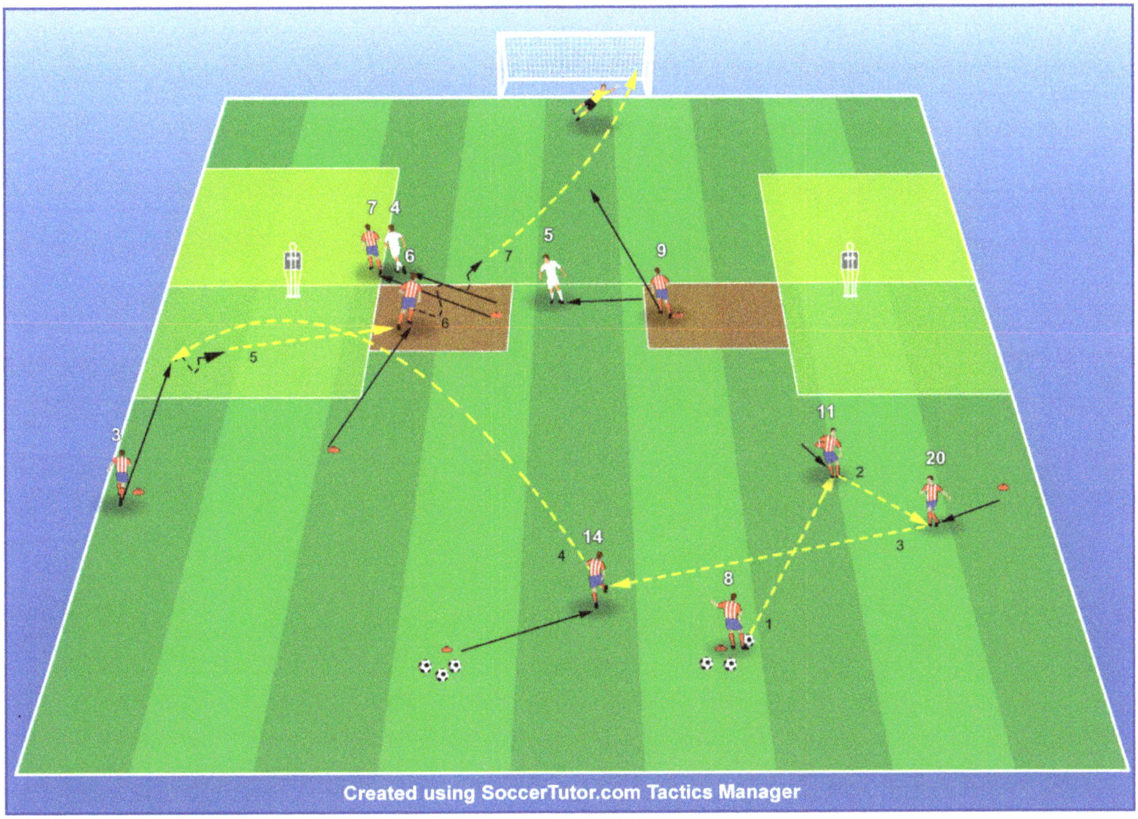

Description (Scenario C)

- In this third scenario, it is the forward **(7)** who makes the run in behind and drags the white centre back No.4 with him.

- This creates space for the left midfielder **(6)** to receive within the red area and then shoot or play a final pass.

- After practicing these different options on one side (left), switch to practice them on the right side of the pitch.

Coaching Points

1. There needs to be synchronisation in the players' movements (especially the forward and the wide midfielder).

2. Read the specific tactical situation and make the correct decision according to the opposing centre back's reaction.

DIEGO SIMEONE'S ATTACKING TACTICS

Tactical Situation 3 - Options for the Full Back After Receiving High Up the Pitch

PROGRESSION

3. Options for the Full Back After Receiving High Up the Pitch in a Functional Small Sided Game

Scenario A: Full Back Passes in Behind for Run of the Wide Midfielder

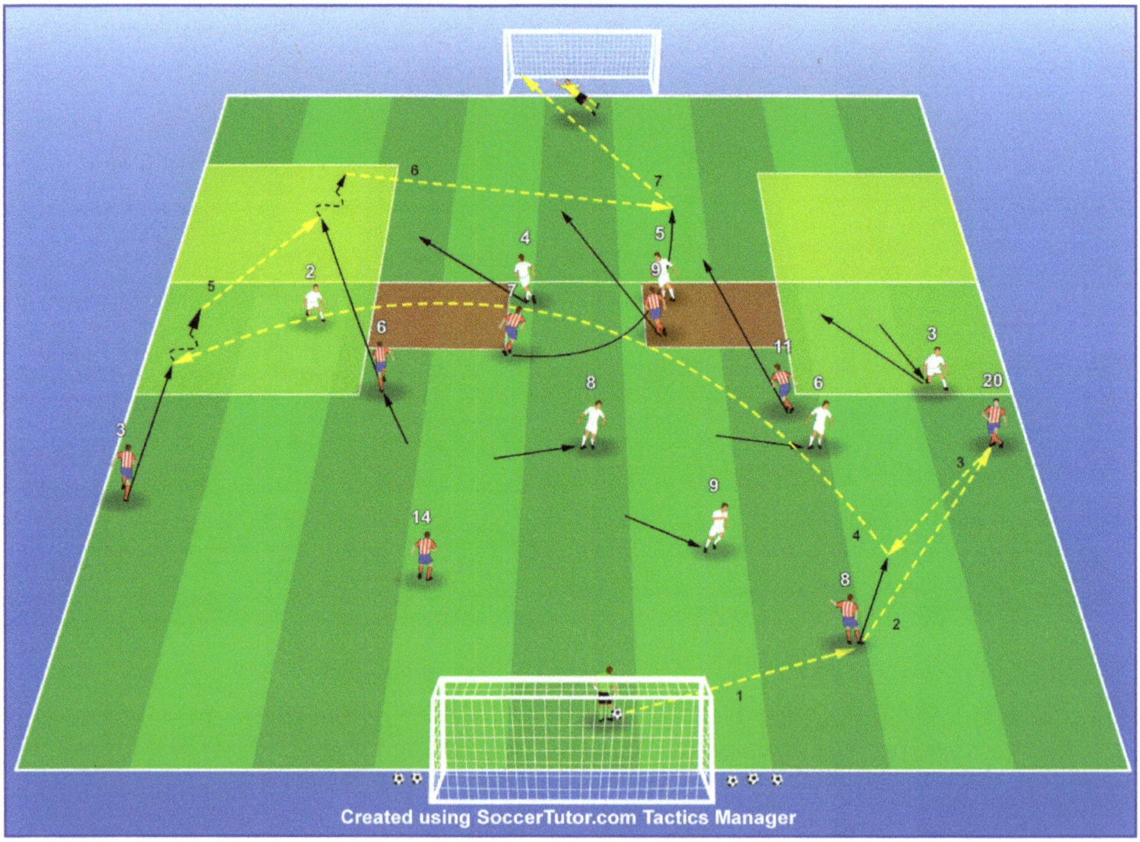

Description (Scenario A)

- Within the same 40 x 50 yard area as the previous practice, we now play a 9 v 8 game.
- The practice starts with the red team's GK and the reds try to score. If the whites win the ball, they try to score within 12-15 seconds.
- If the reds manage to move the ball to a full back **(3 or 20)** in the wide white area, read the tactical situation and make the correct combinations to score, they score 3 goals.

- Please **see the previous practices and analysis pages** for the correct decision making.
- If the red team's combination play is unsuccessful, the Coach throws a new ball in for the whites, who must score within 12-15 seconds.

Restriction: The white full backs (No.2 and No.3) must stay within the wide white areas throughout.

©SOCCERTUTOR.COM

DIEGO SIMEONE'S ATTACKING TACTICS

Tactical Situation 3 - Options for the Full Back After Receiving High Up the Pitch

Scenario B: Wide Midfielder Receives in Space Created by Forward's Run

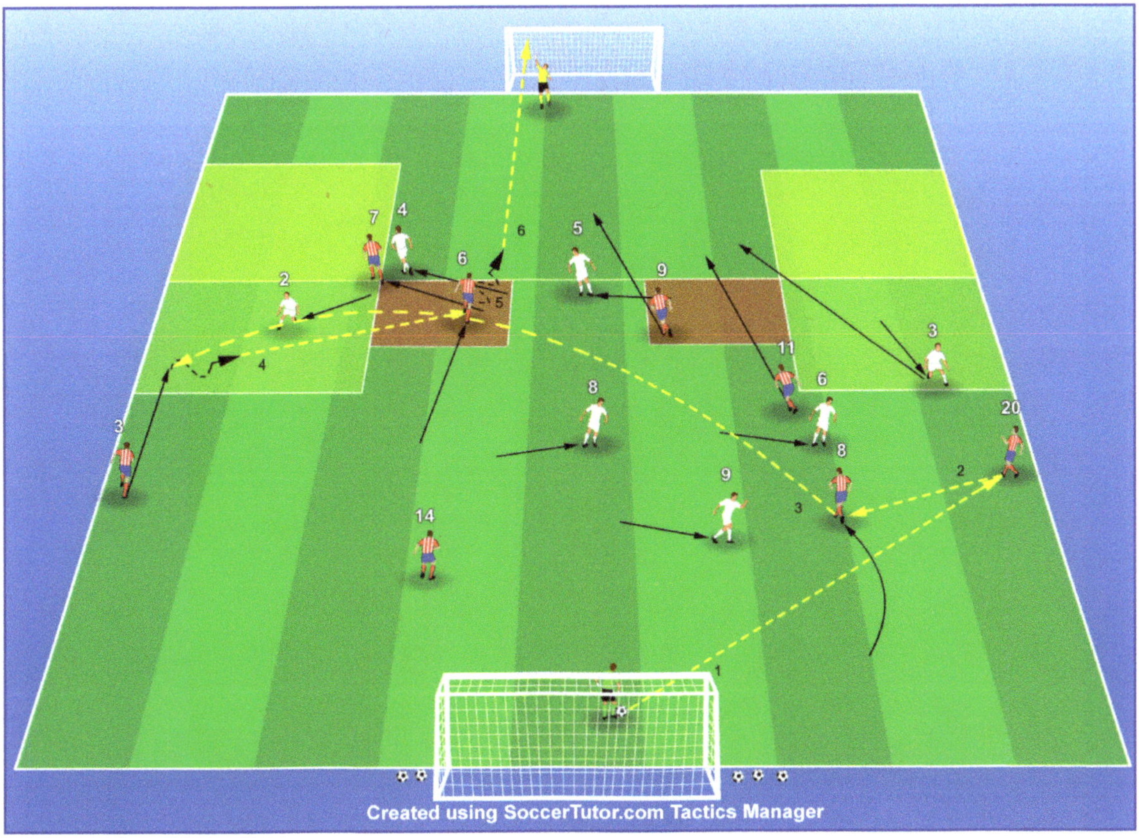

Description (Scenario B)

- In the first scenario (**see previous page**), the white centre back No.4 is too far away to track the red wide midfielder's **(6)** run, so the full back **(3)** passes in behind for him to receive and cross.

- In this second scenario, the white centre back No.4 tracks the red forward's **(7)** run. This creates space for the left midfielder **(6)** to move forward and receive from the left back **(3)** within the small red area.

The left midfielder **(6)** has 2 options:

1. Shoot at goal.
2. Pass in behind for the run of the other forward **(9)**, who tries to score.

Coaching Points

1. There needs to be synchronisation in the players' movements (especially the forward and the wide midfielder).

2. Read the specific tactical situation and make the correct decision according to the opposing centre back's reaction.

©SOCCERTUTOR.COM　　　DIEGO SIMEONE'S ATTACKING TACTICS

Tactical Situation 3 - Options for the Full Back After Receiving High Up the Pitch

PROGRESSION

4. Options for the Full Back After Receiving High Up the Pitch in a Conditioned Game

Description

- In the final practice of this session, the 2 teams play an 11 v 11 game in 2/3 of the pitch with areas marked out, as shown.

- If the red players are familiar enough with reading the tactical situation properly, the areas can be removed.

- The practice starts with the red team's GK and the reds try to score in a specific way. The focus is on reading the opposing centre back's reaction.

- If the reds manage to move the ball to the full back in the wide white area, read the tactical situation and make the correct combinations to score, they score 3 goals.

- Please **see the previous practices and analysis pages** for the correct decision making.

Coaching Points: Same as previous practice.

TACTICAL SITUATION 4

Synchronised Movements of the Full Back and Wide Midfielder

The content in this section is from analysis of Diego Simeone's Atlético Madrid teams during the 2017/2018 and 2018/2019 seasons.

The analysis is based on recurring patterns of play observed within the Atlético Madrid team. Once the same phase of play occurred several times (at least 10), the tactics would be seen as a pattern. The analysis on the following pages are examples of the team's tactics being used effectively.

Each action, pass, individual movement with or without the ball, and the positioning of each player on the pitch including their body shape, are presented.

The analysis is then used to create a session to coach this specific tactical situation.

Tactical Situation 4 - Synchronised Movements of the Full Back and Wide Midfielder

SYNCHRONISED MOVEMENTS OF THE FULL BACK AND WIDE MIDFIELDER

1a. Creating a 2v1 Situation within the Opposing Full Back's Zone of Responsibility with Synchronised Movements

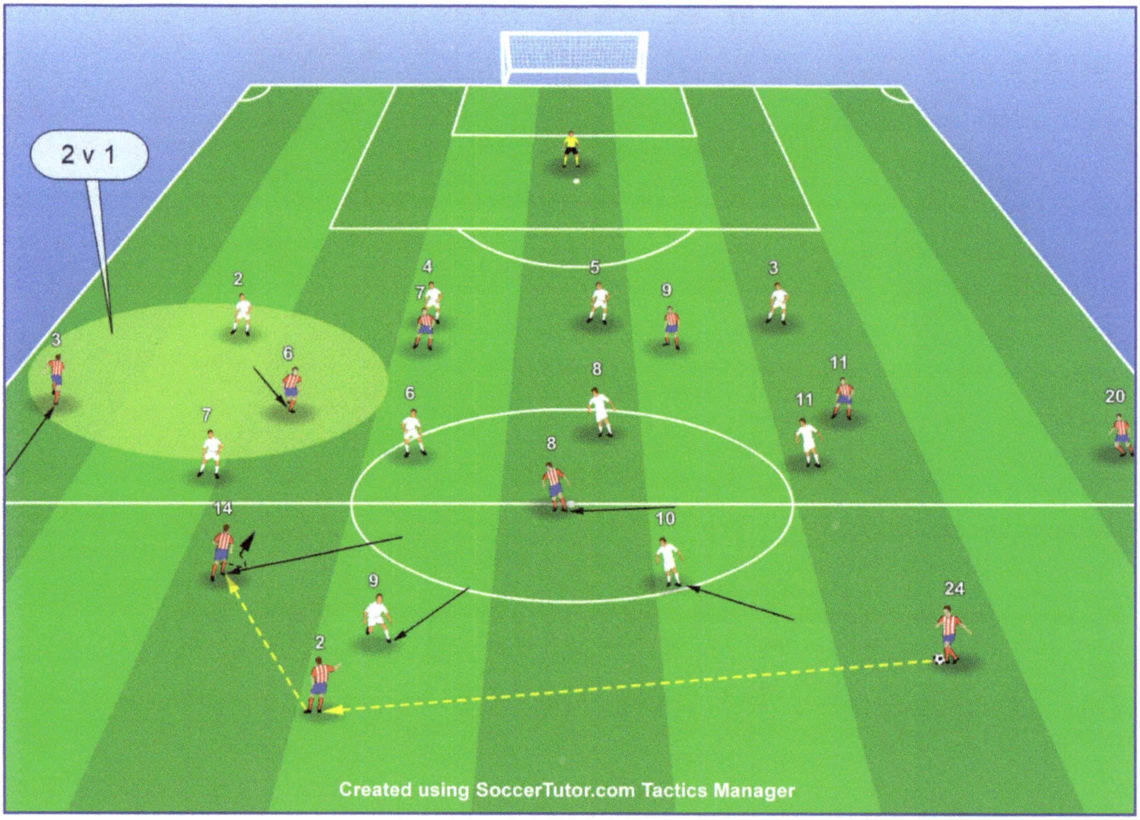

The synchronised movements of the full back and the wide midfielder can lead to 2v1 situation being created within the opposing full back's zone of responsibility.

In this tactical example, the Atlético left midfielder **Koke (6)** drops back into a central position between the opposition's midfield and defensive lines.

The Atlético left back **F. Luis (3)** makes a forward run at the same time to enter the opposing full back's zone of responsibility, and a 2v1 situation is created out wide (see highlighted area).

©SOCCERTUTOR.COM

DIEGO SIMEONE'S ATTACKING TACTICS

Tactical Situation 4 - Synchronised Movements of the Full Back and Wide Midfielder

1b. Opposing Full Back Retains Position and the Wide Midfielder Receives Unmarked Between the Lines

This 2v1 situation can be exploited in 2 different ways, depending on the reaction of the opposing full back.

In this tactical example, the white right back No.2 decides not to follow the dropping back movement of the Atlético Madrid left midfielder **Koke (6)**.

Therefore, **Koke (6)** is free of marking and able to receive the pass from the central midfielder **Gabi (14)** between the opposition's midfield and defensive lines.

Koke (6) is able to turn and has 3 options for a pass in behind the defensive line:

1. The forward **Griezmann (7)**.
2. The other forward **Torres (9)**.
3. Switch of play to the full back on the weak side **Juanfran (20)**.

DIEGO SIMEONE'S ATTACKING TACTICS

Tactical Situation 4 - Synchronised Movements of the Full Back and Wide Midfielder

2. Opposing Full Back Follows the Wide Midfielder's Movement and Creates Space for the Full Back to Receive High Up the Flank

In this variation, the white right back No.2 follows the dropping back movement of the Atlético left midfielder **Koke (6)**.

This creates space in behind white No.2 (see highlighted area).

The Atlético left back **F. Luis (3)** can receive from the central midfielder **Gabi (14)** via an aerial pass.

The Atlético left back **F. Luis (3)** receives within the created space, dribbles forward and delivers a cross for his oncoming team mates.

DIEGO SIMEONE'S ATTACKING TACTICS

SESSION (4 PRACTICES) FOR "SYNCHRONISED MOVEMENTS OF THE FULL BACK AND WIDE MIDFIELDER"

Tactical Situation 4 - Synchronised Movements of the Full Back and Wide Midfielder

SESSION FOR THIS TACTICAL SITUATION (4 PRACTICES)

1. Synchronised Movements of the Full Back and Wide Midfielder in a Technical Practice

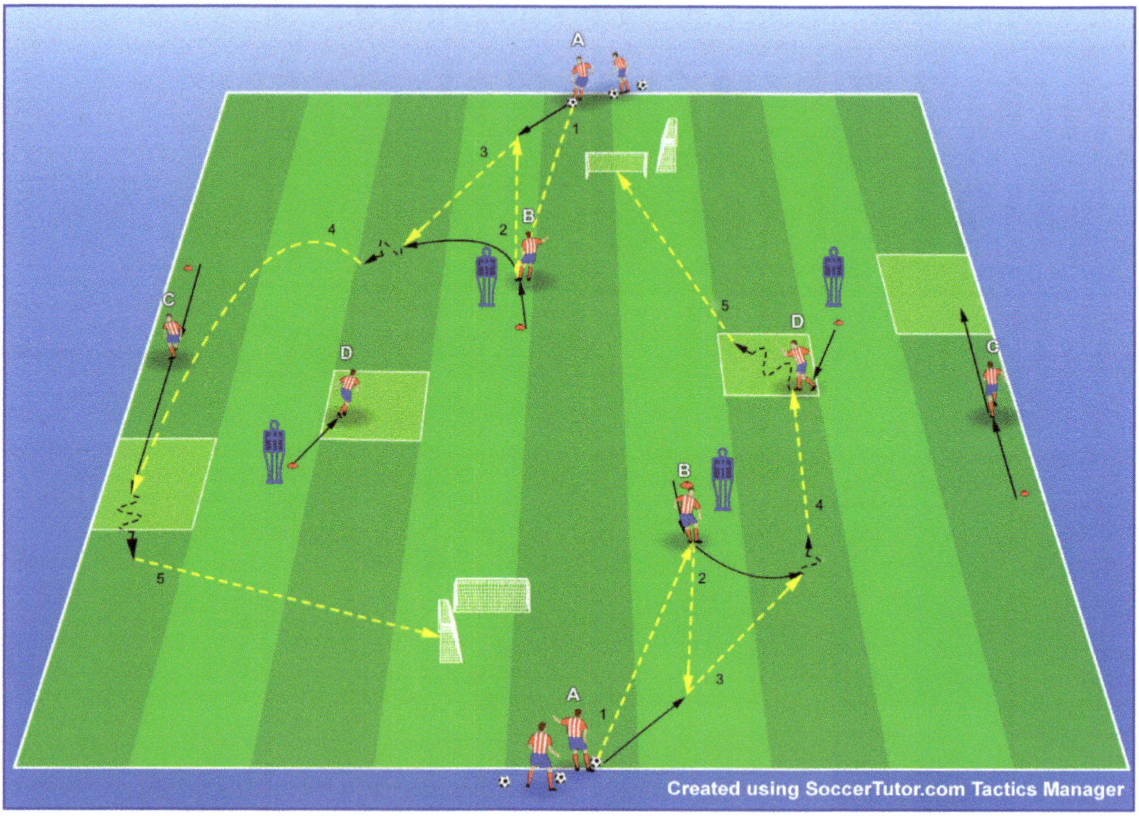

A = Centre back, **B** = Central midfielder, **C** = Full back, **D** = Wide midfielder.

Description (1/2)

- Within a 35 x 45 yard area, the wide areas are 5 x 8 yards and the central areas are 4 x 4 yards. The practice starts at both ends simultaneously with Player A.

- A starts by passing to B, who drops back. B then plays a 1-2 with A, opens up and turns.

- As soon as B receives the third pass, D drops back, and C moves forward.

Player B has 2 options for where to direct the ball:

1. On the left side, the ball is passed to C in the wide area, who dribbles the ball forward and crosses into the mini goal.

2. On the right side, the ball is passed to D in the central area, who receives, turns, and passes into the mini goal.

Each player moves to the next position (A -> B -> C -> D -> A). After practicing these different options on one side of the pitch (right), switch to practice them on the left side.

©SOCCERTUTOR.COM

DIEGO SIMEONE'S ATTACKING TACTICS

Tactical Situation 4 - Synchronised Movements of the Full Back and Wide Midfielder

PROGRESSION
2. Synchronised Movements of the Full Back and Wide Midfielder in a Functional Practice with Finish

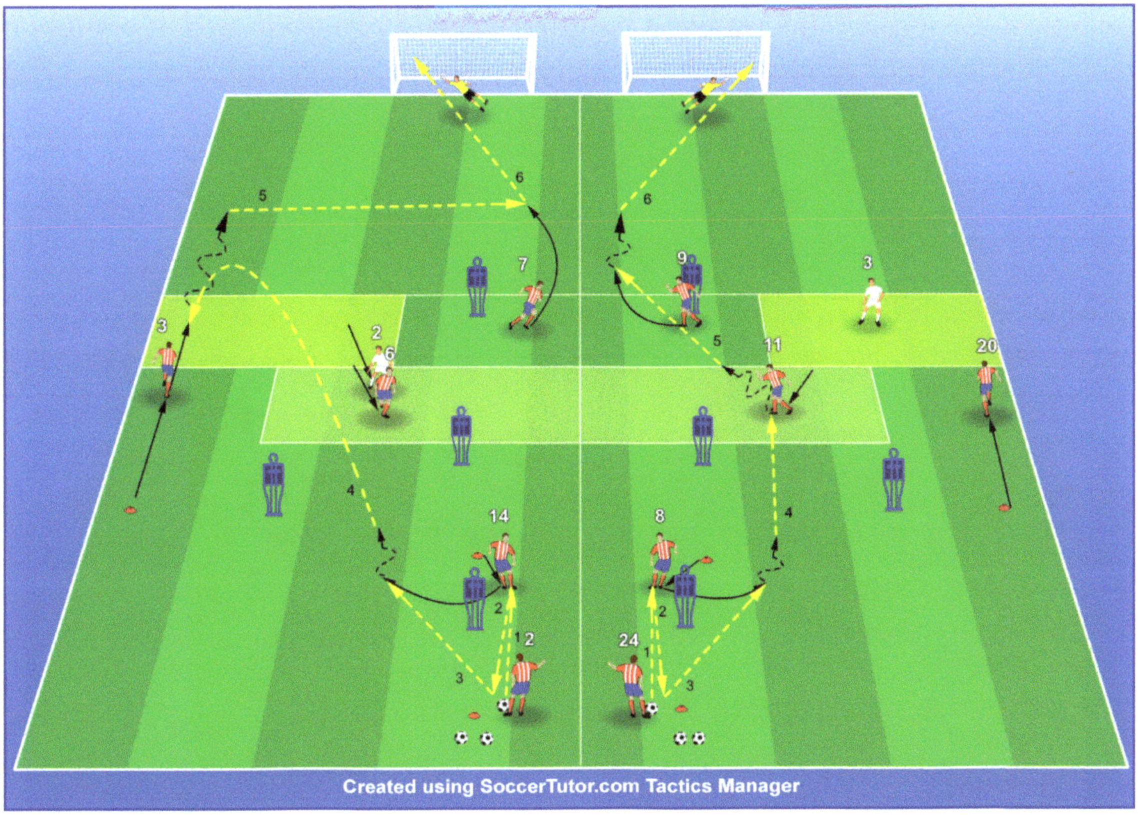

There can be 2 players in the wide midfielder and forward positions to keep a high tempo. The centre back and central midfielder switch positions after each repetition.

Description

- Within a 40 x 50 yard area, there are 12 x 5 yard wide areas and a 25 x 5 yard central area. The practice is played simultaneously in the 2 equal halves.

- The centre back (2/24) starts by passing to the central midfielder (14/8), who drops back. The central midfielder then plays a 1-2 with the centre back, opens up and turns.

- As soon as the central midfielder (14/8) receives the third pass, the wide midfielder (6/11) drops back and the full back (3/20) moves forward.

- LEFT SIDE: If the white full back No.2 follows the red left midfielder's (6) movement, the central midfielder (14) passes to the left back (3) in the wide area, who dribbles forward and delivers a cross for the forward (7) to score.

- RIGHT SIDE: If the white full back No.2 doesn't follow, the pass is played to the right midfielder's (11) feet in the central area. He turns and plays a final pass for the forward (9).

©SOCCERTUTOR.COM

DIEGO SIMEONE'S ATTACKING TACTICS

Tactical Situation 4 - Synchronised Movements of the Full Back and Wide Midfielder

PROGRESSION

3. Synchronised Movements of the Full Back and Wide Midfielder in a 10 v 4 (+GK) Functional Practice

Scenario A: Opposing Full Back Follows the Wide Midfielder's Movement

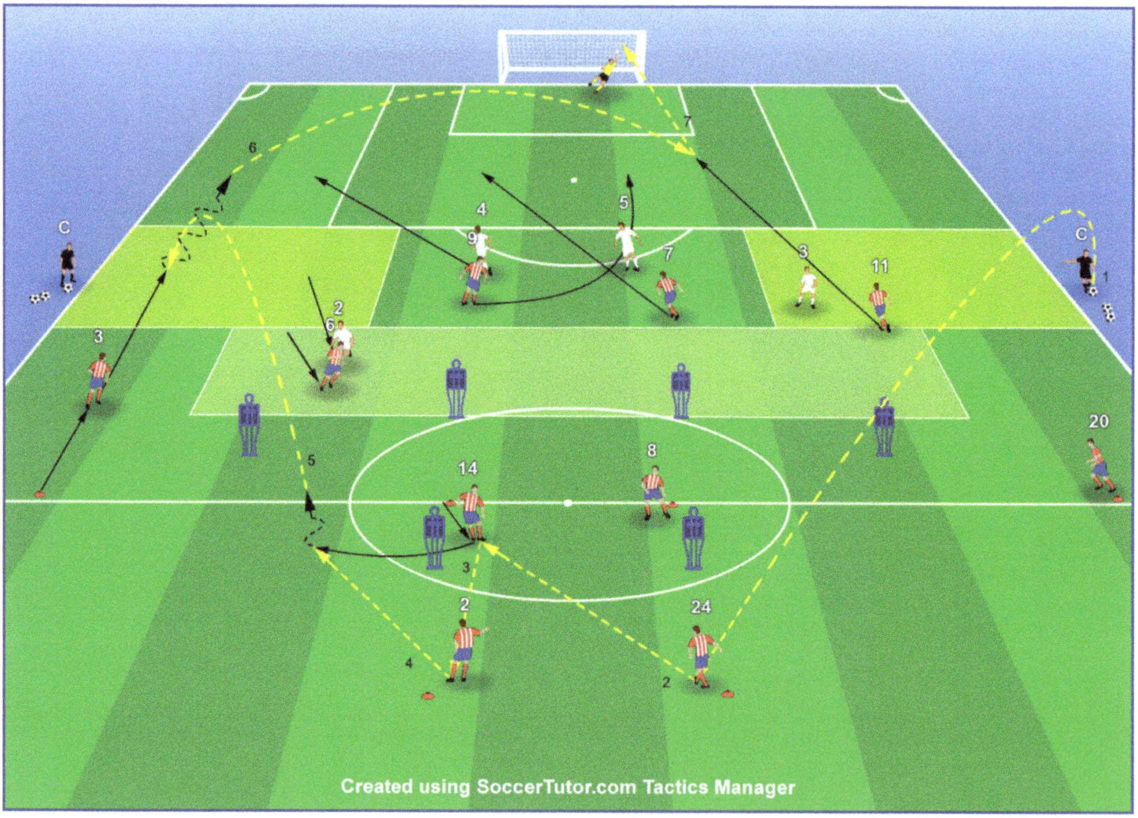

Description (Scenario A)

- In this progression of the previous practice, we add 2 white centre backs to increase the difficulty and play in 2/3 of a full pitch.

- The reds again aim to create and exploit an overload out wide.

- The practice starts with the Coach's long pass to a centre back **(2/24)**. The players combine until the central midfielder **(14/8)** opens up to receive and play forward.

- Decision making is extremely important, as the central midfielder **(14/8)** reads the reaction of the opposing full backs in order to direct the ball towards the right area.

- In this first example, the white right back No.2 follows the red left midfielder's **(6)** movement back into the central area.

- Therefore, the central midfielder **(14)** passes to the left back **(3)** in the wide area, who dribbles forward and delivers a cross.

©SOCCERTUTOR.COM

DIEGO SIMEONE'S ATTACKING TACTICS

Tactical Situation 4 - Synchronised Movements of the Full Back and Wide Midfielder

Scenario B: Opposing Full Back Retains Position

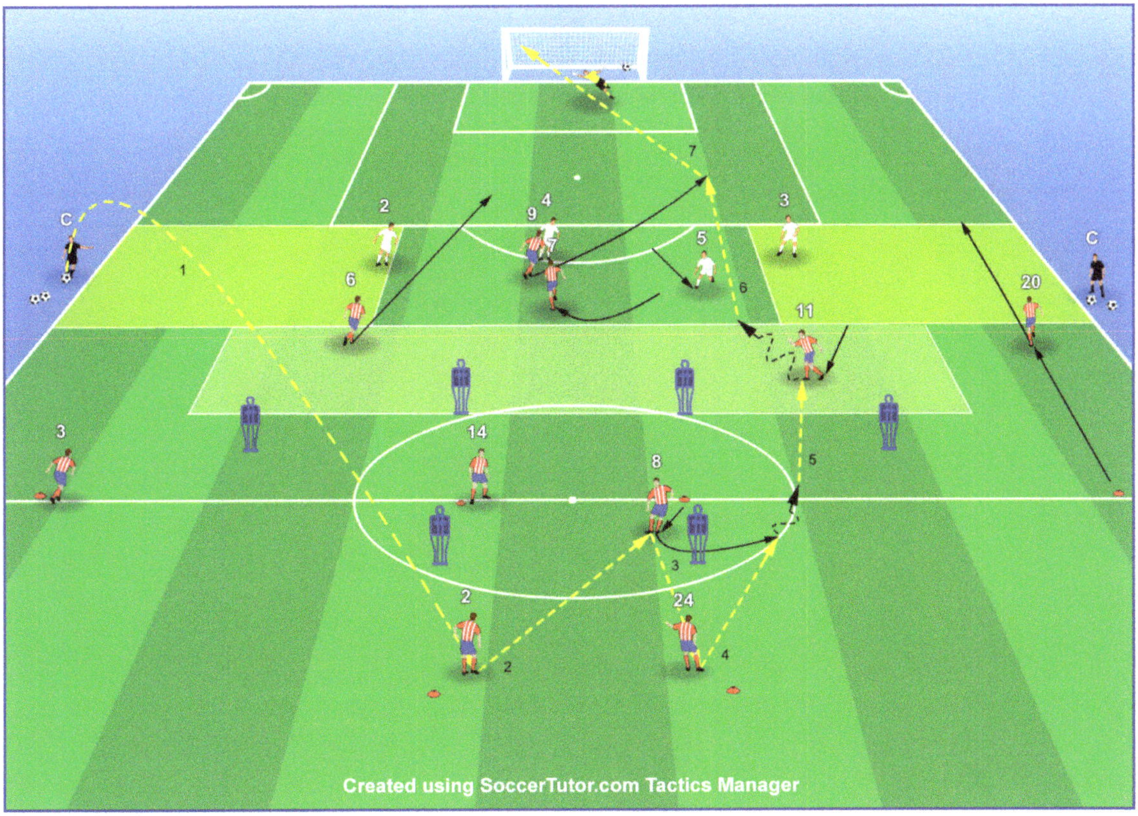

Description (Scenario B)

- In this second scenario, the red team create and exploit an overload on the right side of the pitch.

- The white left back No.3 doesn't follow the red right midfielder's **(11)** movement back into the central area.

- Therefore, the central midfielder's **(8)** pass is played to the right midfielder's **(11)** feet in the central area. He turns and plays a final pass for the forward **(9)** to score.

Coaching Points

1. There needs to be synchronisation in the players' movements (wide midfielder and full back).

2. Read the specific tactical situation and make the correct decision according to the opposing full back's reaction.

3. Accurate passes and crosses are needed, as the reds have to score against 4 defenders.

4. Accurate and quick finishing.

DIEGO SIMEONE'S ATTACKING TACTICS

Tactical Situation 4 - Synchronised Movements of the Full Back and Wide Midfielder

PROGRESSION

4. Synchronised Movements of the Full Back and Wide Midfielder in a Conditioned Game

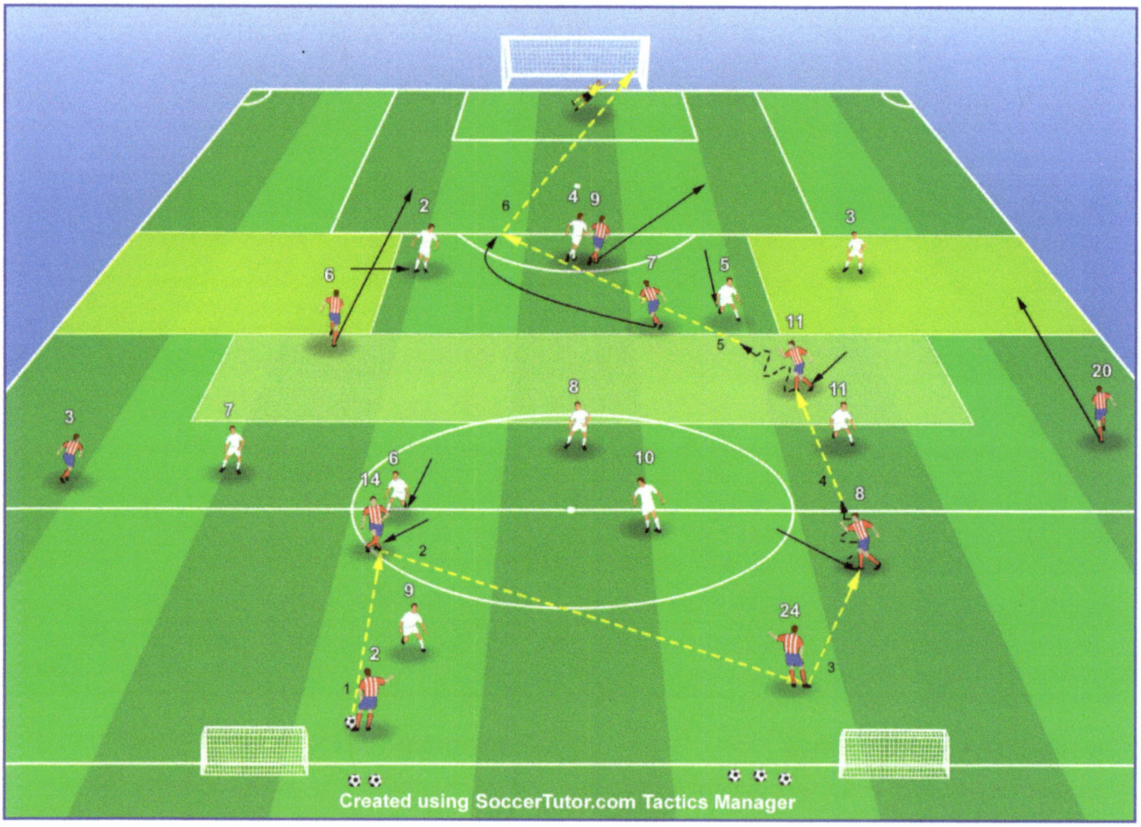

Description

- In the final practice of this session, the 2 teams play a 10v10 (+GK) game. The areas can be kept, or they can be removed.

- The reds try to create and exploit an overload out wide and score, while the whites try to win the ball and then score in the 2 mini goals.

- Please **see the previous practices and analysis pages** for the correct tactical solutions depending on the opposing full back's reactions.

Restriction: In the first 5 minutes of the game, the white central midfielders are not allowed to enter the central area unless there is a pass directed towards a red wide midfielder (**6 or 11**) or a full back (**3 or 20**).

Progression: 11v11 game using 2/3 of a full pitch. The reds can score in any way but if they do it after using synchronised movements of the wide midfielder and full back to create an overload out wide, they score 3 goals.

DIEGO SIMEONE'S ATTACKING TACTICS

TACTICAL SITUATION 5

Forward Exploits Space Behind the Opposing Full Back

The content in this section is from analysis of Diego Simeone's Atlético Madrid teams during the 2017/2018 and 2018/2019 seasons.

The analysis is based on recurring patterns of play observed within the Atlético Madrid team. Once the same phase of play occurred several times (at least 10), the tactics would be seen as a pattern. The analysis on the following pages are examples of the team's tactics being used effectively.

Each action, pass, individual movement with or without the ball, and the positioning of each player on the pitch including their body shape, are presented.

The analysis is then used to create a session to coach this specific tactical situation.

Tactical Situation 5 - Forward Exploits Space Behind the Opposing Full Back

FORWARD EXPLOITS SPACE BEHIND THE OPPOSING FULL BACK WITH WIDE MIDFIELDERS CENTRAL

1. Available Space for the Forwards to Exploit Behind the Opposing Full Backs with the Wide Midfielders in Central Positions

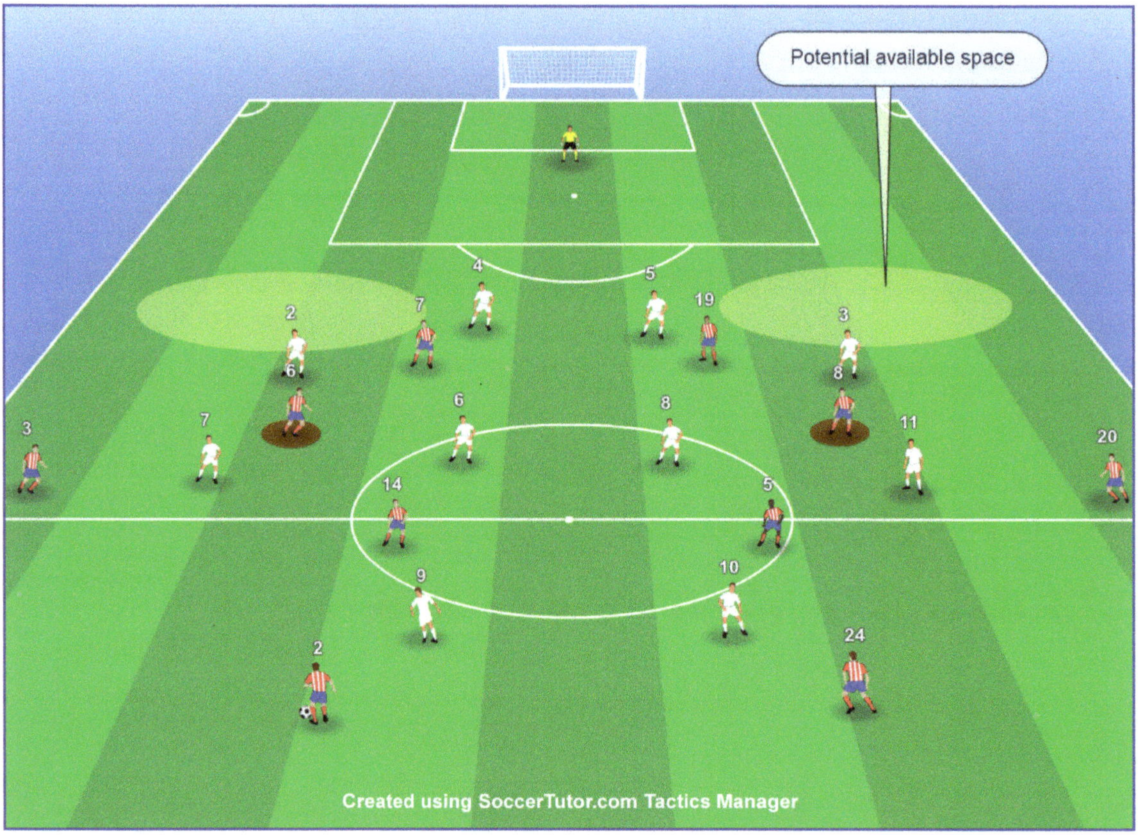

The central and deep positioning of the Atlético Madrid's wide midfielders is likely to force the opposing full backs to take up more advanced positions.

As the Atlético full backs **F. Luis (3)** and **Juanfran (20)** were in deep positions, they were unable to exploit the potential available space behind the opposing full backs.

This potential available space is exploited by the Atlético forwards **Griezmann (7)** and **D. Costa (19)**.

DIEGO SIMEONE'S ATTACKING TACTICS

Tactical Situation 5 - Forward Exploits Space Behind the Opposing Full Back

2a. Opposing Full Back Moves Forward to Mark the Wide Midfielder and Space is Created Behind Him

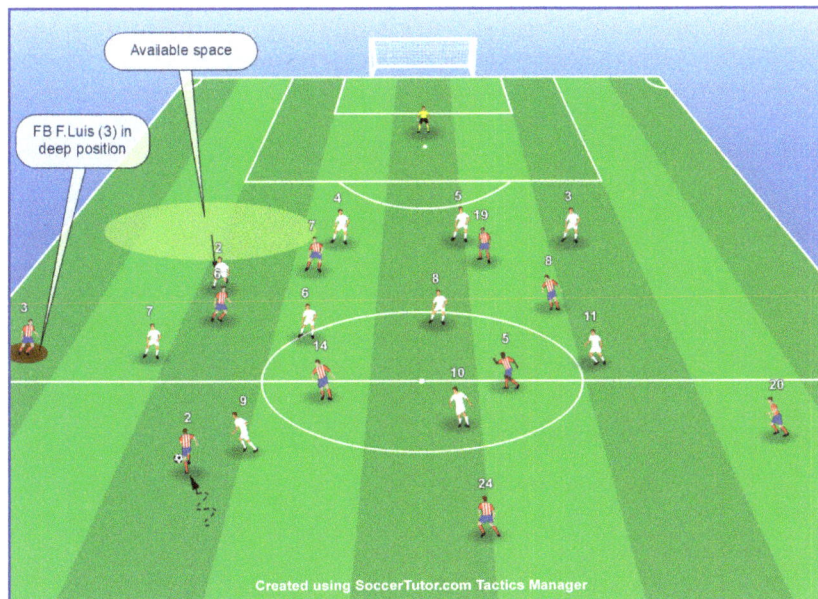

The characteristics of the forwards enables them to exploit the space behind the full backs as they are quick.

The centre back **Godín (2)** has space to move forward. The white right back No.2 notices the deep position of the Atlético left back **F. Luis (3)** and moves close to the left midfielder **Koke (6)** to prevent him from receiving unmarked.

This action creates space behind white No.2.

2b. Centre Back Plays a Direct Pass into the Space Behind the Opposing Full Back

The space behind the opposing right back No.2 is exploited with a diagonal run from the forward on that side **Griezmann (7)**.

The centre back **Godín (2)** sees the opportunity and plays a long pass into the available space for the Atlético forward to exploit.

DIEGO SIMEONE'S ATTACKING TACTICS

Tactical Situation 5 - Forward Exploits Space Behind the Opposing Full Back

3. Passing to the Wide Midfielder to Drag the Opposing Full Back Out of Position and Create Space in Behind

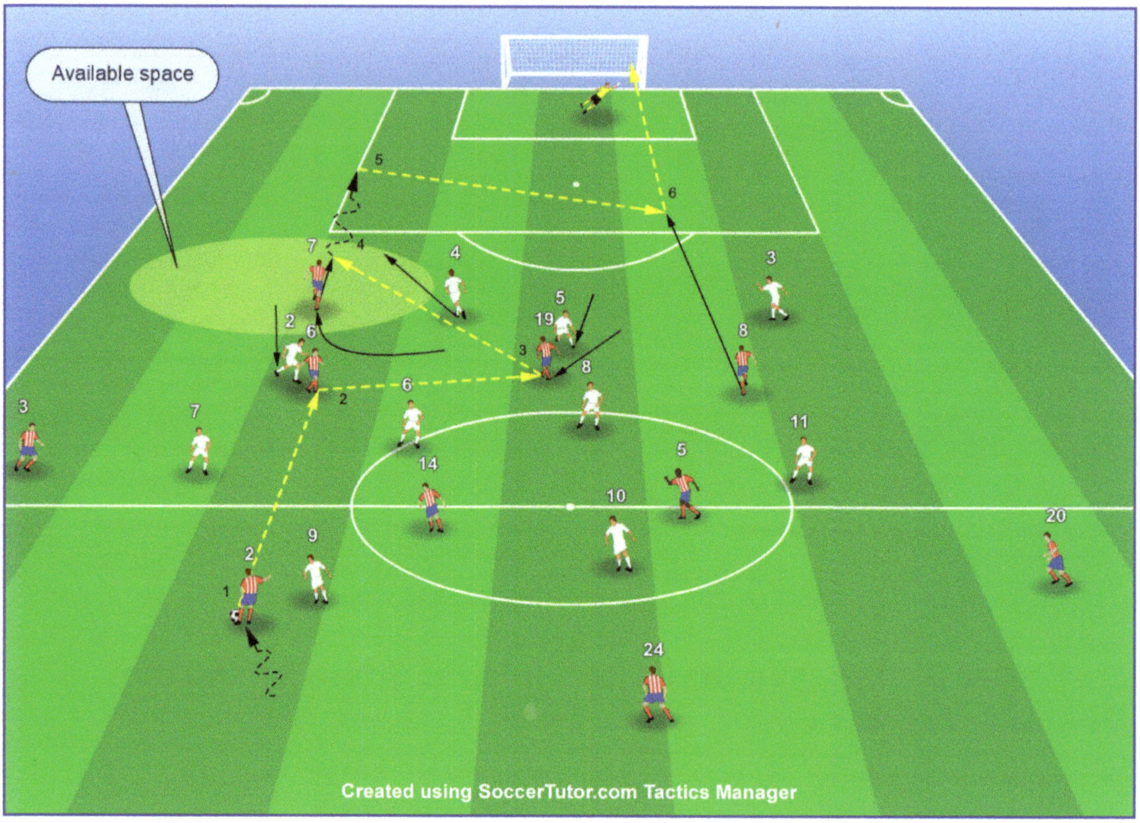

If the opposing full back is not in an advanced position close to the Atlético wide midfielder, he could be dragged out of position by passing the ball to the wide midfielder.

As soon as the ball is passed by **Godín (2)** towards the left midfielder **Koke (6)**, the white right back No.2 moves forward to put him under pressure. The available space behind No.2 can be exploited with a passing combination.

The forward on the weak side **D. Costa (19)** moves to provide a passing option and **Koke (6)** passes inside to him. **D. Costa (19)** can then pass the ball into the available space behind the white No.2.

In this situation, another benefit is created with the forward on the strong side **Griezmann (7)** dragging the opposing centre back No.4 out of position.

This means that **Griezmann (7)** has a 1v1 situation against white No.4 after receiving from **D. Costa (19)** because the other white centre back No.5 is too far away to provide support.

NOTE: Both **Griezmann (7)** and **D. Costa (19)** have been capable of exploiting situations like this in the best possible way. It would most often end in them delivering a cross for a team-mate to shoot at goal.

Tactical Situation 5 - Forward Exploits Space Behind the Opposing Full Back

4. Forward on the Weak Side Moves to Receive Unmarked Between the Lines and Turn for a 3 v 3 Attack in the Final Third

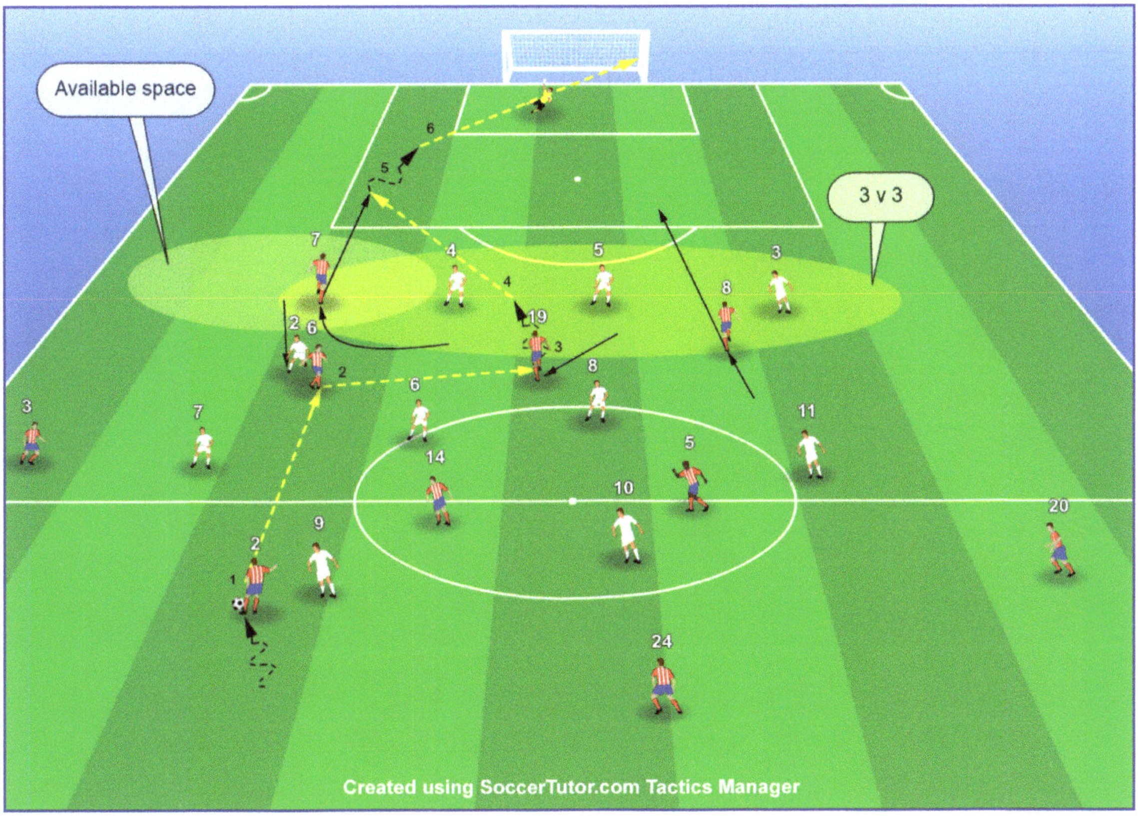

In this variation, the white centre back No.5 does not move to contest the forward **D. Costa (19)** when the pass from the right midfielder **Koke (6)** is played.

Therefore, **D. Costa (19)** is able to receive unmarked between the lines and turn towards goal.

Diego Simeone's Atlético Madrid team then look to exploit a 3 v 3 situation to try and score, with the same space available towards the left side again.

The forward on the weak side **D. Costa (19)** again moves to provide a passing option and **Koke (6)** passes inside to him. **D. Costa (19)** can then pass the ball in behind for the run of the other forward **Griezmann (7)**.

DIEGO SIMEONE'S ATTACKING TACTICS

Tactical Situation 5 - Forward Exploits Space Behind the Opposing Full Back

5. Full Back Plays a Direct Pass into the Space Behind the Opposing Full Back After Receiving Wide from the Centre Back

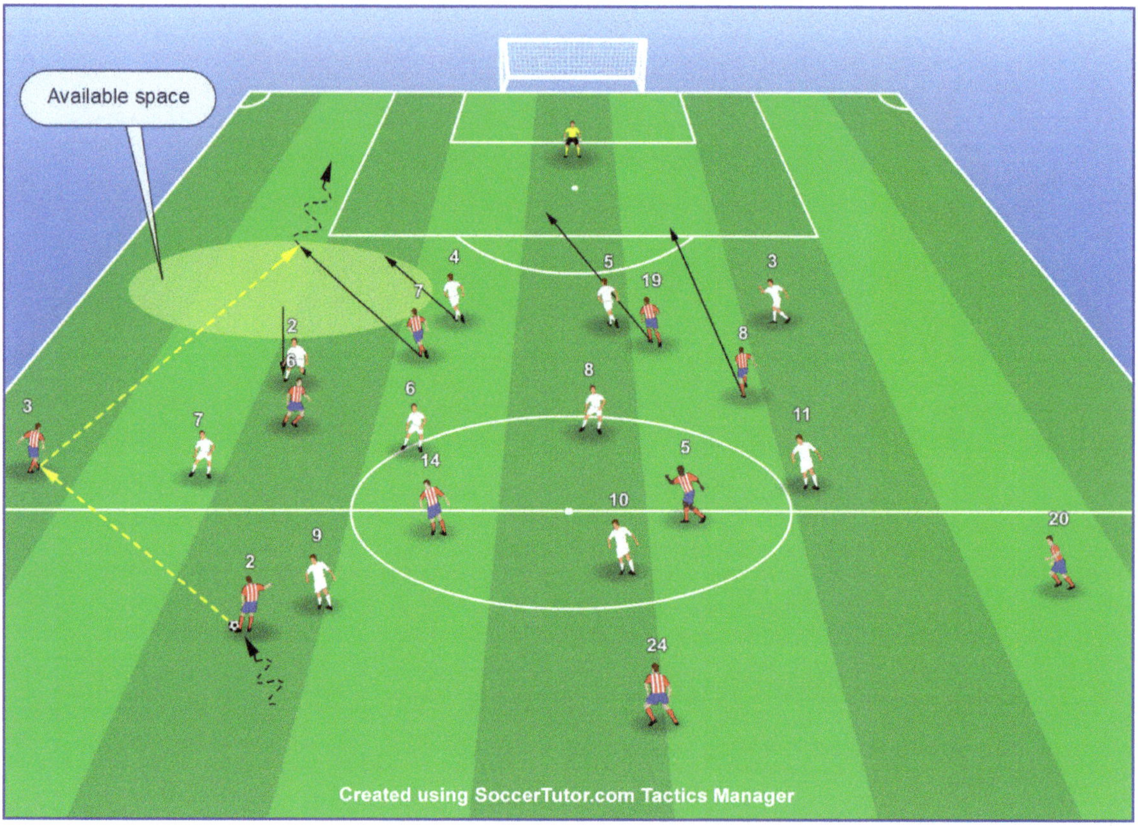

Here is another option to exploit the space behind the opposing full back.

As soon as the centre back **Godín (2)** dribbles the ball forward and the left midfielder **Koke (6)** is in a favourable position between the lines to receive a pass from him, the opposing right back No.2 moves close to him. This reaction creates available space in behind white No.2.

Instead of passing directly into the space, **Godín (2)** decides to move the ball wide to the left back **F. Luis (3)**.

F. Luis (3) then directs the ball towards the available space with a ground pass for the forward **Griezmann (7)** to receive in a dangerous position.

 **ASSESSMENT**

All options displayed have proved highly effective for Atlético to create scoring chances. If the opposing full back doesn't follow the wide midfielder and defends the space, the wide midfielder can receive free of marking and turn between the lines (4v4 attack).

Tactical Situation 5 - Forward Exploits Space Behind the Opposing Full Back

VARIATION: FORWARD CREATES SPACE FOR THE WIDE MIDFIELDER IN THE CENTRE

Forward Drags the Centre Back Wide to Create Space for the Wide Midfielder's Forward Run in the Centre

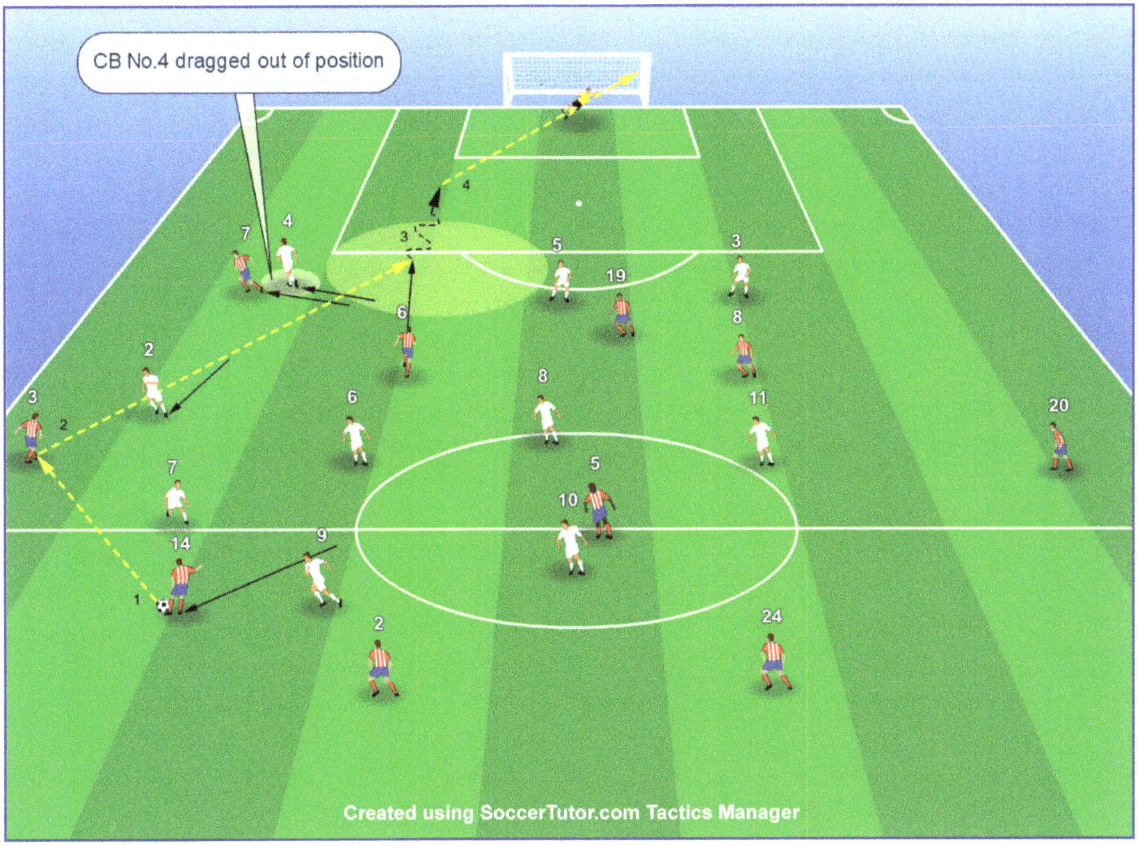

There were situations for Atlético when the ball was moved to the full back in a wide position and the forward made a movement towards the side-line. This action forced the opposing centre back to follow him (dragged out of position).

This created space in the centre for the wide midfielder, who was already in a central position.

In this example, the ball is passed to the left back **F. Luis (3)**, who is in a high position.

As soon as **F. Luis (3)** receives, the white right back No.2 moves to press him, so the forward **Griezmann (7)** makes a run towards the side-line and into the space behind white No.2.

The white centre back No.4 follows **Griezmann (7)** and space is created in the centre. This is exploited by the left midfielder **Koke (6)**, who receives the diagonal pass from **F. Luis (3)** in a favourable position to shoot at goal.

DIEGO SIMEONE'S ATTACKING TACTICS

Tactical Situation 5 - Forward Exploits Space Behind the Opposing Full Back

FORWARD EXPLOITS SPACE BEHIND THE FULL BACK WITH WIDTH CREATED BY WIDE MIDFIELDER

1. Left Midfielder Provides the Width Due to the Central Positioning of the Left Back

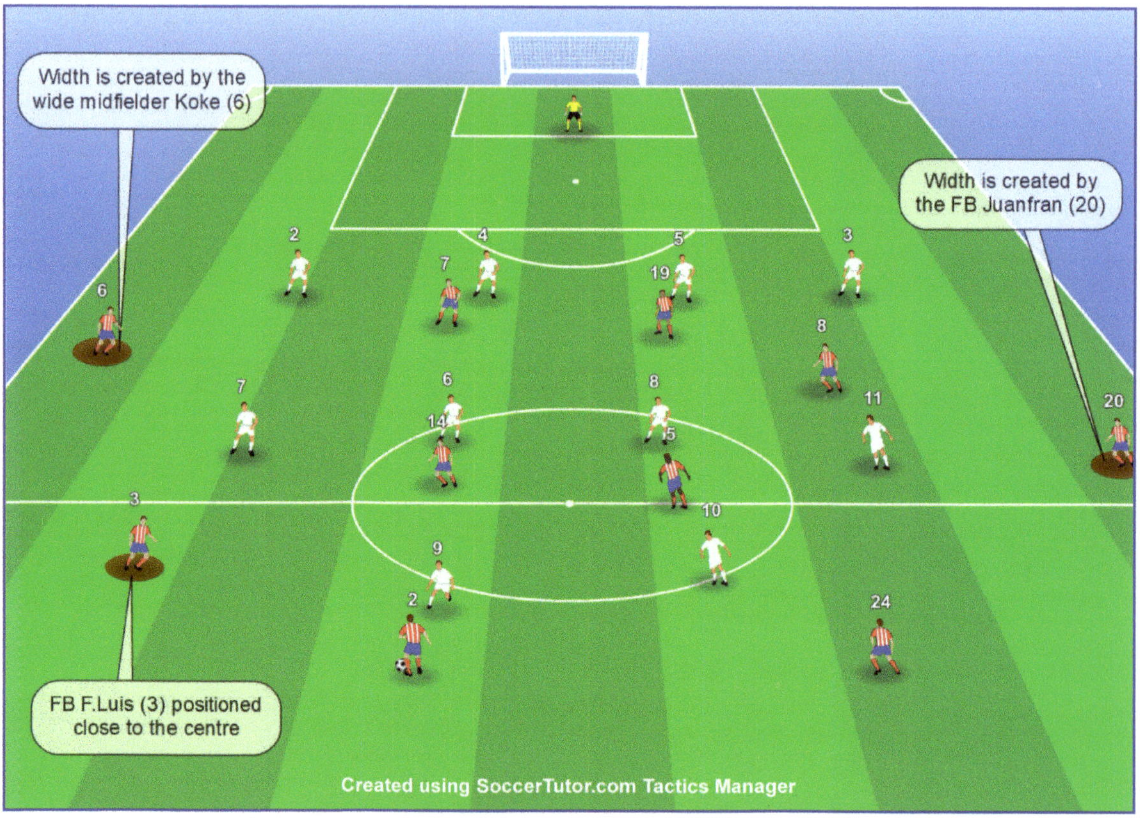

On the previous pages in this section, we have shown tactical examples where the Atlético wide midfielders are both positioned centrally and the full backs provide the width. This is the most common occurrence.

However, there are situations when an Atlético full back is more centrally positioned. When this happens, the wide midfielder must react and move towards the side-line to create the width on that side.

In this example, the Atlético left back **F. Luis (3)** is positioned closer to the centre than usual.

Therefore, the left midfielder **Koke (6)** provides the width on the left side of the pitch.

The potential available space to exploit behind the opposing full back is now different and is explained on the **next 2 pages**.

DIEGO SIMEONE'S ATTACKING TACTICS

Tactical Situation 5 - Forward Exploits Space Behind the Opposing Full Back

2a. Wide Midfielder Drops Back to Receive in the Best Possible Position with Time and Space Available

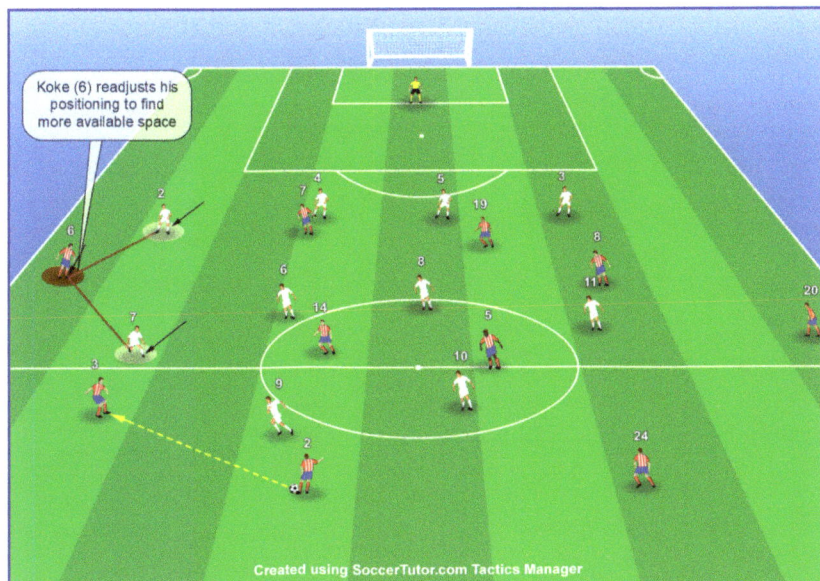

When the ball is passed to the left back **F. Luis (3)** and he is pressed by white No.7, the left midfielder **Koke (6)** drops back a few yards to take up the best possible position, which is in the middle of the white right back No.2 and the right midfielder No.7.

This positioning ensures **Koke (6)** has more available time and space if he receives a pass.

2b. Opposing Full Back Presses After the Pass is Played and the Wide Midfielder is Able to Receive, Turn and Pass

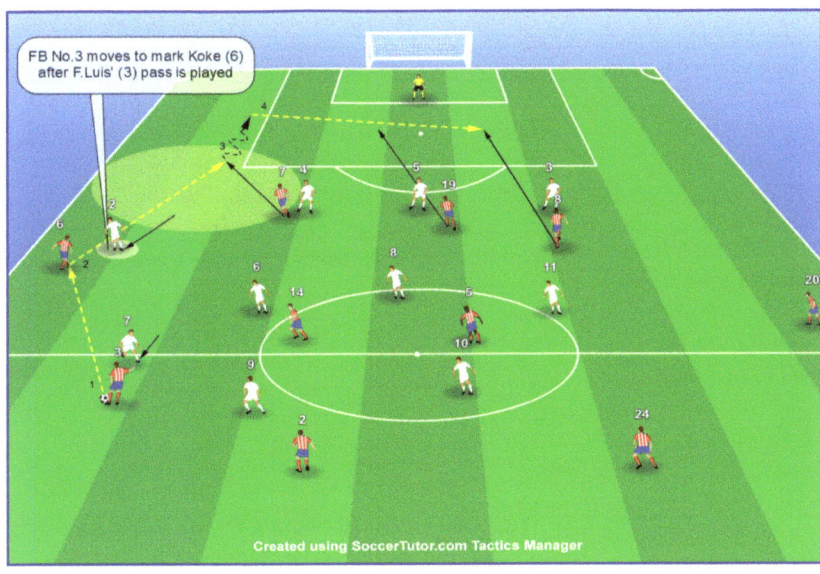

When the ball is passed to **Koke (6)**, he has time to turn and face the opposition's goal before white No.2 is able to close him down.

As white No.2 moves forward after the pass has been played by **F. Luis (3)** to press **Koke (6)**, space is created behind him.

The space is exploited by the forward **Griezmann (7)**, who makes a run and receives the pass in behind from **Koke (6)**.

©SOCCERTUTOR.COM   DIEGO SIMEONE'S ATTACKING TACTICS

Tactical Situation 5 - Forward Exploits Space Behind the Opposing Full Back

3. Opposing Full Back Moves Forward to Mark the Wide Midfielder Early and the Forward Exploits the Space Created Behind

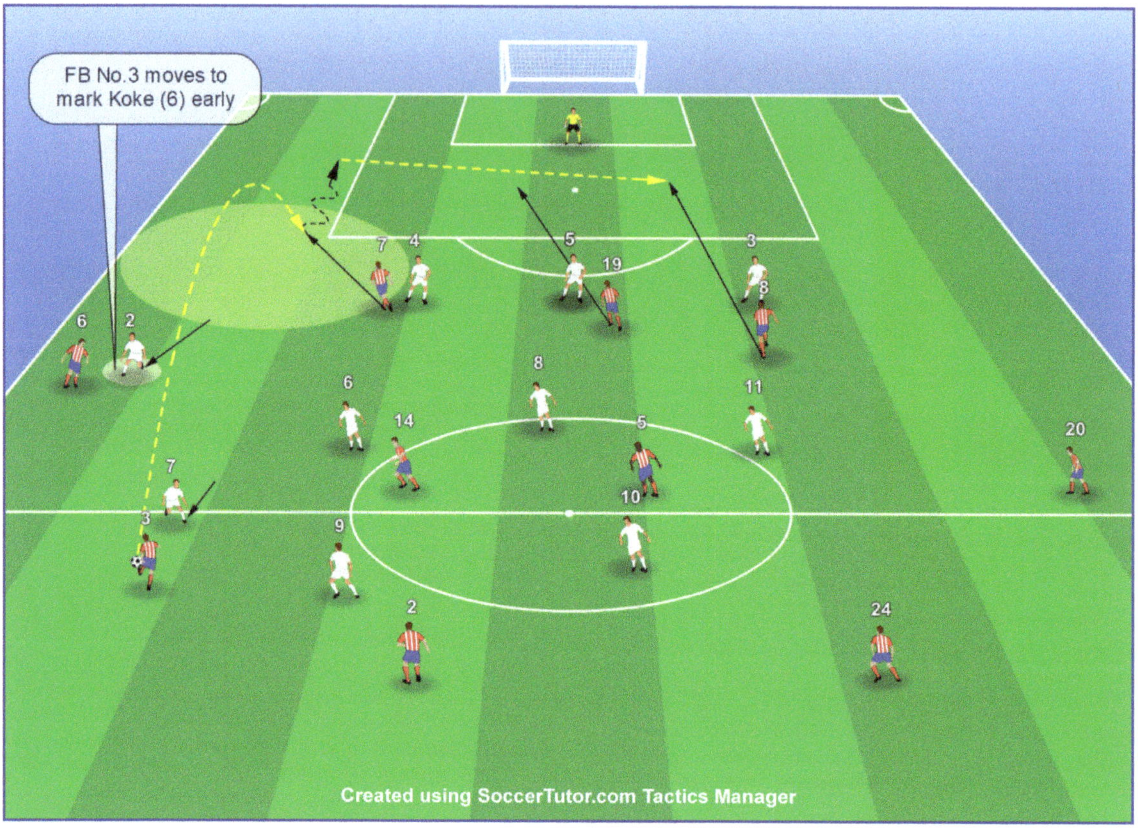

This is a variation of the previous tactical example. This time, the white right back No.2 moves forward to mark **Koke (6)** before any pass is played towards him.

If a pass is played towards **Koke (6)**, then white No.2 will be able to prevent him from turning. However, space is created behind white No.2, which the forward **Griezmann (7)** can exploit.

Griezmann (7) makes a run into the available space. Instead of passing to **Koke (6)**, the left back **F. Luis (3)** directs the ball towards the available space with a direct long pass for the forward **Griezmann (7)** to receive in a dangerous position.

ASSESSMENT

The characteristics of the Atlético forwards were all suited to take advantage of the situations described in this section. **Griezmann**, **Diego Costa**, **Kevin Gameiro**, **Angel Correa**, and **Fernando Torres** are all quick and able to exploit the available spaces.

©SOCCERTUTOR.COM   DIEGO SIMEONE'S ATTACKING TACTICS

SESSION (4 PRACTICES) FOR "FORWARD EXPLOITS SPACE BEHIND THE OPPOSING FULL BACK"

Tactical Situation 5 - Forward Exploits Space Behind the Opposing Full Back

SESSION FOR THIS TACTICAL SITUATION (4 PRACTICES)
1. Forward Exploits Space Behind the Opposing Full Back in a Technical Practice with Finish
Options 1 & 2: Long Passes into the Available Space

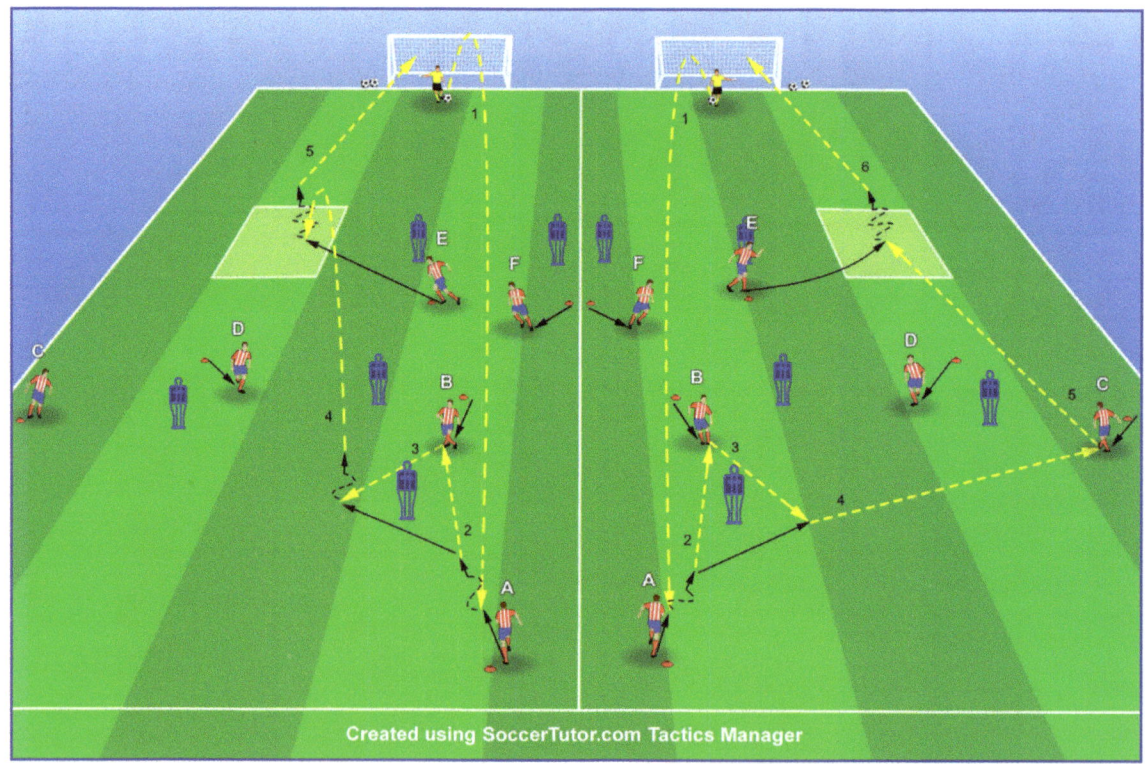

A = Centre back, **B** = Central midfielder,
C = Full back, **D** = Wide midfielder,
E = Strong side forward, **F** = Weak side forward

Description (Options 1 & 2)
- The practice starts with a long pass from the GK to the centre back (**A**) on both sides simultaneously.
- The centre back (**A**) plays a 1-2 with the central midfielder (**B**) and receives on the other side of the mannequin.
- The wide midfielder (**D**) drops back. From this point, Player A has 4 options. The aim is for a forward to receive in the white area and score.

In this first diagram, options 1 and 2 are shown:

1. On the left side of the diagram, the centre back (**A**) plays a long aerial pass into the white area for the forward on the strong side (**E**) to receive and score.

2. On the right side of the diagram, the centre back (**A**) passes to the full back (**C**), who drops back. **C** receives and hits a ground pass towards the same area for the forward (**E**).

©SOCCERTUTOR.COM   DIEGO SIMEONE'S ATTACKING TACTICS

Tactical Situation 5 - Forward Exploits Space Behind the Opposing Full Back

Options 3 & 4: Forward on the Weak Side Moves to Receive

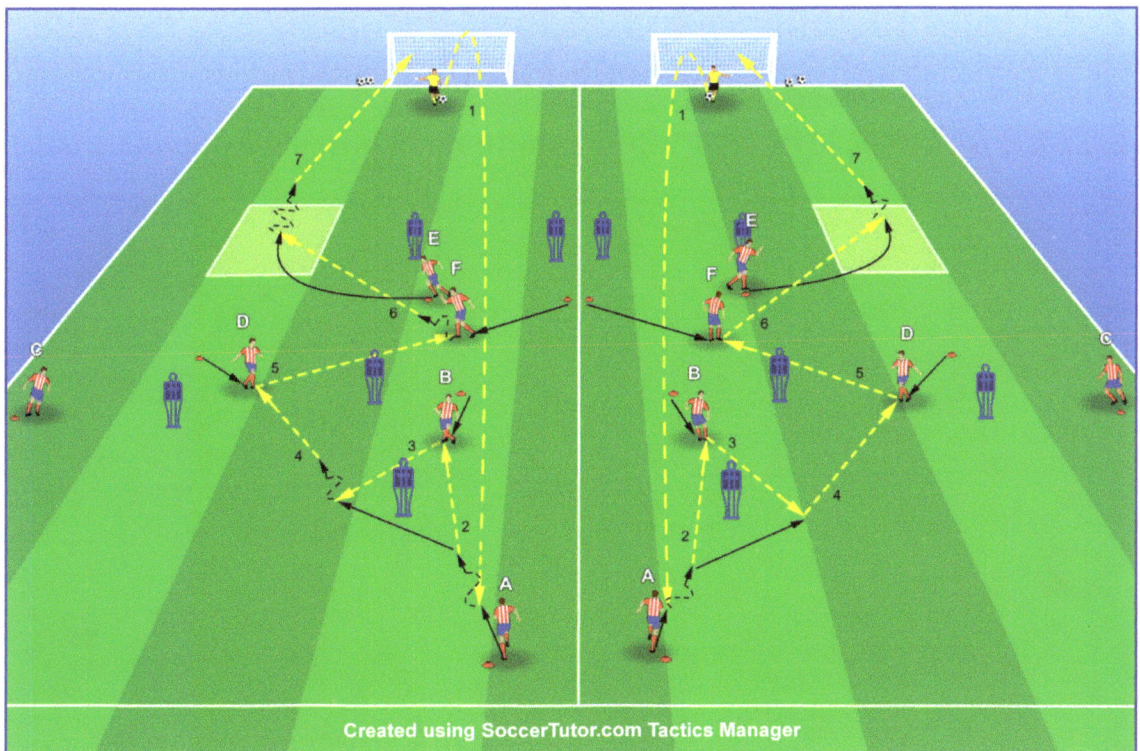

Description (Options 3 & 4)

On this second diagram, options 3 and 4 are shown:

3. On the left side of this second diagram, the centre back's **(A)** pass is directed to the wide midfielder **(D)** who passes first-time inside to the forward on the weak side **(F)**. Player **F** receives, turns, and passes into the path of the other forward **(E)** to receive within the white area and score.

4. On the right side of the diagram, the forward on the weak side **(F)** does not receive and turn. Instead, he passes first-time into the white area for the other forward **(E)**.

After each repetition, A switches positions with B, C switches positions with D and E switches positions with F.

Coaching Points

1. There needs to be synchronisation in the players' movements (wide midfielder and forward).
2. Accurate and well timed passes.
3. Accurate finishing.

DIEGO SIMEONE'S ATTACKING TACTICS

Tactical Situation 5 - Forward Exploits Space Behind the Opposing Full Back

PROGRESSION
2. Forward Exploits Space Behind the Opposing Full Back in a Functional Practice with Finish

Scenario A: Direct Aerial Pass from Centre Back into the Available Space

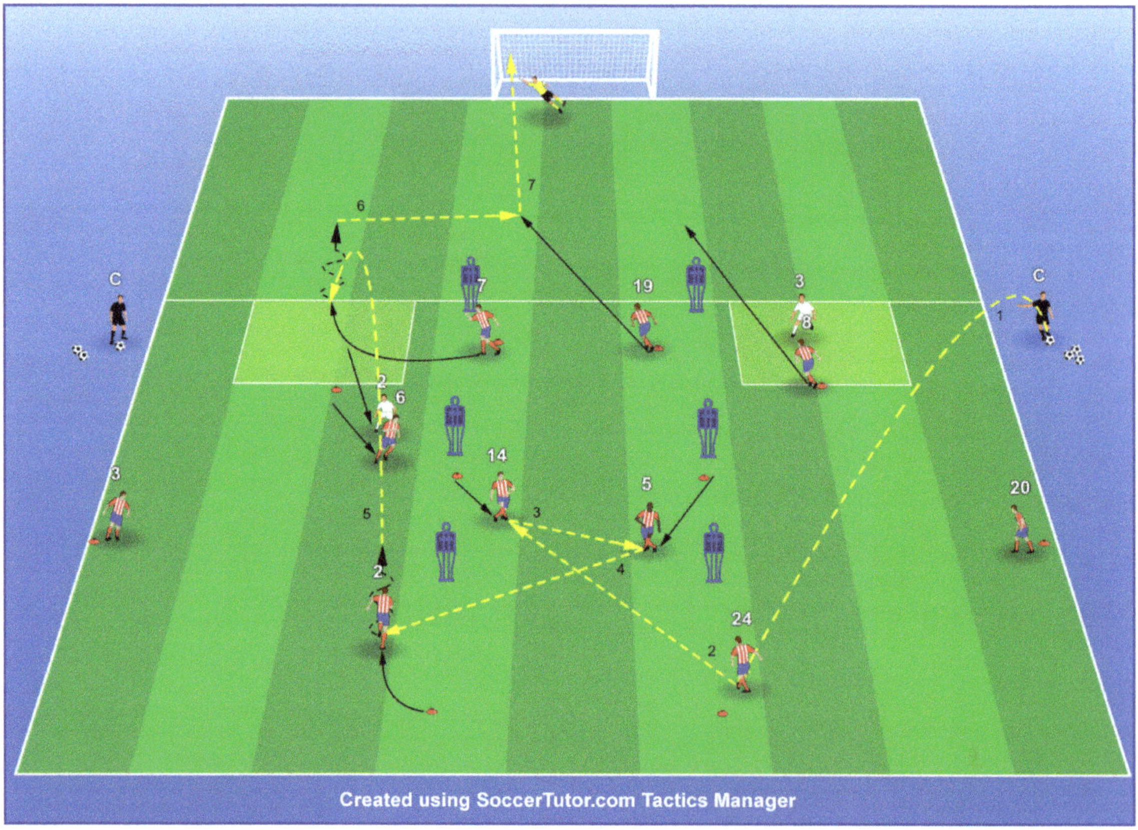

Created using SoccerTutor.com Tactics Manager

Description (Scenario A)

- In a 40 x 50 yard area, the 2 small wide areas are 8 x 7 yards.

- The 2 white full backs are coached to follow the red wide midfielders **(6 and 8)** each time they drop back to receive a pass.

- The practice starts with the Coach's pass to a centre back **(24** in diagram), who passes to the central midfielder on the weak side **(14)**.

- The other central midfielder **(5)** drops back to receive the lay-off and pass to the other centre back **(2)**, who receives and dribbles the ball forward.

- The wide midfielder **(6)** then drops back and is followed by the white right back No.2.

- In this example, the centre back **(2)** plays an aerial pass into the wide area for the forward **(7)** to receive in the space behind white No.2.

DIEGO SIMEONE'S ATTACKING TACTICS

Tactical Situation 5 - Forward Exploits Space Behind the Opposing Full Back

Scenario B: Ground Pass from Full Back into the Available Space

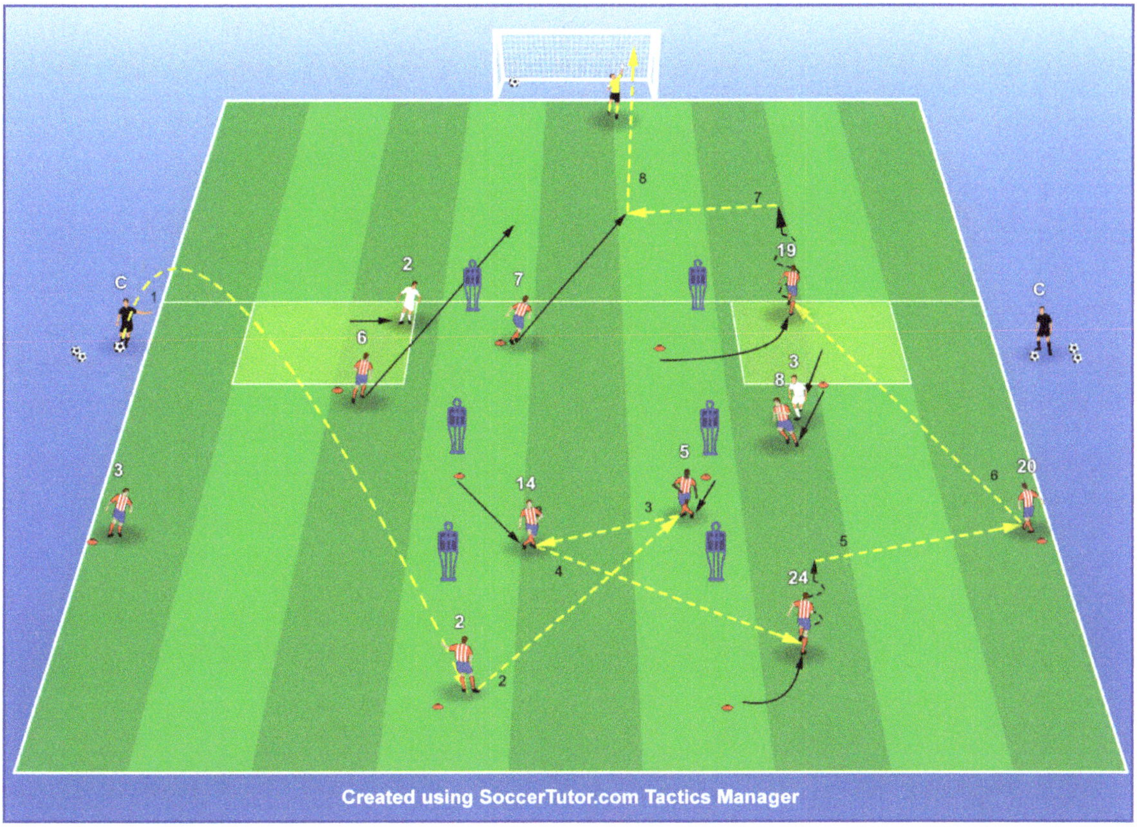

Description (Scenario B)

- In this second scenario, the ball is moved from left to right and the other centre back **(24)** dribbles the ball forward.

- The wide midfielder **(8)** has dropped back and is followed by the white left back No.3.

- The centre back **(24)** does not pass directly to the forward this time and instead passes out wide to the full back **(20)**.

- The full back **(20)** drills a ground pass into the wide area for the forward **(19)** to receive in the space behind white No.3.

DIEGO SIMEONE'S ATTACKING TACTICS

Tactical Situation 5 - Forward Exploits Space Behind the Opposing Full Back

Scenario C: Forward on the Weak Side Moves to Receive

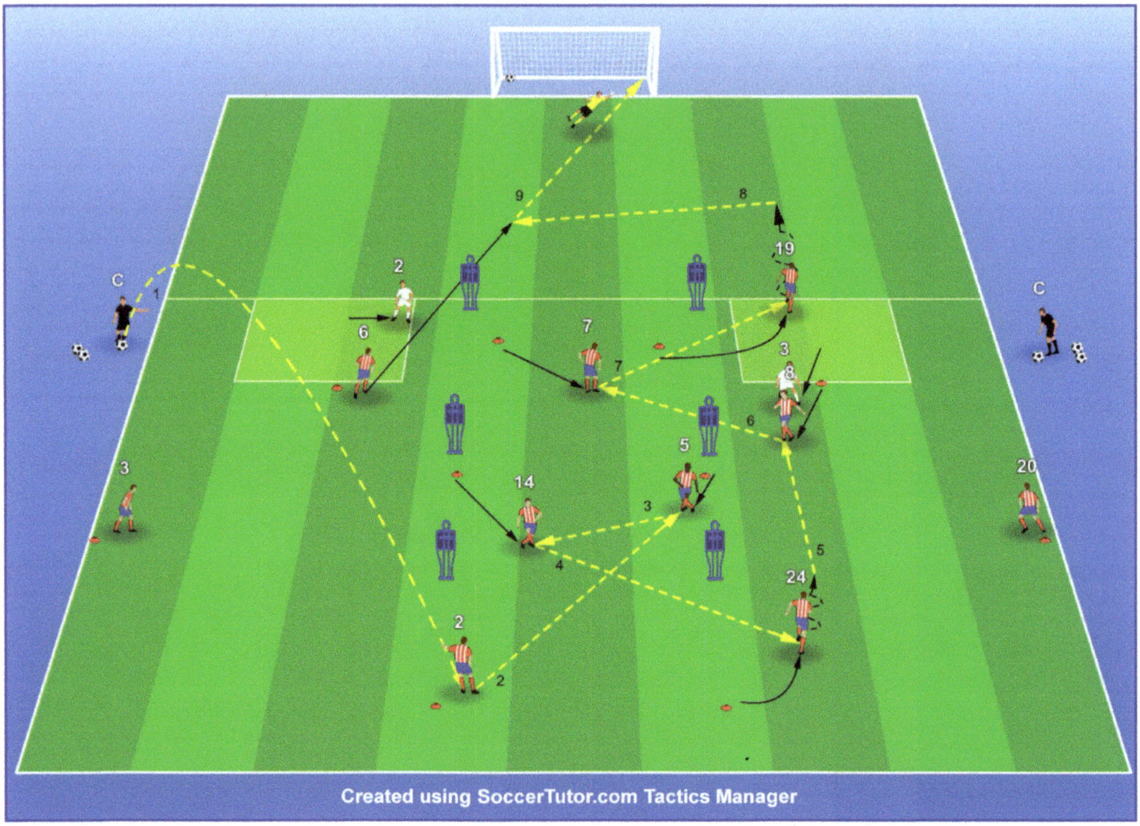

Description (Scenario C)

- In this third scenario, combination play is used to move the ball into the space behind the opposing full back.

- In the previous 2 examples, the centre back passes directly to the forward or to the full back. This time, the centre back **(24)** passes to the wide midfielder **(11)**, who is being marked by the white left back No.3.

- The wide midfielder **(8)** passes inside to the forward on the weak side **(7)**, who moves across to receive and passes to the other forward within the wide area behind white No.3.

Progressions

1. The white full backs decide whether they follow the red wide midfielders or not. The red players then have to use the correct reactions (**see analysis in this section**).

2. Add 2 centre backs to make it more difficult for the reds to score.

Coaching Points

1. There needs to be synchronisation in the players' movements (wide midfielder and forward).

2. Read the situation and make decisions according to the opposing full back's reaction.

DIEGO SIMEONE'S ATTACKING TACTICS

Tactical Situation 5 - Forward Exploits Space Behind the Opposing Full Back

PROGRESSION

3. Forward Exploits Space Behind the Opposing Full Back in a Functional Game

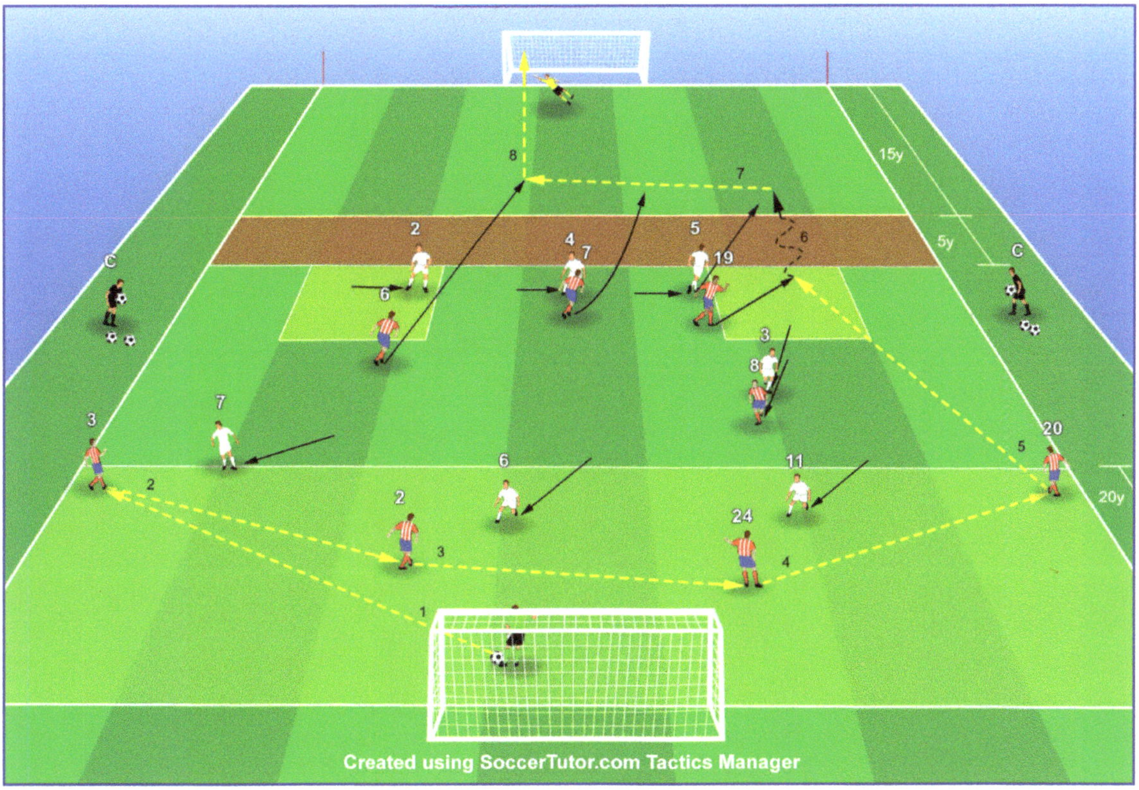

Description

In a 40 x 50 yard area, we play a 9v8 game. There is a 40 x 20 yard white low zone and a red high zone which is 40 x 5 yards. There are also 2 small yellow areas, which represent the potential space behind the full backs.

The 2 white full backs are coached to follow the red wide midfielders **(6/8)** each time they drop back.

The red GK starts and the reds aim to drag an opposing full back out of position, exploit the space created behind him and score.

- Please **see the previous practices and analysis pages** for the correct decision making.

If the reds choose the wrong decision or make an unsuccessful pass, the Coach throws a new ball in for the whites to score within 12-15 seconds.

Restrictions

1. The white centre backs and full backs cannot enter the red zone.
2. The red full backs **(3/20)** always stay inside the white low zone (deep positions), so that the white full backs always follow the wide midfielders **(6/8)**.

DIEGO SIMEONE'S ATTACKING TACTICS

Tactical Situation 5 - Forward Exploits Space Behind the Opposing Full Back

PROGRESSION
4. Forward Exploits Space Behind the Opposing Full Back in a Conditioned Game

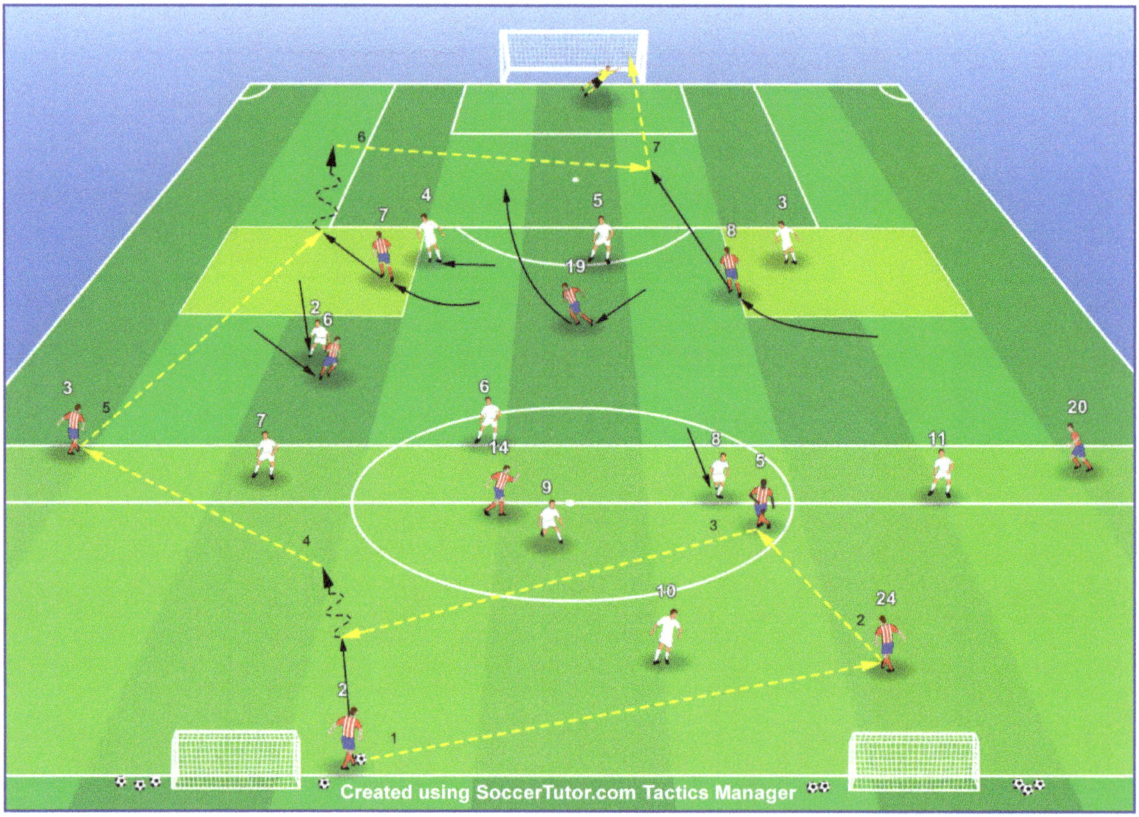

Description

- In the final practice of this session, the 2 teams play a 10 v 10 (+GK) game in 2/3 of the pitch. You can have the areas marked out to help the players or not.

- The practice starts with the reds in a 6 v 5 situation in the low white zone, as 1 of the white central midfielders has to always stay outside of it (No.6 in diagram example).

- The reds can score in any way, but if they score after a forward successfully exploits space created behind an opposing full back, they score 3 goals.

- Please **see the previous practices and analysis pages** for the correct decision making.

- The red full backs stay within the white low zone in the first phase and they can be used to move the ball behind the opposing full back (as shown in the diagram example). As soon as a forward pass is made, then the full backs can move forward and support their team-mates.

- The white team try to win the ball and then score in the mini goals within 12-15 seconds.

Coaching Points: Same as previous practice.

DIEGO SIMEONE'S ATTACKING TACTICS

TACTICAL SITUATION 6

Forward Drops Back to Receive or Create Space in Behind

The content in this section is from analysis of Diego Simeone's Atlético Madrid teams during the 2017/2018 and 2018/2019 seasons.

The analysis is based on recurring patterns of play observed within the Atlético Madrid team. Once the same phase of play occurred several times (at least 10), the tactics would be seen as a pattern. The analysis on the following pages are examples of the team's tactics being used effectively.

Each action, pass, individual movement with or without the ball, and the positioning of each player on the pitch including their body shape, are presented.

The analysis is then used to create a session to coach this specific tactical situation.

Tactical Situation 6 - Forward Drops Back to Receive or Create Space in Behind

FORWARD DROPS BACK TO RECEIVE OR CREATE SPACE IN BEHIND

1. Opposing Centre Back Retains Position and the Forward Drops Back to Receive Unmarked Between the Lines

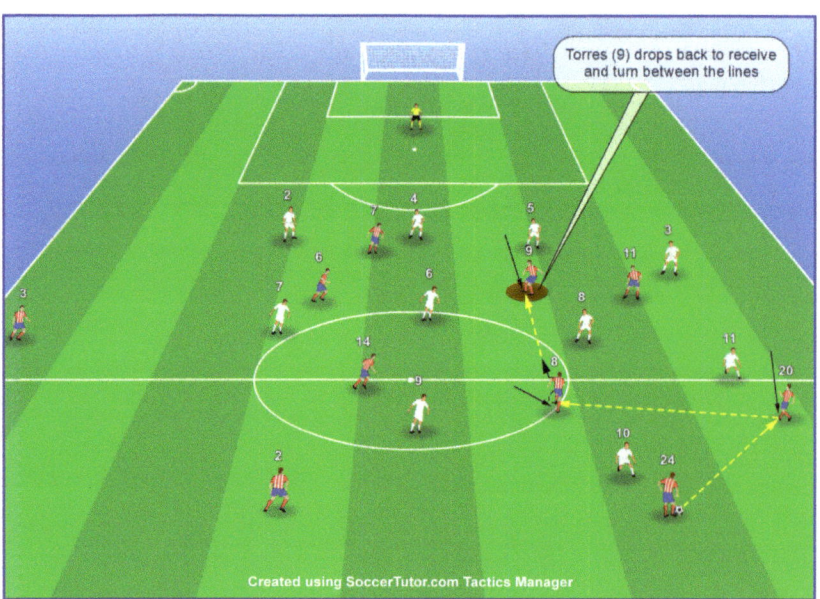

When the Atlético central midfielders manage to receive unmarked or the defenders found space to move forward with the ball in a central area, the forward closest to the ball usually dropped back between the lines to receive.

This action creates a dilemma for the opposing centre back, who must decide whether to follow the movement.

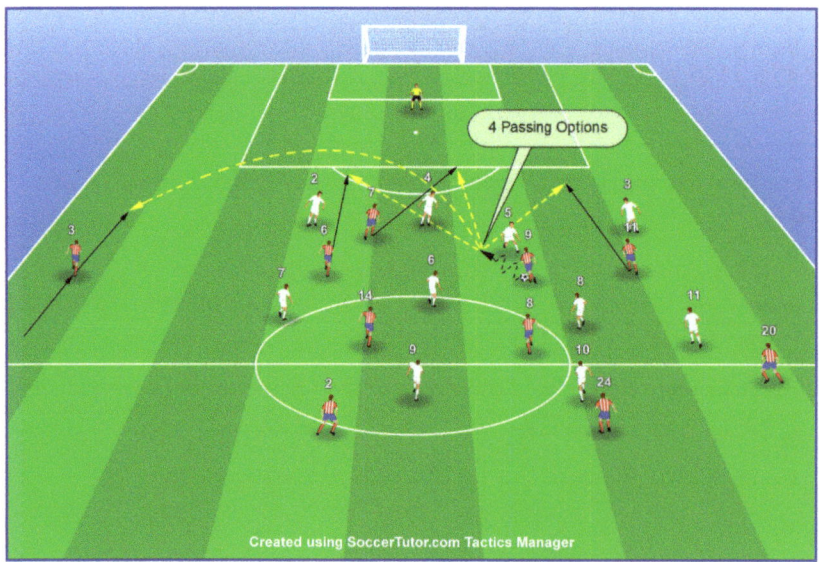

Atlético tried to take advantage of this situation but the correct option depended on the reaction of the opposing centre back.

In this first example, the white centre back No.5 initially decides to defend the space rather than follow the forward **Torres (9)**.

Torres (9) is then able to receive and turn free of marking between the lines.

©SOCCERTUTOR.COM   DIEGO SIMEONE'S ATTACKING TACTICS

Tactical Situation 6 - Forward Drops Back to Receive or Create Space in Behind

2. Opposing Centre Back Follows the Forward Dropping Back and the Other Forward Exploits the Space Created in Behind

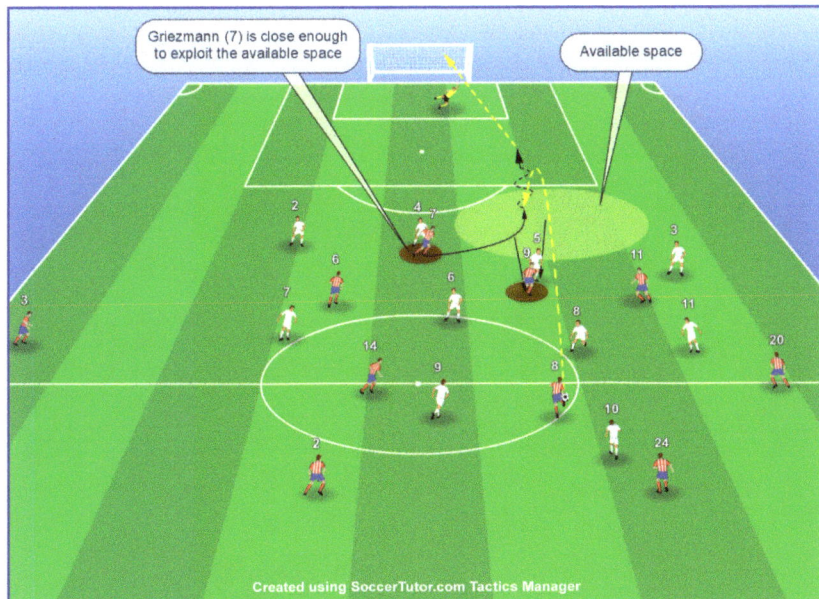

If the opposing centre back No.5 follows the Atlético forward **Torres' (9)** dropping back movement, then space is created in behind immediately.

If the other forward **Griezmann (7)** was close enough, this space was exploited by him.

The central midfielder **Saúl (8)** plays a long aerial pass into the created space for **Griezmann (7)** to receive in behind.

3. Opposing Centre Back Moves to Press the Forward when the Pass is Made, and the Space is Exploited with a Passing Combination

If white No.5 only presses after the pass is played to prevent the turn, **Torres (9)** passes inside to the wide midfielder **Koke (6)**, who is already in a central position between the lines.

Koke (6) receives unmarked inside the **Crucial Central Area**. His best option is to direct the ball into the available space behind white No.5. This is for **Griezmann (7)** in this example.

©SOCCERTUTOR.COM   DIEGO SIMEONE'S ATTACKING TACTICS

Tactical Situation 6 - Forward Drops Back to Receive or Create Space in Behind

4. Wide Midfielder Makes Run to Exploit the Space Created when the Forward on the Weak Side is Too Far Away

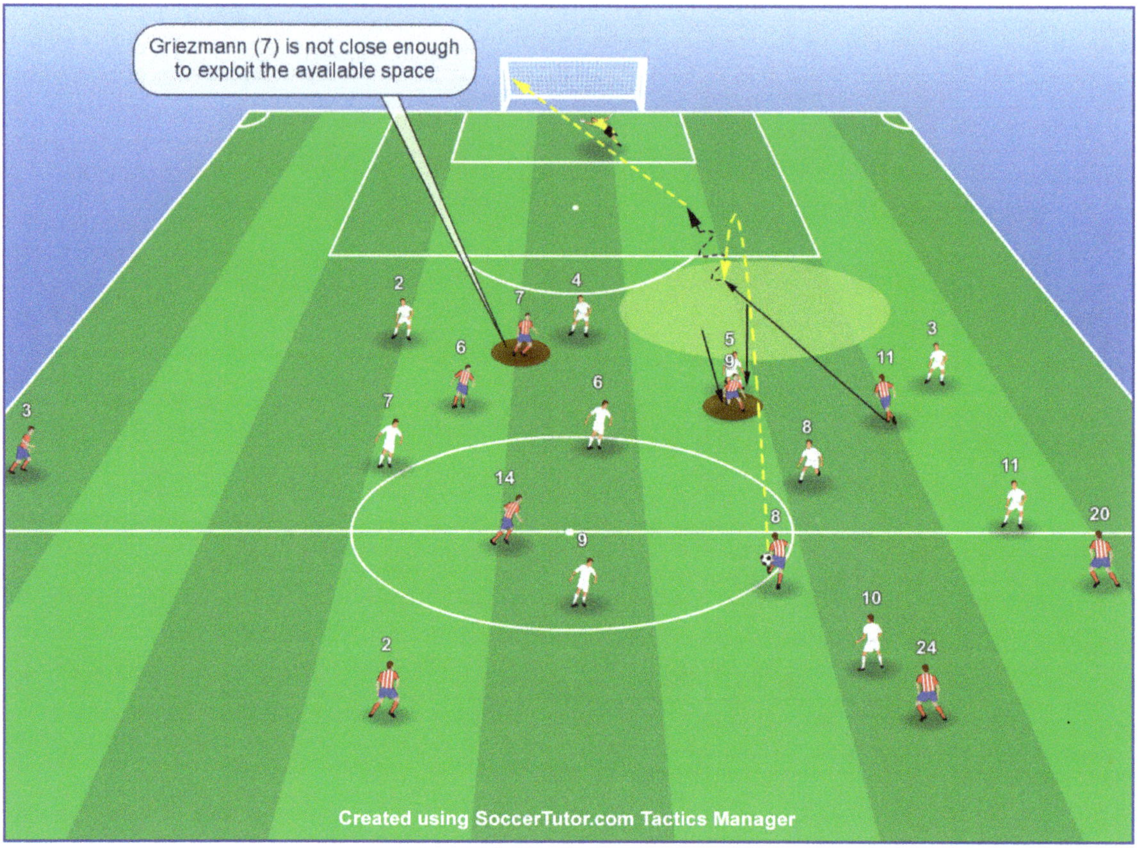

There were also situations when the forward on the weak side was too far away to take advantage of the space behind the centre back.

Depending on the reaction of the opposing centre back, the space created behind him was exploited by the wide midfielder with a direct pass in behind or via a passing combination.

In this example, white No.5 follows the dropping back movement of the forward **Torres (9)**.

As the other forward **Griezmann (7)** is too far away to exploit the space behind white No.5 it is the right midfielder **Correa (11)** who runs into the available space and receives the direct aerial pass from the central midfielder **Saúl (8)**.

 **ASSESSMENT**

The Atlético right midfielder **Correa (11)** was highly effective when exploiting these kinds of situations, as the Argentine has the required speed to take advantage of the space. In contrast, the left midfielder **Koke (6)** isn't the perfect option to exploit a situation like this, as his characteristics are different.

©SOCCERTUTOR.COM — DIEGO SIMEONE'S ATTACKING TACTICS

Tactical Situation 6 - Forward Drops Back to Receive or Create Space in Behind

5. Wide Midfielder Makes Run to Exploit the Space Created After a Passing Combination

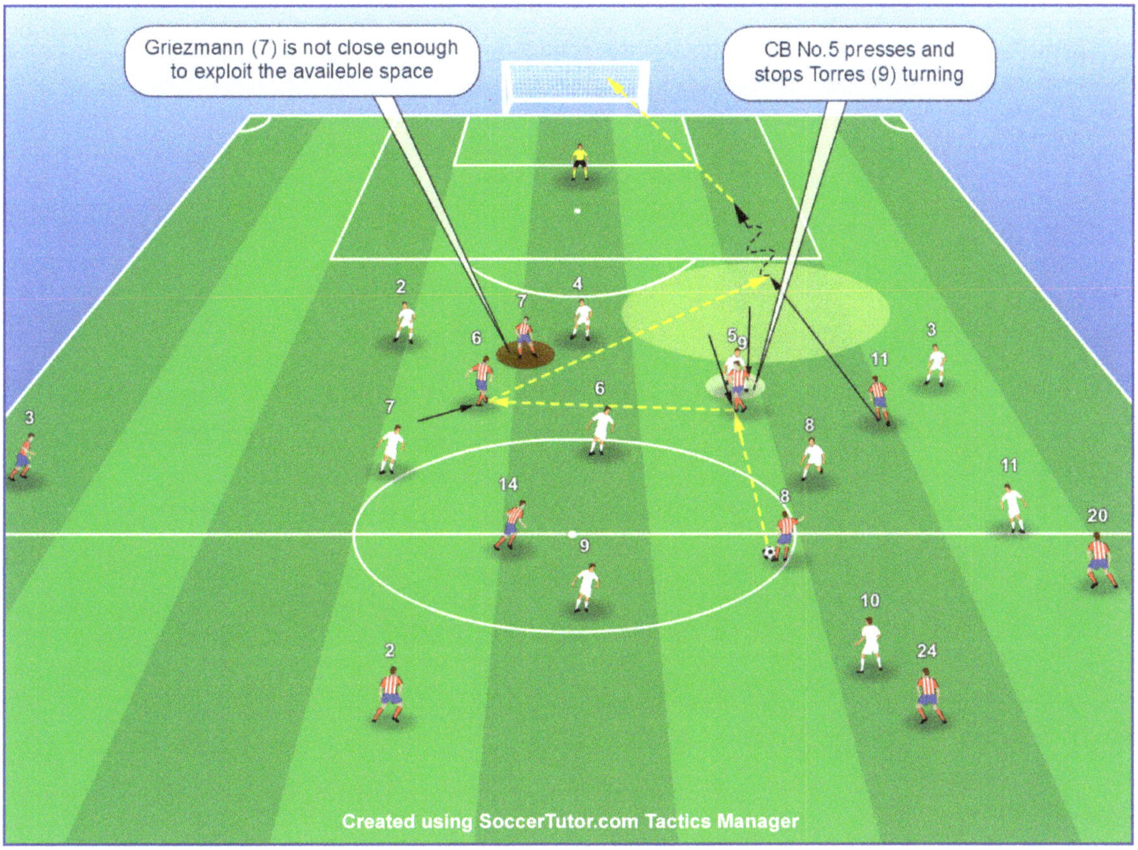

This is a similar situation to the previous one, but with a different reaction from the opposing centre back No.5, who waits for the pass to be played before moving to press **Torres (9)**.

In this situation, Atlético use combination play and a third man run.

As soon as the inside pass from **Torres (9)** to **Koke (6)** is played, the right midfielder **Correa (11)** starts his forward run into the available space behind white No.5.

The ball is then passed to him by **Koke (6)**, who uses a maximum of 1 or 2 touches.

ASSESSMENT

Be aware that the right midfielder **Correa (11)** can also receive a square pass from **Torres (9)**. It is very important for **Koke (6)** and **Correa (11)** to read his body shape.

If **Torres (9)** is half-turned towards **Koke (6)**, then **Correa (11)** should be ready to start his forward run. If **Torres (9)** is half-turned towards **Correa (11)**, then he should expect a pass from him and search for another option as soon as he receives.

SESSION (4 PRACTICES) FOR "FORWARD DROPS BACK TO RECEIVE OR CREATE SPACE IN BEHIND"

Tactical Situation 6 - Forward Drops Back to Receive or Create Space in Behind

SESSION FOR THIS TACTICAL SITUATION (4 PRACTICES)
1. Forward Drops Back to Receive or Create Space in Behind in a Technical Practice with Finish

Scenario A: Forward on Weak Side Exploits Space Created in Behind

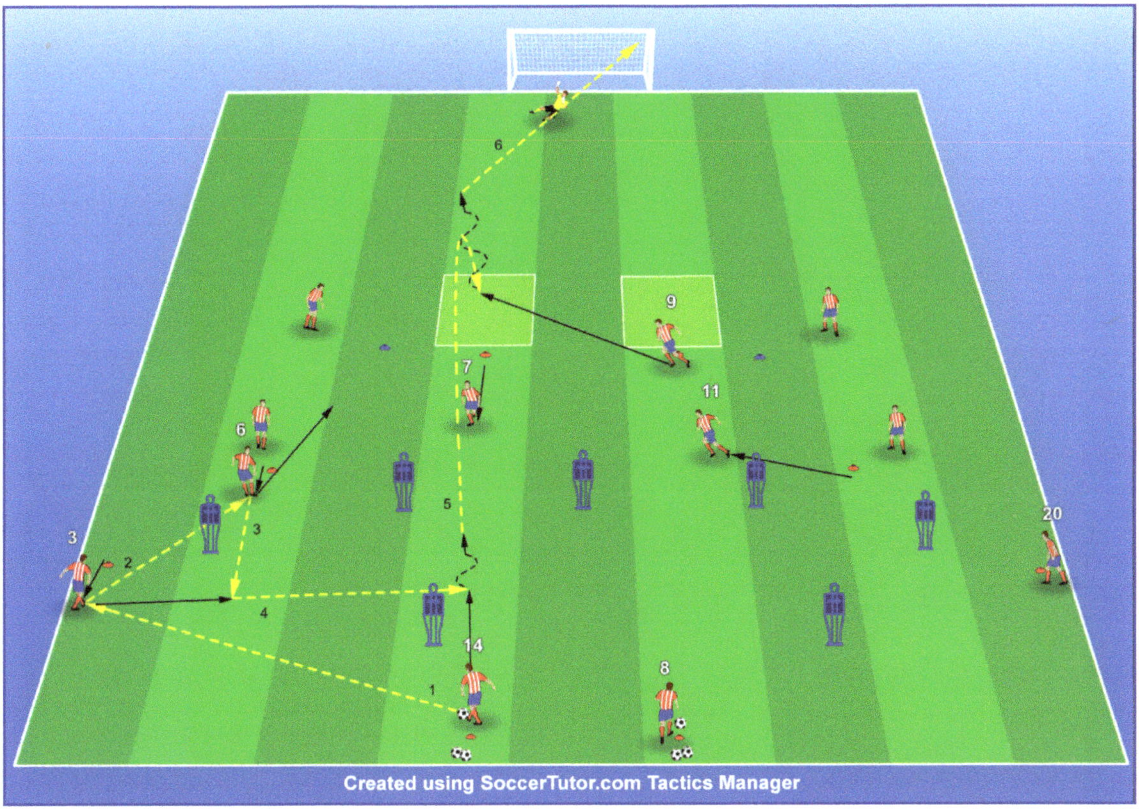

The players need to read the positioning of the forward on the weak side (red cone = close enough, blue cone = too far away).

Description (Scenario A)

- In a 35 x 45 yard area, there are 2 small central areas of 5 x 8 yards. The practice starts on either side with a central midfielder. In this example, the left central midfielder **(14)** passes to the left back **(3)**, who drops back a few yards to receive and combine with the left midfielder **(6)** round the mannequin.

- The next pass is to the central midfielder **(14)** in front of the mannequin, who must decide whether to pass into the small central area or to the forward's **(7)** feet.

- In this first example, we imagine the opposing centre back follows **No.7's** movement. The forward on the weak side **(9)** is positioned on the red cone and therefore close enough to receive the central midfielder's **(14)** aerial pass within the small central area and try to score a goal past the GK.

DIEGO SIMEONE'S ATTACKING TACTICS

Tactical Situation 6 - Forward Drops Back to Receive or Create Space in Behind

Scenario B: Wide Midfielder Exploits Space Created in Behind

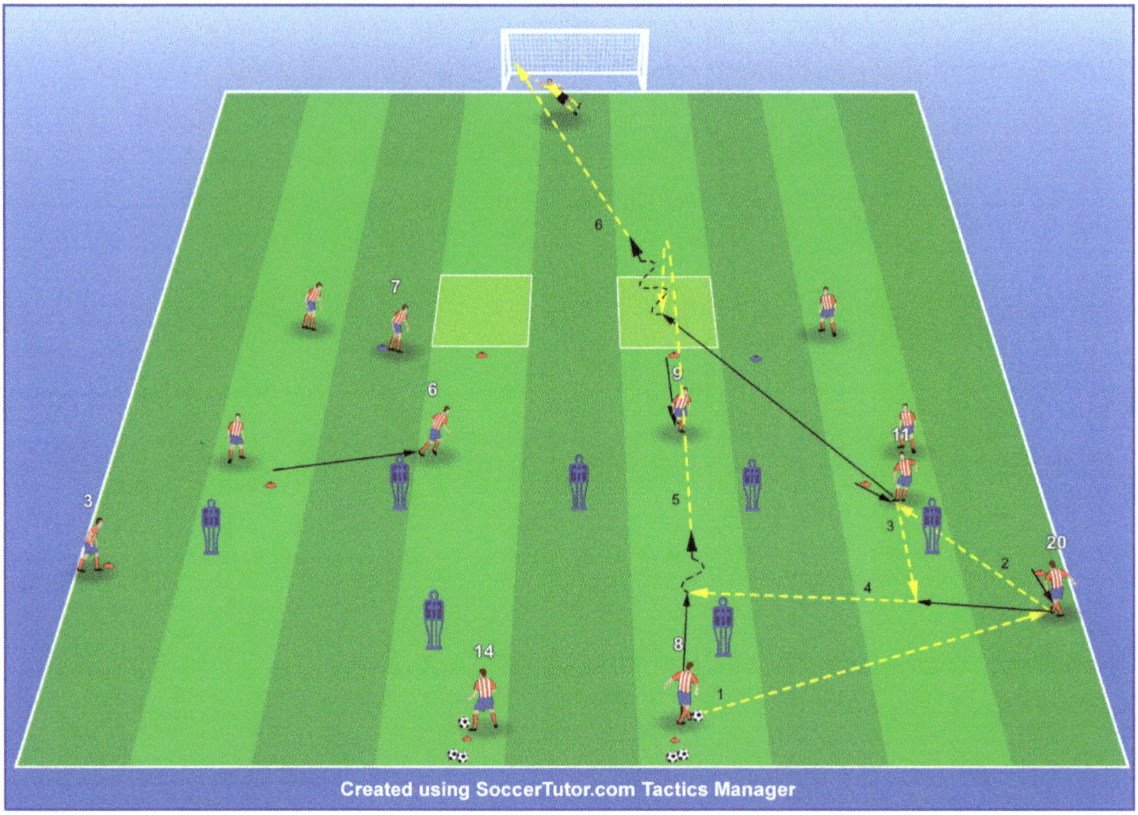

Description (Scenario B)

- In this second scenario, we again imagine that the opposing centre back follows the forward's **(9)** movement.

- The play is now on the right side and the forward on the weak side **(7)** is positioned on the blue cone, so is too far away to exploit the space in behind and receive within the white area.

- The right midfielder **(11)** recognises the situation and makes a forward run to receive the central midfielder's **(8)** aerial pass within the white area and tries to score a goal past the GK.

DIEGO SIMEONE'S ATTACKING TACTICS

Tactical Situation 6 - Forward Drops Back to Receive or Create Space in Behind

Scenario C: Forward Exploits Space After a Passing Combination

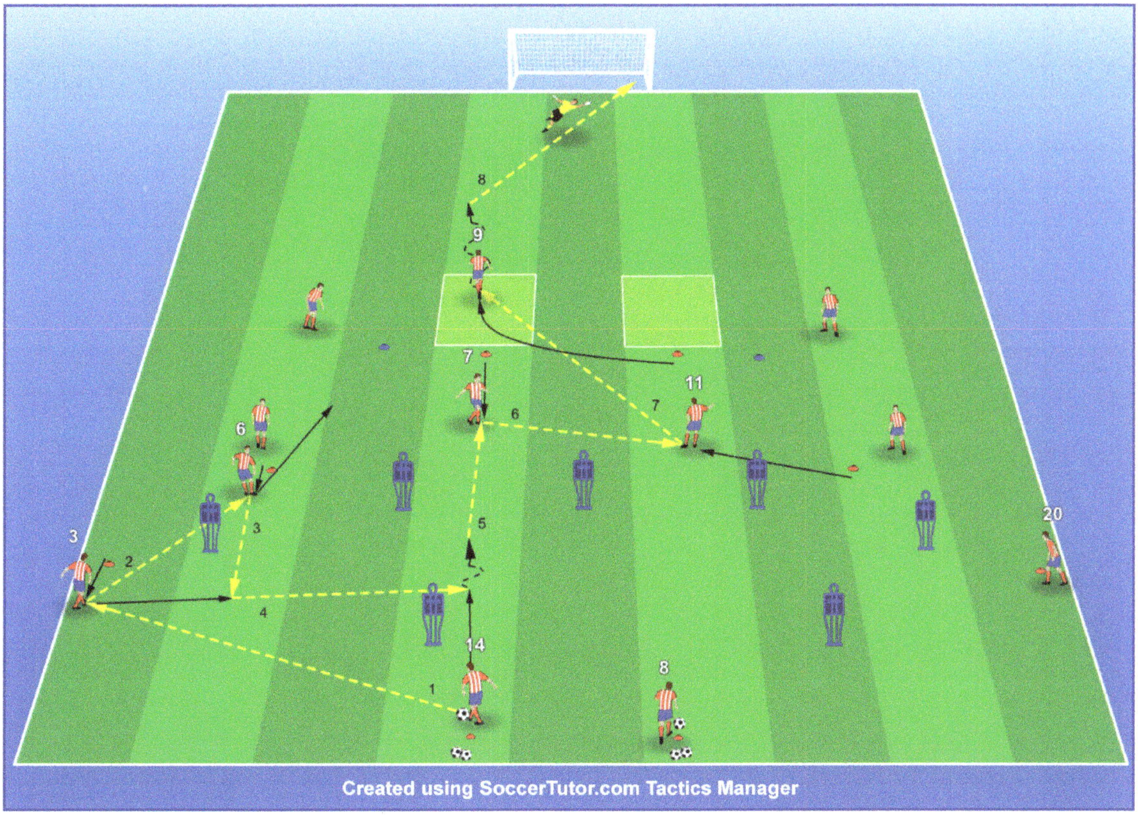

Description (Scenario C)

- In this third scenario, we imagine that the opposing centre back moves to press the forward (7) after the pass from the central midfielder (14) is played.

- The forward on the weak side (9) is positioned on the red cone and is therefore close enough to exploit the available space and receive in the white area.

- The central midfielder (14) passes to the forward's (7) feet, who can either pass to the left midfielder (6) or preferably to the right midfielder (11), as shown in the diagram.

- The forward on the weak side (9) moves into the available space in the white area.

- The right midfielder (11) uses 1 or 2 touches to play the ball into the white area for the run of the forward (9).

- The forward (9) receives within the white area and then tries to score past the GK.

Tactical Situation 6 - Forward Drops Back to Receive or Create Space in Behind

Scenario D: Wide Midfielder Exploits Space After a Passing Combination

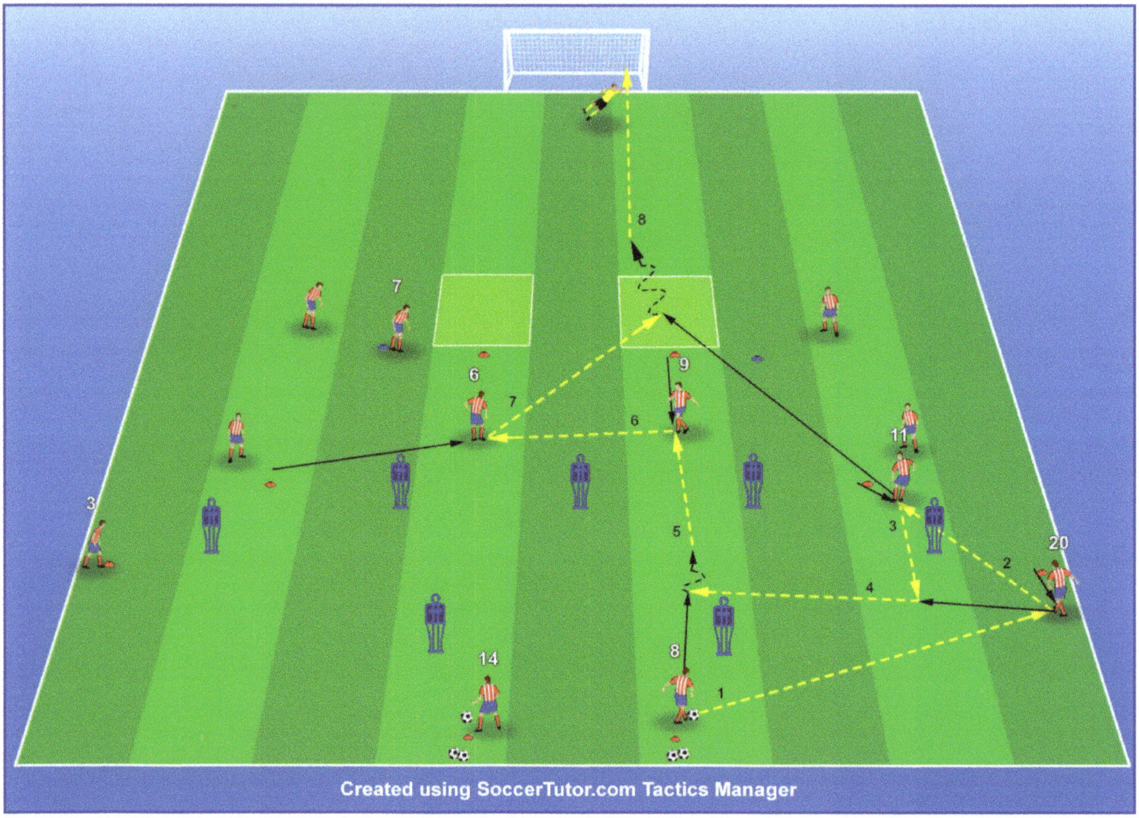

Description (Scenario D)

- In this fourth scenario, we again imagine that the opposing centre back moves to press the forward (9) after the pass from the central midfielder (8) is played.

- However, this time the forward on the weak side (7) is positioned on the blue cone and is too far away to exploit the available space and receive in the white area.

- The right midfielder (11) recognises the situation and makes a forward run to receive the left midfielder's (6) pass into the white area and tries to score a goal past the GK.

- There are 2 players in the wide midfielder and forward positions to keep a high tempo.

Coaching Points

1. There needs to be synchronisation in the players' movements (both forwards and wide midfielders).

2. Read the situation and make decisions according to the positioning of the forward on the weak side (close or too far away).

3. Well-timed and accurate passes with 1 or 2 touches + quick and accurate finishing.

NOTE: If the opposing centre back retains his position to defend the space, the forward can receive, turn, and then play a final pass for a team-mate. The full back on the weak side also joins the attack (**see page 92 for full analysis**).

©SOCCERTUTOR.COM

DIEGO SIMEONE'S ATTACKING TACTICS

Tactical Situation 6 - Forward Drops Back to Receive or Create Space in Behind

PROGRESSION

2. Forward Drops Back to Receive or Create Space in Behind in a Functional Practice

Scenario A: Forward on Weak Side Exploits Space Created in Behind

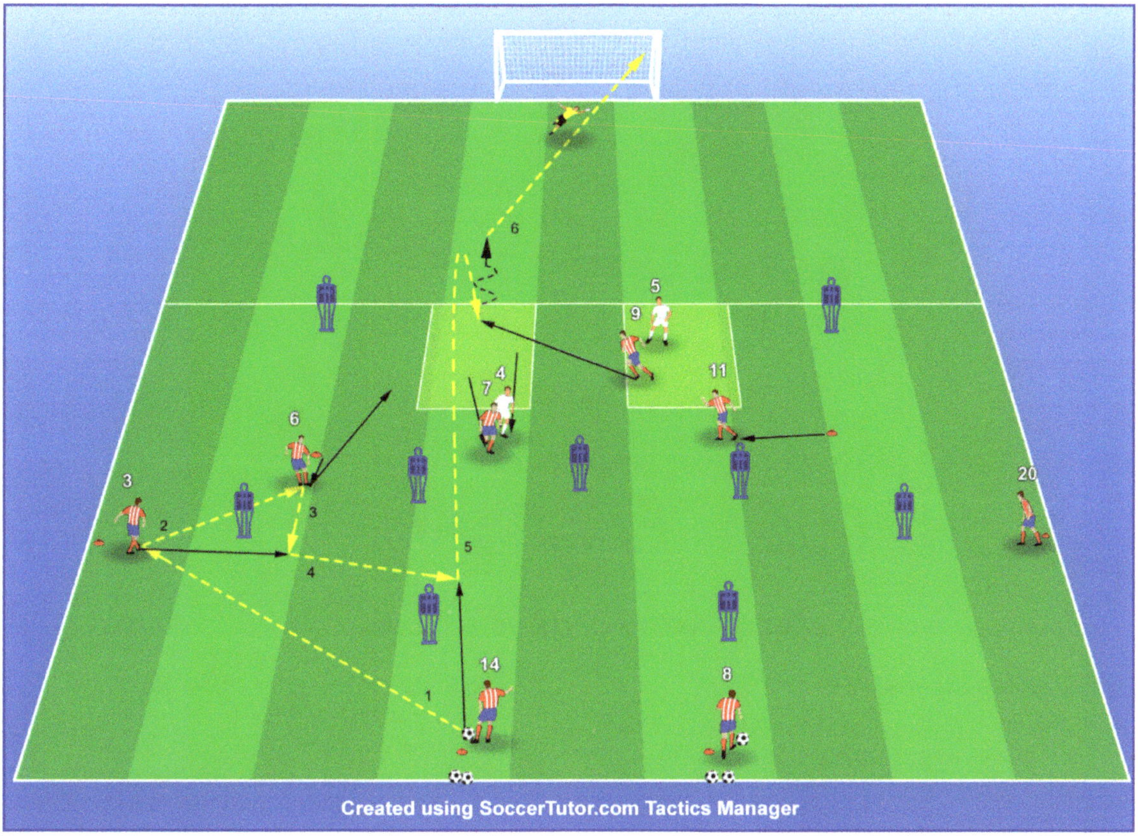

Description (Scenario A)

- In a 40 x 50 yard area, the 2 white central areas are 5 x 8 yards.

- The 2 white centre backs can react in any way they want. They can either follow the forward right away, press him as soon as the pass is played or let him receive and turn.

- The red central midfielder (**No.14** in diagram) must read the white centre back's (No.4) reaction and decide where to direct the ball.

- The practice starts on the left or right with the same 4 passes shown, resulting in the central midfielder (**14**) receiving.

- **See the previous practices and analysis pages** for the correct decision making for No.14.

- In this first example, white No.4 follows the red forward (**7**), so the central midfielder (**14**) directs the ball into the available space (white area) for the forward on the weak side (**9**) to receive and try to score past the GK.

DIEGO SIMEONE'S ATTACKING TACTICS

Tactical Situation 6 - Forward Drops Back to Receive or Create Space in Behind

Scenario B: Wide Midfielder Exploits Space Created in Behind

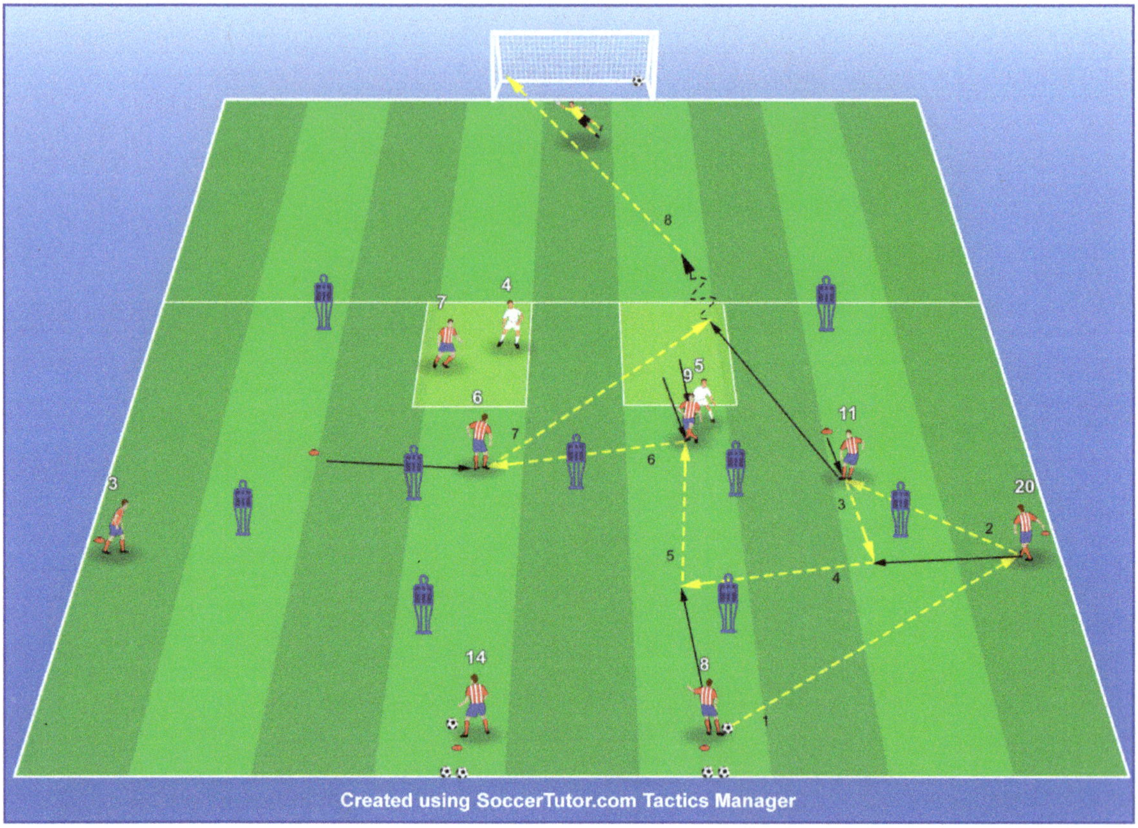

Description (Scenario B)

- In this second scenario, the white centre back No.5 moves to press the red forward (9) as soon as the pass towards him is played to prevent the turn.

- The red forward (9) is aware of the pressure and passes (square) first-time to the wide midfielder on the weak side (6).

- As the forward on the weak side (7) is too far away to exploit the space behind white No.5, the wide midfielder on the strong side (11) makes a forward run into the white area to receive from No.6, who uses 1 or 2 touches.

- There can be 2 players in the wide midfielder and forward positions to keep a high tempo.

- The white centre backs are semi-passive throughout the practice.

Progression: Add 2 white full backs.

Coaching Points

1. Synchronisation in player movements (wide midfielders and forwards).
2. Read the situation and make decisions according to the position of the forward on the weak side and the opposing centre back's reaction.
3. Accurate passing and finishing.

DIEGO SIMEONE'S ATTACKING TACTICS

Tactical Situation 6 - Forward Drops Back to Receive or Create Space in Behind

PROGRESSION

3. Forward Drops Back to Receive or Create Space in Behind in a Small Sided Game

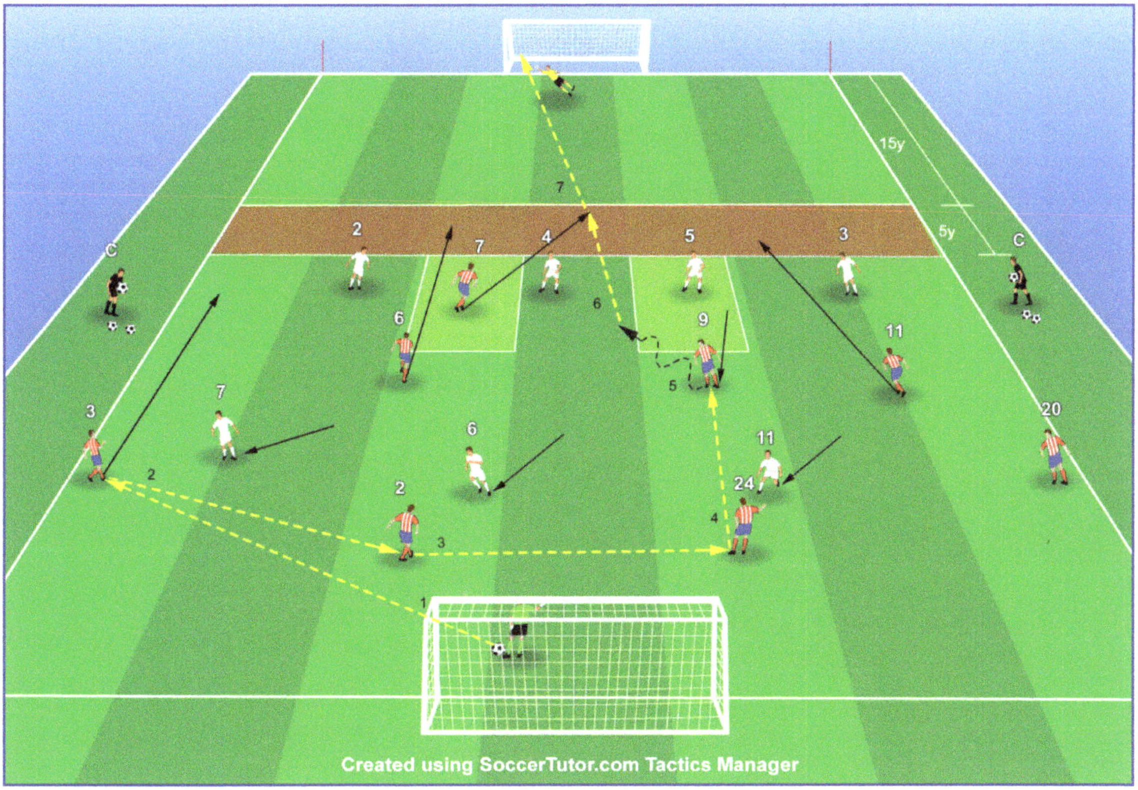

Description

- In a 40 x 50 yard area, we play an 9v8 game. There is a red 40 x 5 yards high zone and 2 small white areas, which represent the potential space behind the centre backs.

- The reds can score in any way, but if they score after successfully exploiting space created behind a centre back, or after one of the forwards receives and turns free of marking (see diagram example), they score 3 goals.

- **See the previous practices and analysis pages** for the correct decision making according to the position of the weak side forward and reaction of the white centre back.

- The whites try to win the ball and score within 10-12 seconds (counter attack).

- If the reds choose the wrong decision or make an unsuccessful pass, the Coach throws a new ball in for the whites to score within 10-12 seconds.

Restrictions

1. The white players cannot enter the red zone unless a red player receives inside it.
2. The white GK cannot enter the red zone.

DIEGO SIMEONE'S ATTACKING TACTICS

Tactical Situation 6 - Forward Drops Back to Receive or Create Space in Behind

PROGRESSION

4. Forward Drops Back to Receive or Create Space in Behind in a Conditioned Game

Description

- In the final practice of this session, the 2 teams play an 11v11 game in 2/3 of the pitch. You can decide whether to have the areas marked out to help the players or not.

- The reds can score in any way, but if they score after successfully exploiting space created behind a centre back, or after one of the forwards receives and turns free of marking, they score 3 goals.

- **See the previous practices and analysis pages** for the correct decision making according to the position of the weak side forward and reaction of the white centre back.

- The whites try to win the ball and score within 10-12 seconds (counter attack).

Coaching Points

1. Synchronisation in player movements (wide midfielders and forwards).

2. Read the situation and make decisions according to the position of the forward on the weak side and the opposing centre back's reaction.

©SOCCERTUTOR.COM

DIEGO SIMEONE'S ATTACKING TACTICS

TACTICAL SITUATION 7

Weak Side Forward Drops Back to Create Space in Behind

The content in this section is from analysis of Diego Simeone's Atlético Madrid teams during the 2017/2018 and 2018/2019 seasons.

The analysis is based on recurring patterns of play observed within the Atlético Madrid team. Once the same phase of play occurred several times (at least 10), the tactics would be seen as a pattern. The analysis on the following pages are examples of the team's tactics being used effectively.

Each action, pass, individual movement with or without the ball, and the positioning of each player on the pitch including their body shape, are presented.

The analysis is then used to create a session to coach this specific tactical situation.

Tactical Situation 7 - Weak Side Forward Drops Back to Create Space in Behind

WEAK SIDE FORWARD DROPS BACK TO CREATE SPACE IN BEHIND FOR WIDE MIDFIELDER

1. Weak Side Forward Drops Back to Drag the Opposing Centre Back Out of Position and Create Space for the Run of the Wide Midfielder

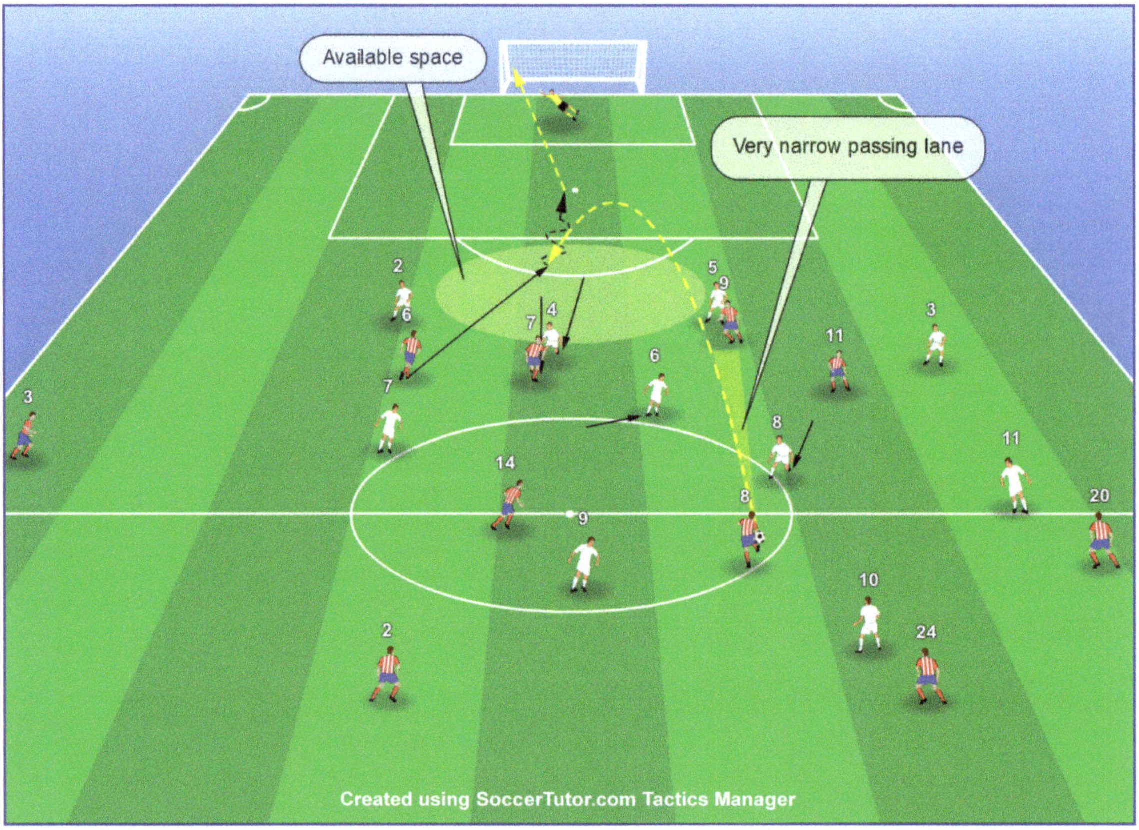

If there is a very narrow passing lane for a through pass to the forward on the strong side, the forward on the weak side drops back to offer a passing option.

Depending to the reaction of the opposing centre back on the weak side, there are specific options that Diego Simeone's Atlético Madrid team use to break through the defence.

In this example, the opposing centre back No.4 follows the dropping back movement of **Griezmann (7)**, therefore the space created behind him can be exploited.

The wide midfielder on that side **Koke (6)** makes a run into the created space and receives a long direct pass from the central midfielder **Saúl (8)**.

DIEGO SIMEONE'S ATTACKING TACTICS

Tactical Situation 7 - Weak Side Forward Drops Back to Create Space in Behind

2. Opposing Full Back Tracks the Wide Midfielder's Movement and Space is Created Out Wide for the Run of the Full Back

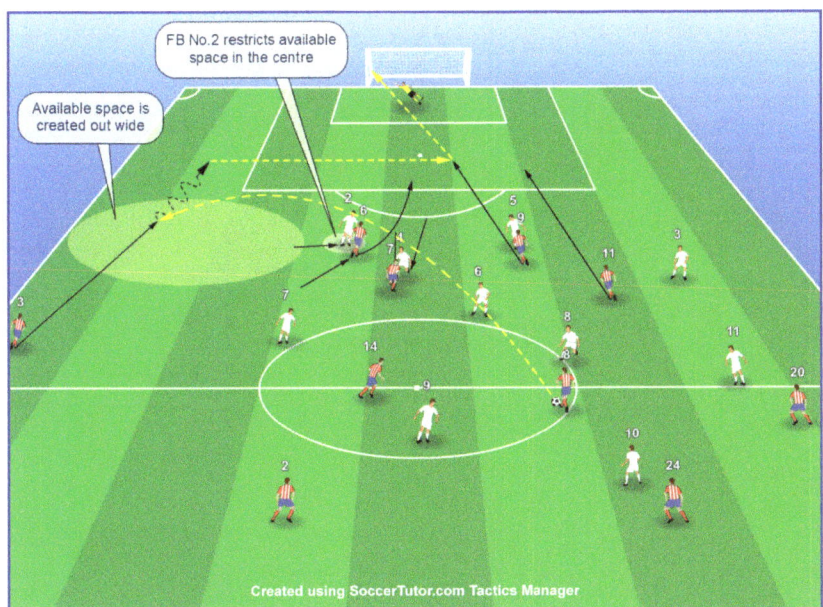

In this second example, the white right back No.2 shifts across to restrict the available space for Atlético's left midfielder **Koke (6)**.

Due to this reaction, space is created out wide for the forward run of the left back **F. Luis (3)**, who receives the long switch of play from the central midfielder **Saúl (8)**.

3. Opposing Centre Back Retains Position and the Weak Side Forward is Able to Receive Between the Lines and Turn

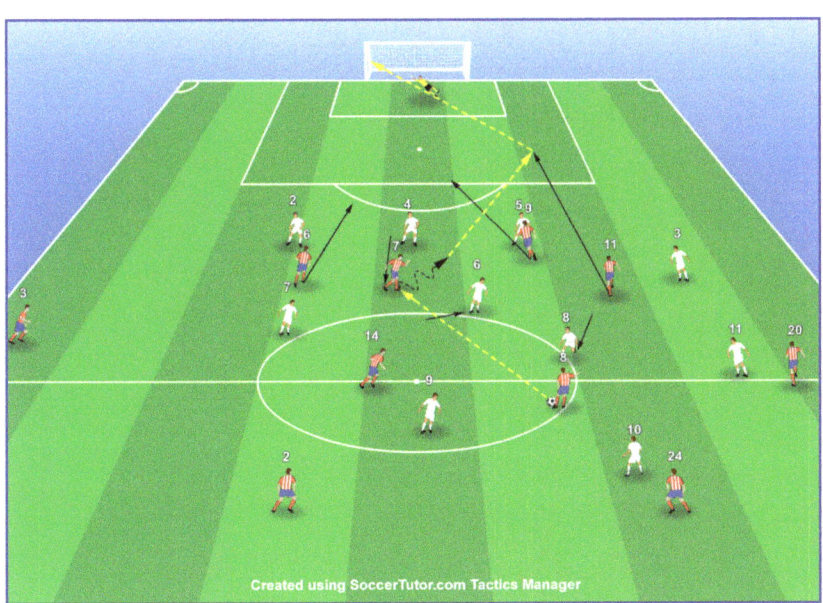

In this third and final example, the white centre back No.4 decides to defend the space and retains his position.

This means that the forward on the weak side **Griezmann (7)** is able to receive unmarked and turn between the opposition's midfield and defensive lines.

From there, **Griezmann (7)** searches for a final pass to one of his teammates.

DIEGO SIMEONE'S ATTACKING TACTICS

SESSION (3 PRACTICES) FOR "WEAK SIDE FORWARD DROPS BACK TO CREATE SPACE IN BEHIND"

Tactical Situation 7 - Weak Side Forward Drops Back to Create Space in Behind

SESSION FOR THIS TACTICAL SITUATION (3 PRACTICES)
1. Weak Side Forward Drops Back to Create Space for Wide Midfielder in a Functional Practice (1)

Scenario A: Opposing Centre Back Follows the Weak Side Forward

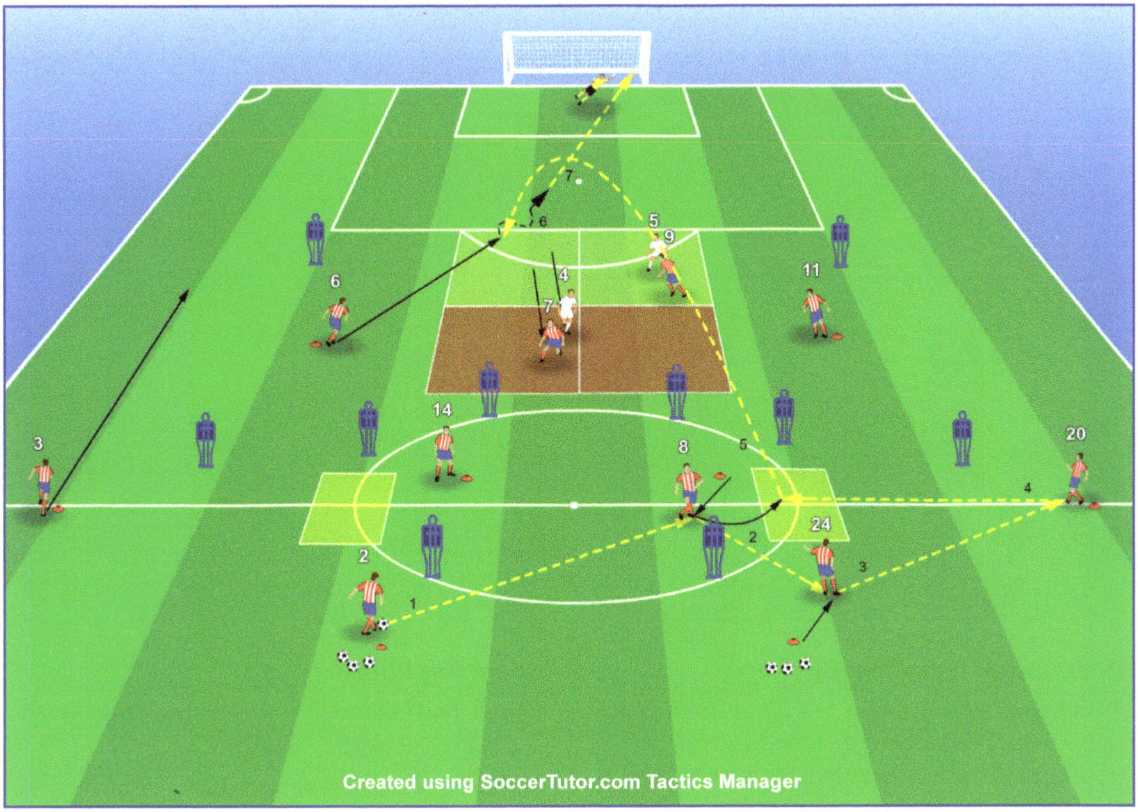

Description (Scenario A)

- The practice starts with either centre back **(2/24)** and after 4 passes, the ball is with a central midfielder **(14/8)** in the small yellow area.

- As soon as the central midfielder **(8)** receives, the forward on the weak side **(7)** drops back to offer a passing option.

- The red central midfielder **(8)** must read the white centre back's (No.4) reaction and decide where to direct the ball.

- **Please see the analysis pages in this section** for the correct decision making for the red central midfielder.

- In this first example, the white centre back No.4 follows the dropping back movement of the forward **(7)** and space is created behind.

- The wide midfielder on that side **(6)** makes a run into the created space (white area), receives a long direct pass from the central midfielder **(8)** and tries to score past the GK.

Tactical Situation 7 - Weak Side Forward Drops Back to Create Space in Behind

Scenario B: Opposing Centre Back Retains Position to Defend the Space

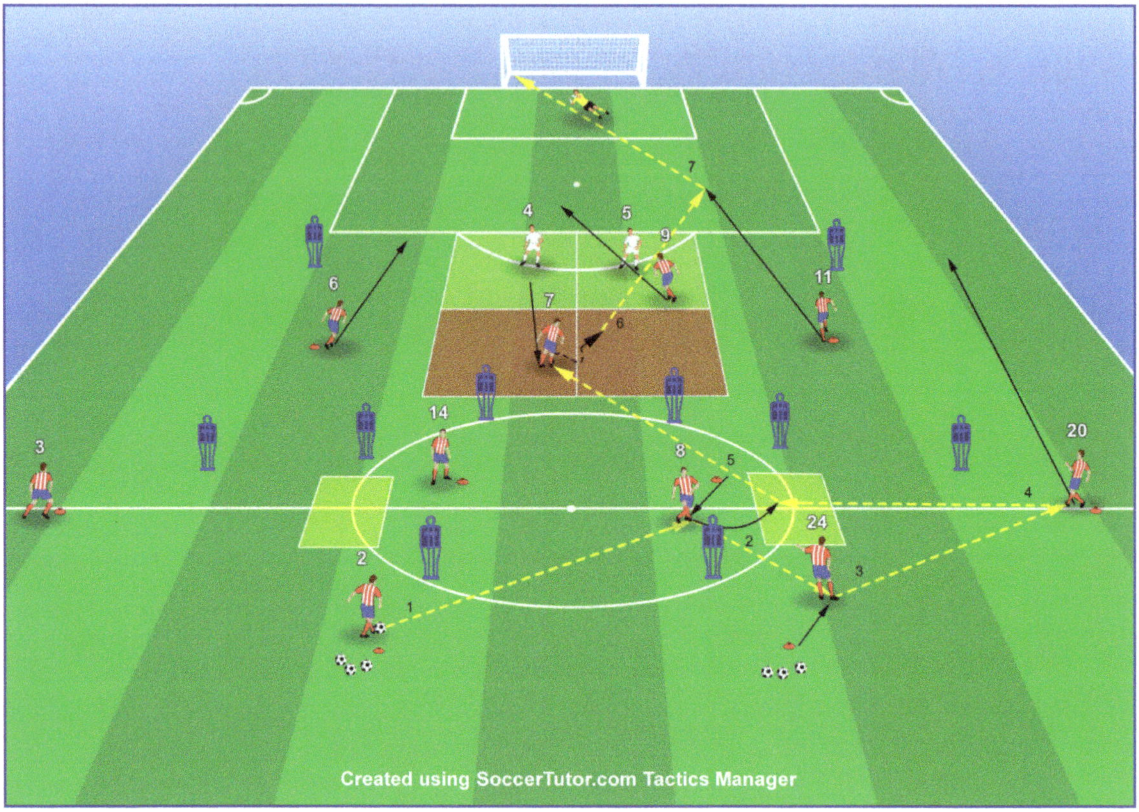

Description (Scenario B)

- In this second scenario, the white centre back No.4 doesn't follow the red forward's **(7)** dropping back movement. He instead retains his position and defends the space.

- This means that the forward on the weak side **(7)** is able to receive unmarked within the red area (in between the lines) from the central midfielder **(8)** and turn.

- From there, the forward **(7)** looks to play a final pass to one of his team-mates. In the diagram example, he passes in behind for the run of the right midfielder **(11)**, who shoots at goal.

Coaching Points

1. Synchronisation in player movements (wide midfielders and forwards).

2. Read the situation and make decisions according to the opposing centre back's reaction.

DIEGO SIMEONE'S ATTACKING TACTICS

Tactical Situation 7 - Weak Side Forward Drops Back to Create Space in Behind

PROGRESSION
2. Weak Side Forward Drops Back to Create Space for Wide Midfielder in a Functional Practice (2)

Scenario A: Opposing Centre Back Follows the Weak Side Forward

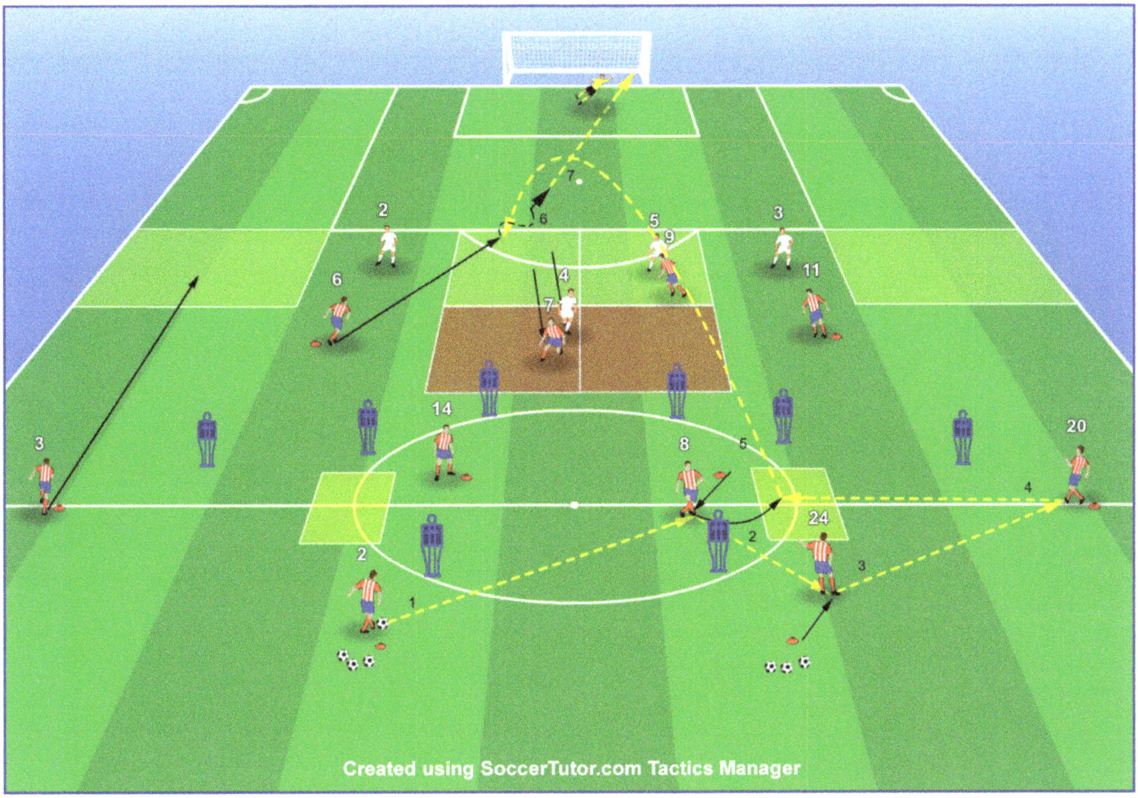

Description (Phase 1 - Scenario A)

- In this progression, we add 2 white full backs and 2 wide areas for the red full backs.

- In the first phase (5-6 min), the white centre backs are coached to follow the red forward's dropping back movement every time.

- As the red weak side wide midfielder **(6)** moves to exploit the space created behind the white centre back No.4 (white area), the white full back on that side (No.2) decides whether to cover this movement or not.

- In this first example, the white right back No.2 decides to retain his position and does not shift across to provide cover and track the red left midfielder's **(6)** movement.

- Therefore, the red central midfielder **(8)** plays a direct aerial pass for the run of the left midfielder **(6)** to receive within the white area and try to score past the GK.

DIEGO SIMEONE'S ATTACKING TACTICS

Tactical Situation 7 - Weak Side Forward Drops Back to Create Space in Behind

Scenario B: Opposing Full Back Covers and Space is Created Wide

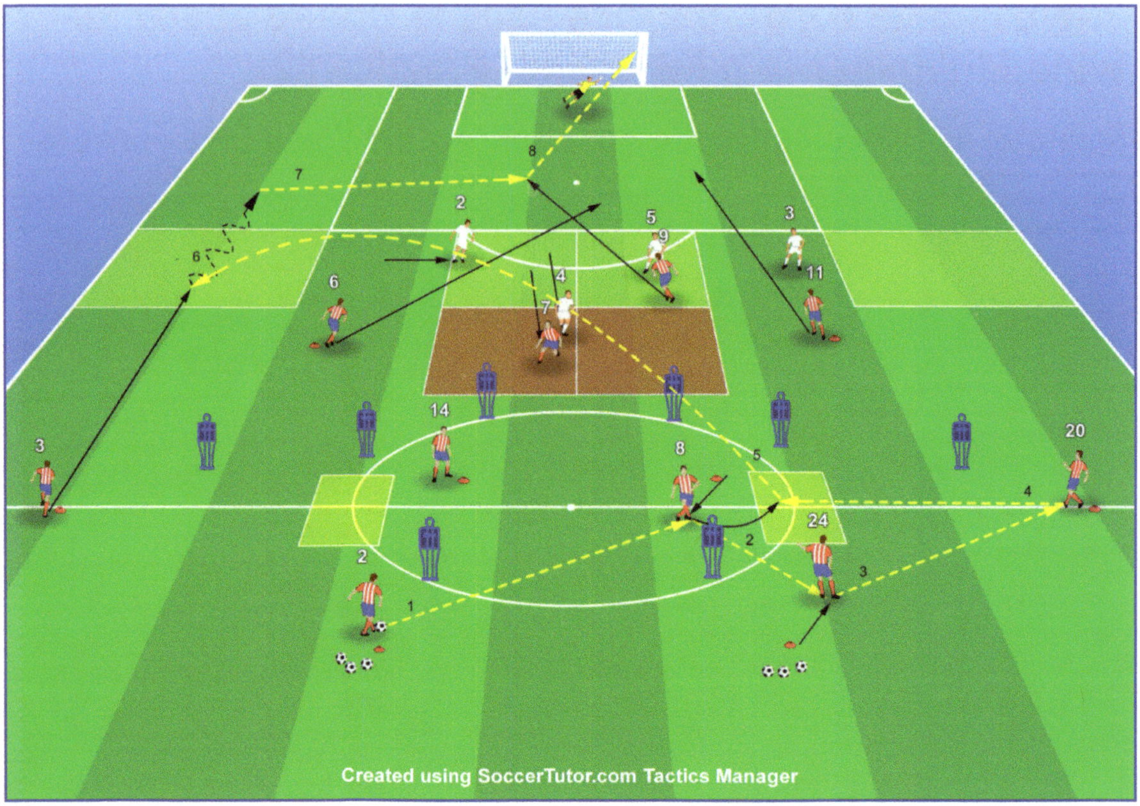

Description (Phase 1 - Scenario B)

- In this second scenario, the white full back No.2 shifts across to restrict the available space for the red wide midfielder (**6**).

- Due to this reaction, space is created out wide for the forward run of the full back (**3**), who receives the long switch of play from the central midfielder (**8**) within the wide area.

- After a pass to the wide midfielder (**previous page**) or full back (**diagram above**), the reds try to score against 4 white defenders and GK.

Description (Phase 2)

- After the first phase (5-6 min) is complete, the white centre backs are free to decide whether or not to follow the red forward's dropping back movement.

- If the white centre back does follow the red forward's dropping back movement, he chooses the passing options displayed in the 2 diagrams.

- If the white centre back decides not to follow the red forward's movement, then the central midfielder can pass to the forward's feet, who can receive and turn for a 4v4 attack.

Coaching Points

1. Synchronisation in player movements (wide midfielders and forwards).

2. Read the situation and make decisions according to the defensive reactions of the opposing centre backs and full backs.

©SOCCERTUTOR.COM   DIEGO SIMEONE'S ATTACKING TACTICS

Tactical Situation 7 - Weak Side Forward Drops Back to Create Space in Behind

PROGRESSION
3. Weak Side Forward Drops Back to Create Space for Wide Midfielder in a Conditioned Game

Description
- In the final practice of this session, the 2 teams play an 11v11 game in 2/3 of the pitch. You can decide whether to have the areas to help the players or not.
- The reds can score in any way, but if they score after successfully exploiting space created by a forward dropping back, they score 3 goals.
- The forward on the weak side or strong side can drop back so the play isn't predictable.
- The whites try to win the ball and score within 12-15 seconds (counter attack).

Coaching Points
1. Synchronisation in player movements (wide midfielders and forwards).
2. Read the situation and make decisions according to the defensive reactions of the opposing centre backs and full backs.

TACTICAL SITUATION 8

Creating an Overload and Attacking Through the Centre

The content in this section is from analysis of Diego Simeone's Atlético Madrid teams during the 2017/2018 and 2018/2019 seasons.

The analysis is based on recurring patterns of play observed within the Atlético Madrid team. Once the same phase of play occurred several times (at least 10), the tactics would be seen as a pattern. The analysis on the following pages are examples of the team's tactics being used effectively.

Each action, pass, individual movement with or without the ball, and the positioning of each player on the pitch including their body shape, are presented.

The analysis is then used to create a session to coach this specific tactical situation.

Tactical Situation 8 - Creating an Overload and Attacking Through the Centre

CREATING AN OVERLOAD AND ATTACKING THROUGH THE CENTRE

1a. Wide Midfielder Creates an Overload by Moving into the Centre of the Pitch to Receive

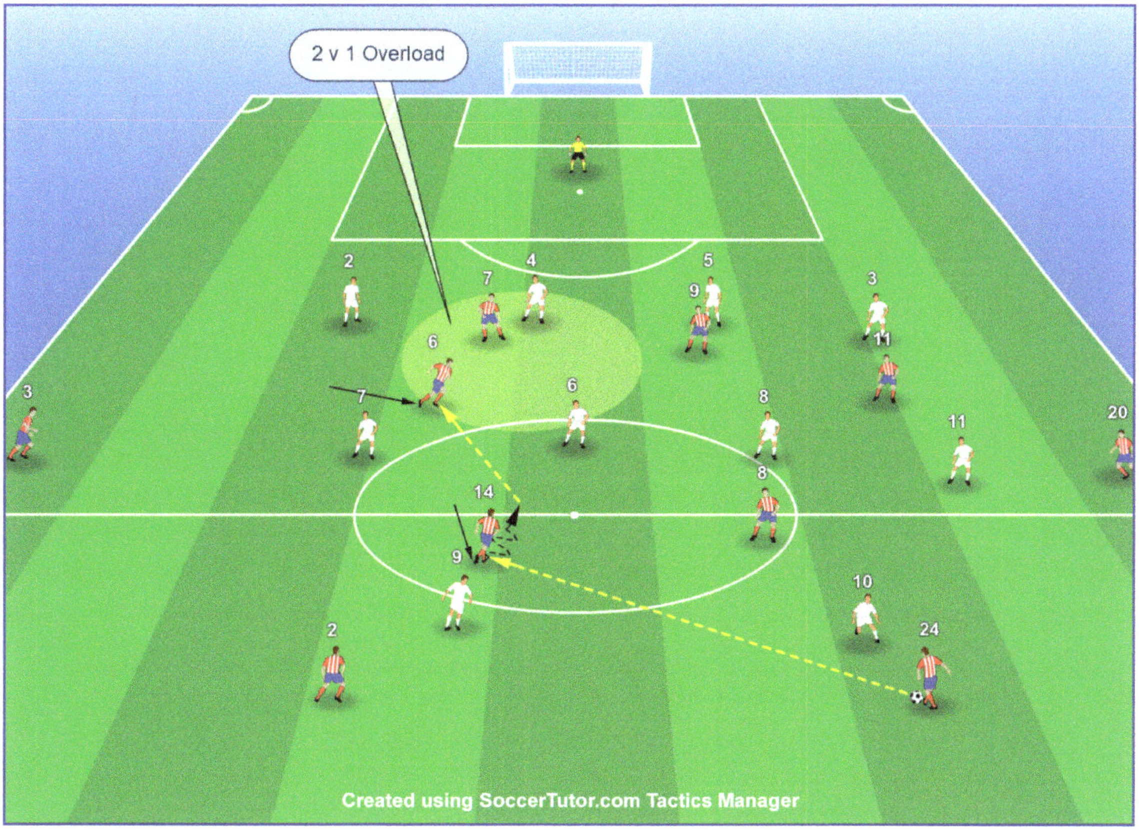

The central positioning of Atlético's wide midfielders helps create overloads in specific areas. Attacking through the centre is a popular tactic for Diego Simeone's team.

The wide midfielder moves towards the centre in between the opposition's midfield and defensive lines and enters the zone of responsibility of the opposing centre back, who then has 2 players to deal with (see highlighted area).

This prevents the opposing centre back (white No.4 in diagram) from moving forward to press Atlético's left midfielder **Koke (6)**.

As soon as central midfielder **Gabi (14)** receives from the centre back **Giménez (24)** in this example, the left midfielder **Koke (6)** moves towards the centre and creates a 2v1 overload in a crucial area, as shown.

©SOCCERTUTOR.COM

DIEGO SIMEONE'S ATTACKING TACTICS

Tactical Situation 8 - Creating an Overload and Attacking Through the Centre

1b. Opposing Centre Back Retains Position and the Wide Midfielder is Able to Receive, Turn and Look for a Final Pass

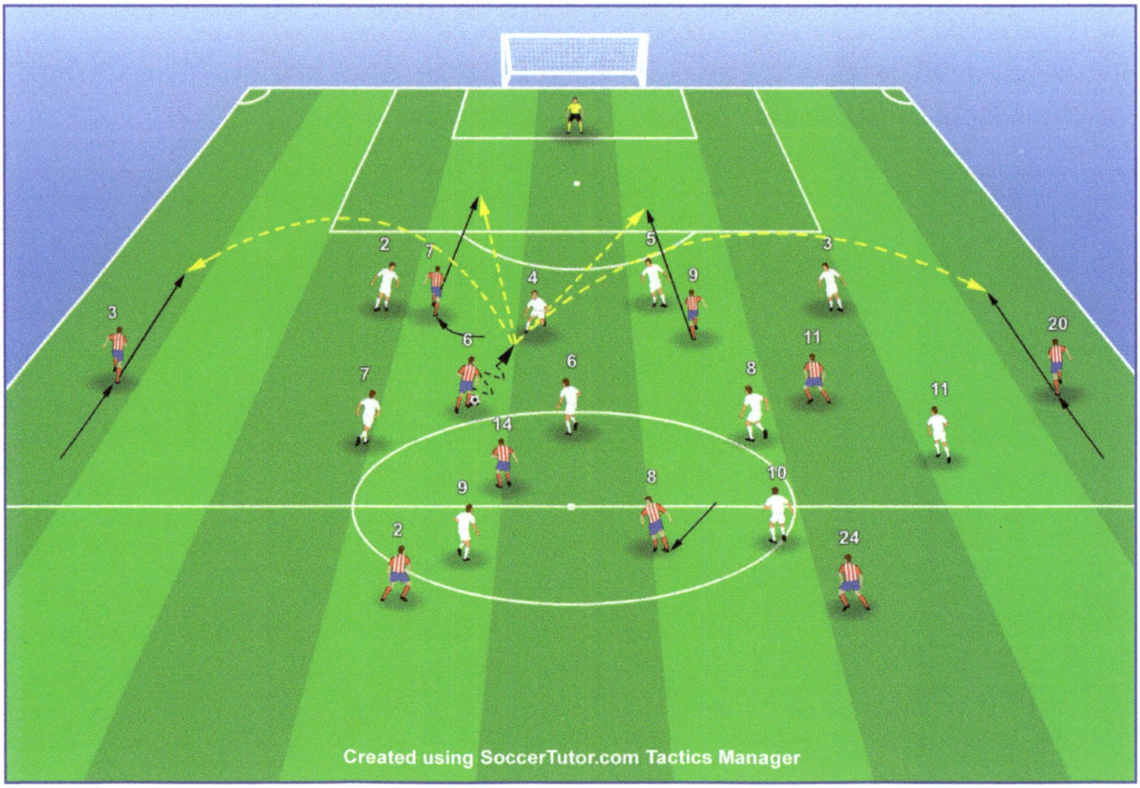

This situation enables the left midfielder **Koke (6)** to receive free of marking and turn facing the opponent's goal.

As soon as the turn is carried out, the 2 forwards **Griezmann (7)** and **Torres (9)** move to receive a potential final pass, as do both full backs **F. Luis (3)** and **Juanfran (20)**, who are positioned near the side-lines to retain width.

The forward movement of both full backs triggers the central midfielder **Saúl (8)** to drop back and help retain a numerical advantage at the back.

DIEGO SIMEONE'S ATTACKING TACTICS

Tactical Situation 8 - Creating an Overload and Attacking Through the Centre

2. Opposing Centre Back Tracks the Wide Midfielder's Movement, who Plays First-time Pass in Behind

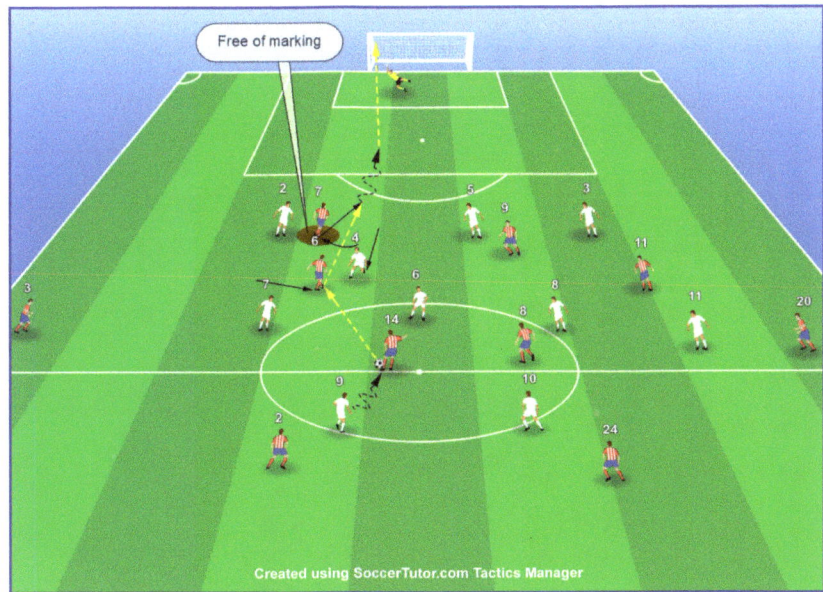

In a similar situation to the previous one, **Koke (6)** receives a forward pass from **Gabi (14)**, but the reaction from the white defenders is different.

Specifically, the white centre back No.4 decides to step forward and put **Koke (6)** under pressure, which leaves **Griezmann (7)** free of marking. **Griezmann (7)** opens up to receive a first-time pass from **Koke (6)**.

3. Opposing Centre Back Tracks the Wide Midfielder's Movement, who Uses a Link Player to Pass in Behind

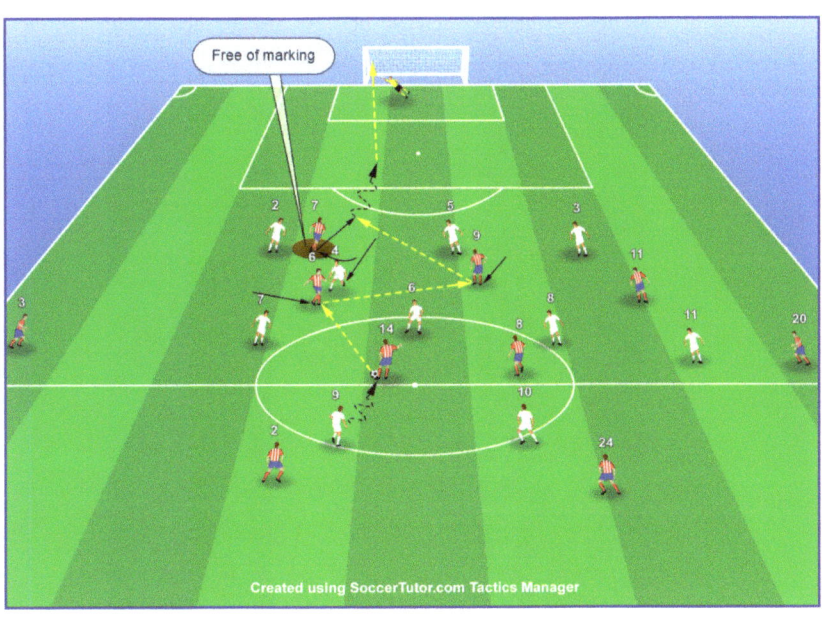

This shows another option for how Atlético deal with the same situation using a passing combination.

As soon as **Koke (6)** receives under pressure from the white centre back No.4, the ball is directed to **Griezmann (7)** via the other forward **Torres (9)**, who moves close to **Koke (6)** to offer him a passing option.

DIEGO SIMEONE'S ATTACKING TACTICS

SESSION (3 PRACTICES) FOR "CREATING AN OVERLOAD AND ATTACKING THROUGH THE CENTRE"

Tactical Situation 8 - Creating an Overload and Attacking Through the Centre

SESSION FOR THIS TACTICAL SITUATION (3 PRACTICES)
1. Creating an Overload and Attacking Through the Centre in a Technical Practice

Phase 1: Opposing Centre Back Tracks Wide Midfielder's Movement

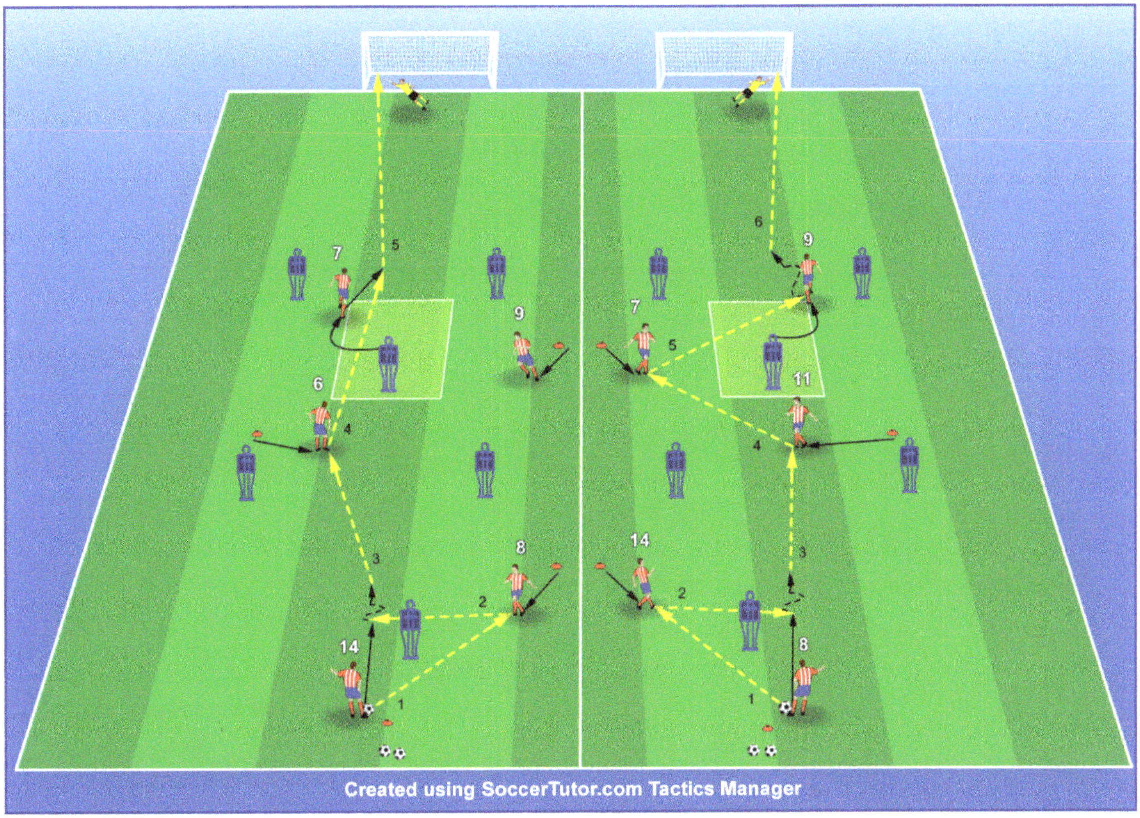

In the first phase of this practice (5-6 min), we assume the opposing centre back moves forward to press the wide midfielder (6 or 11), which is why the 3 mannequins are in a triangle.

Description (Phase 1)

- The central midfielders (**14 or 8**) start by playing a 1-2 with the other central midfielder to receive beyond the first mannequin. As soon as the central midfielder receives the return pass, the wide midfielders (**6/11**) move inside to offer a passing option.

- The next pass is directed to the wide midfielders (**6/11**) and both forwards (**7/9**) open up to make themselves available for a pass.

- On the left side of this first diagram, the wide midfielder (**6**) plays a first-time pass between the mannequins for the strong side forward (**7**), who tries to score past the GK.

- On the right side, the wide midfielder (**11**) uses the weak side forward (**7**) as a link player to play in behind to **No.9**.

©SOCCERTUTOR.COM DIEGO SIMEONE'S ATTACKING TACTICS

Tactical Situation 8 - Creating an Overload and Attacking Through the Centre

Phase 2: Opposing Centre Back Retains Position and Defends Space

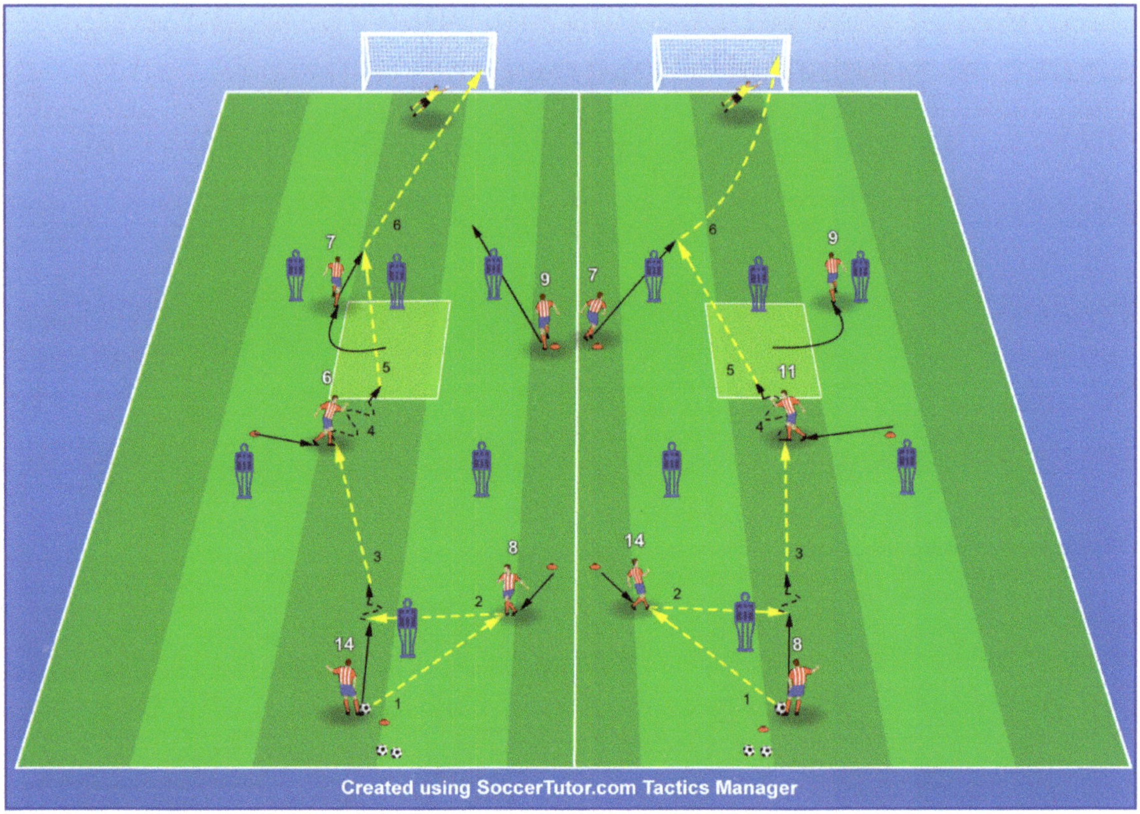

After the first phase (5-6 min) is complete, we start with Phase 2 and move 1 mannequin forward, as shown. We assume the opposing centre back doesn't track the wide midfielder's movement and therefore retains his position to defend the space.

Description (Phase 2)

- The red wide midfielders **(6/11)** now practice receiving from the central midfielders **(14/8)**, turning quickly and then playing a final pass in behind.

- On the left side of this second diagram, the wide midfielder **(6)** receives, turns, and plays a final pass in behind for the strong side forward **(7)**, who tries to score past the GK.

- On the right side, the wide midfielder **(11)** plays a final pass to the weak side forward **(7)**.

Progression

Replace the central mannequin with a passive white centre back. The wide midfielder then has to read his reaction and decide whether to play a first-time pass (**previous page**) or receive and turn (**diagram above**).

Coaching Points

1. There needs to be synchronisation in the players' movements (forwards and wide midfielders).
2. Accurate and well-timed passing.
3. Open body shape and fast turns.
4. Accurate finishing.

DIEGO SIMEONE'S ATTACKING TACTICS

Tactical Situation 8 - Creating an Overload and Attacking Through the Centre

PROGRESSION
2. Creating an Overload and Attacking Through the Centre in a Dynamic Zonal Practice

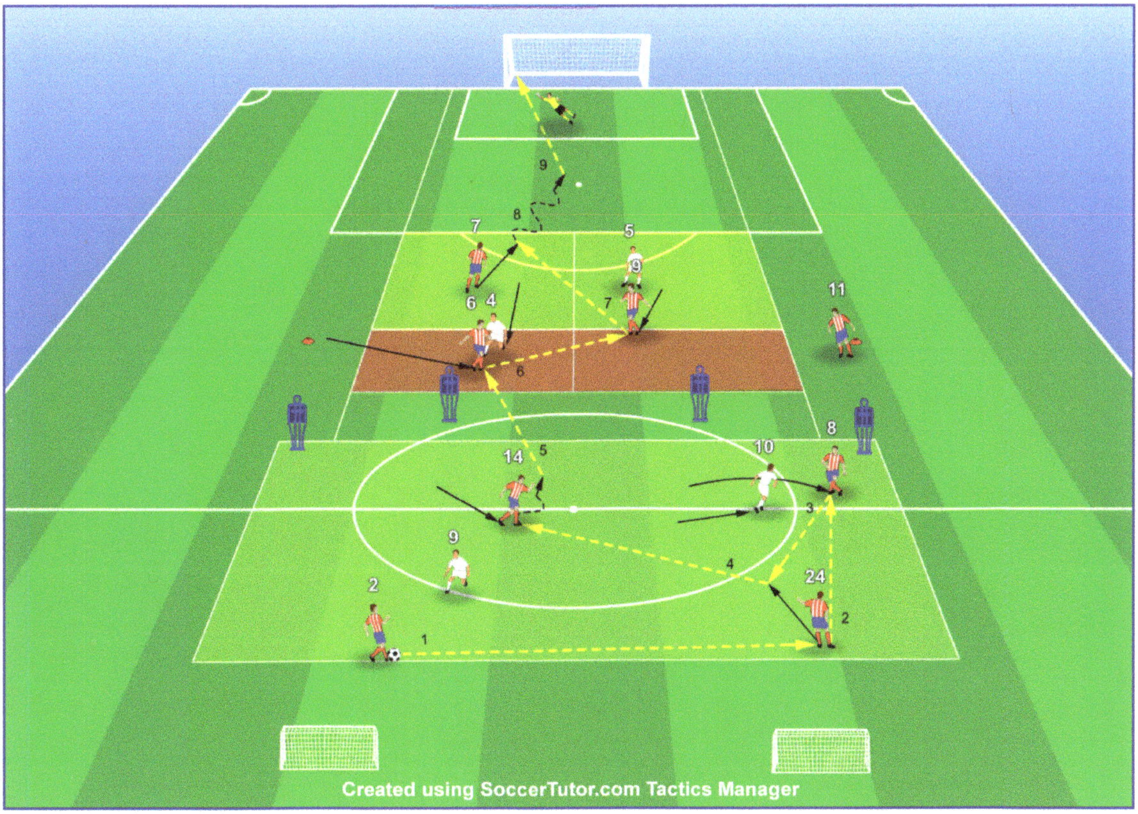

Description
- The practice starts within the marked-out low zone and the reds play 4v2 with the aim of moving the ball to a central midfielder unmarked beyond the white forwards.
- As soon as this happens, the wide midfielder on that side (6) moves towards the centre to create an overload and receive from the central midfielder (14).
- The wide midfielder (6) must decide whether to play a first-time pass in behind or receive and turn, depending on the white centre back's reaction.

- Please **see the previous practices and analysis pages** in this section for the correct decision making for the red wide midfielder.
- In this example, the opposing centre back No.4 moves forward to press the wide midfielder (6), so he uses the weak side forward (9) as a link player to pass to the other forward (7) in the space created behind No.4.
- If the white centre backs win the ball, they move the ball to the forwards and try to score in the mini goals within 12-15 seconds. If the white forwards win the ball within the low zone, they try and score within 6 seconds.

©SOCCERTUTOR.COM — DIEGO SIMEONE'S ATTACKING TACTICS

Tactical Situation 8 - Creating an Overload and Attacking Through the Centre

PROGRESSION
3. Creating an Overload and Attacking Through the Centre in a Conditioned Game

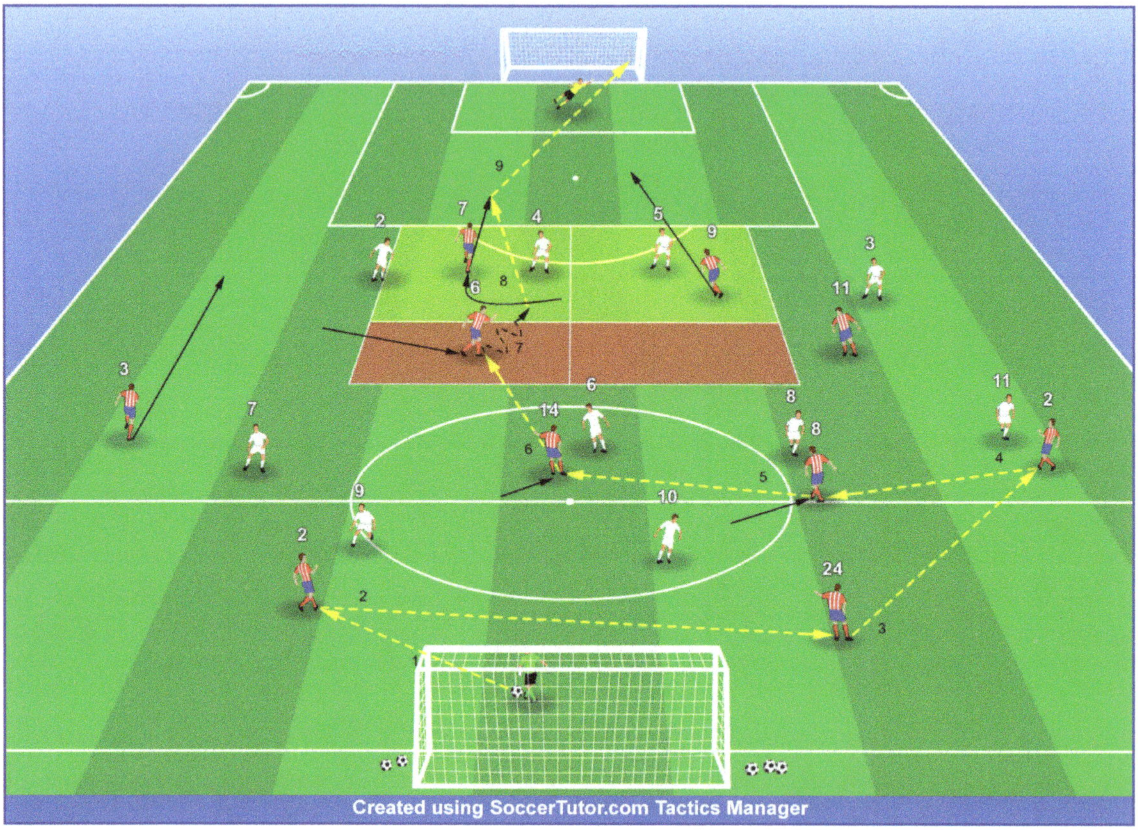

Description
- In the final practice of this session, the 2 teams play an 11v11 game in 2/3 of the pitch. You can decide whether to have the areas to help the players or not.
- The reds can score in any way but if they score after successfully exploiting an overload in the centre, they score 3 goals.
- The red wide midfielder has to read the tactical situation and make the right decision about where to direct the ball and create a scoring chance (**see previous practices and analysis pages**).
- In the diagram example, the white centre back retains his position, so the wide midfielder **(6)** can receive, turn, and play a final pass.
- The white team try to win the ball and then score (counter attack) within 10-12 seconds.

Coaching Points
1. There needs to be synchronisation in the players' movements (forwards and wide midfielders).
2. Read the situation and make decisions according to the opposing centre back's reaction.

DIEGO SIMEONE'S ATTACKING TACTICS

©SOCCERTUTOR.COM

TACTICAL SITUATION 9

Making a Run on Blind Side of Defender to Receive a Long Pass in Behind

The content in this section is from analysis of Diego Simeone's Atlético Madrid teams during the 2017/2018 and 2018/2019 seasons.

The analysis is based on recurring patterns of play observed within the Atlético Madrid team. Once the same phase of play occurred several times (at least 10), the tactics would be seen as a pattern. The analysis on the following pages are examples of the team's tactics being used effectively.

Each action, pass, individual movement with or without the ball, and the positioning of each player on the pitch including their body shape, are presented.

The analysis is then used to create a session to coach this specific tactical situation.

Tactical Situation 9 - Making a Run on Blind Side of Defender to Receive a Long Pass in Behind

MAKING A RUN ON THE BLIND SIDE OF THE DEFENDER TO RECEIVE A LONG PASS IN BEHIND

Griezmann (7) makes run on blind side of CB No.4

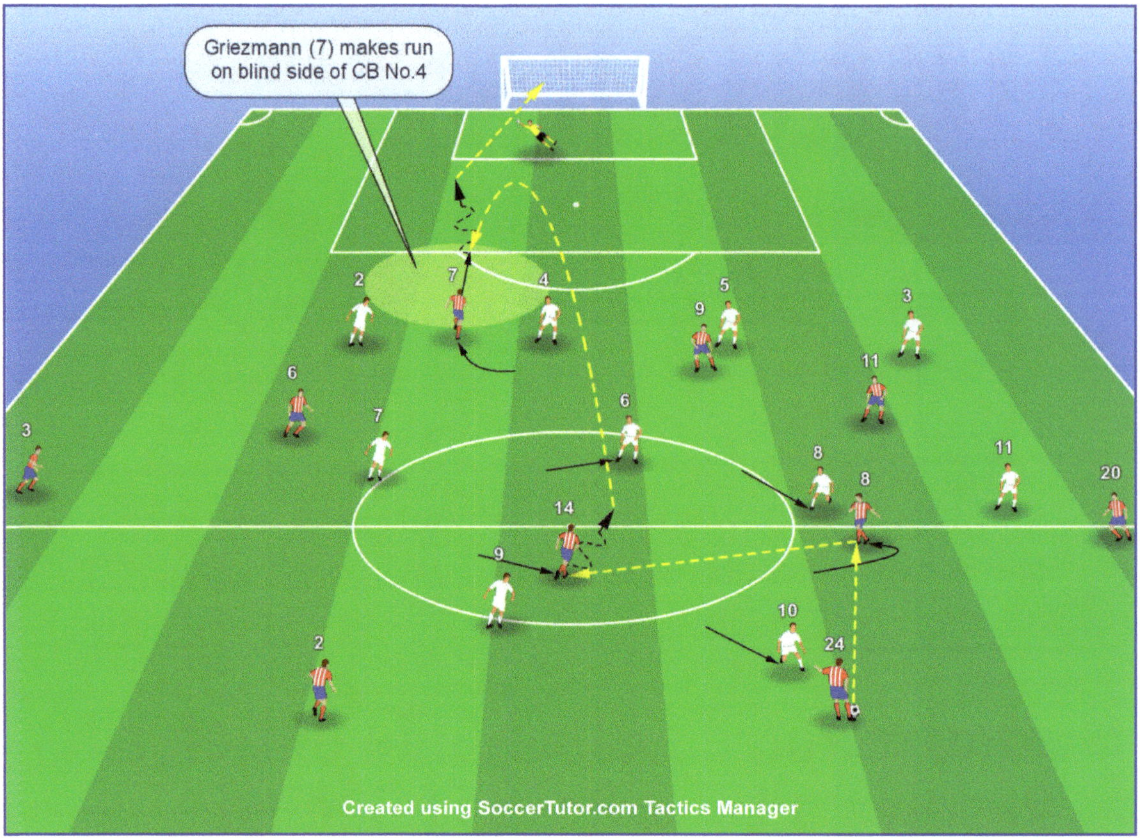

One of the frequent movements for the Atlético forwards that leads to scoring chances is the run on the blind side of the centre backs. This kind of movement creates problems to the opposing centre backs, as they are not able to see both the ball and the forward. One or two seconds out of view can be enough for the forward to receive unmarked on his blind side.

In this example, as soon as the central midfielder **Gabi (14)** receives unmarked in the centre, the forward on the weak side **Griezmann (7)** makes a run on the blind side of white centre back No.4, who can't see both him and the ball. As **Griezmann (7)** gets free of marking for a couple of seconds, he is able to receive a long aerial pass in behind and shoot on goal.

ASSESSMENT

The two most important elements for success in this situation are the well-timed run of the forward (so that he avoids being offside) and the accuracy of the pass from the player in possession.

©SOCCERTUTOR.COM DIEGO SIMEONE'S ATTACKING TACTICS

SESSION (3 PRACTICES) FOR "MAKING A RUN ON BLIND SIDE OF DEFENDER TO RECEIVE A LONG PASS IN BEHIND"

DIEGO SIMEONE'S ATTACKING TACTICS

Tactical Situation 9 - Making a Run on Blind Side of Defender to Receive a Long Pass in Behind

SESSION FOR THIS TACTICAL SITUATION (3 PRACTICES)

1. Making a Run on Blind Side of Defender to Receive a Long Pass in Behind in a Technical Practice

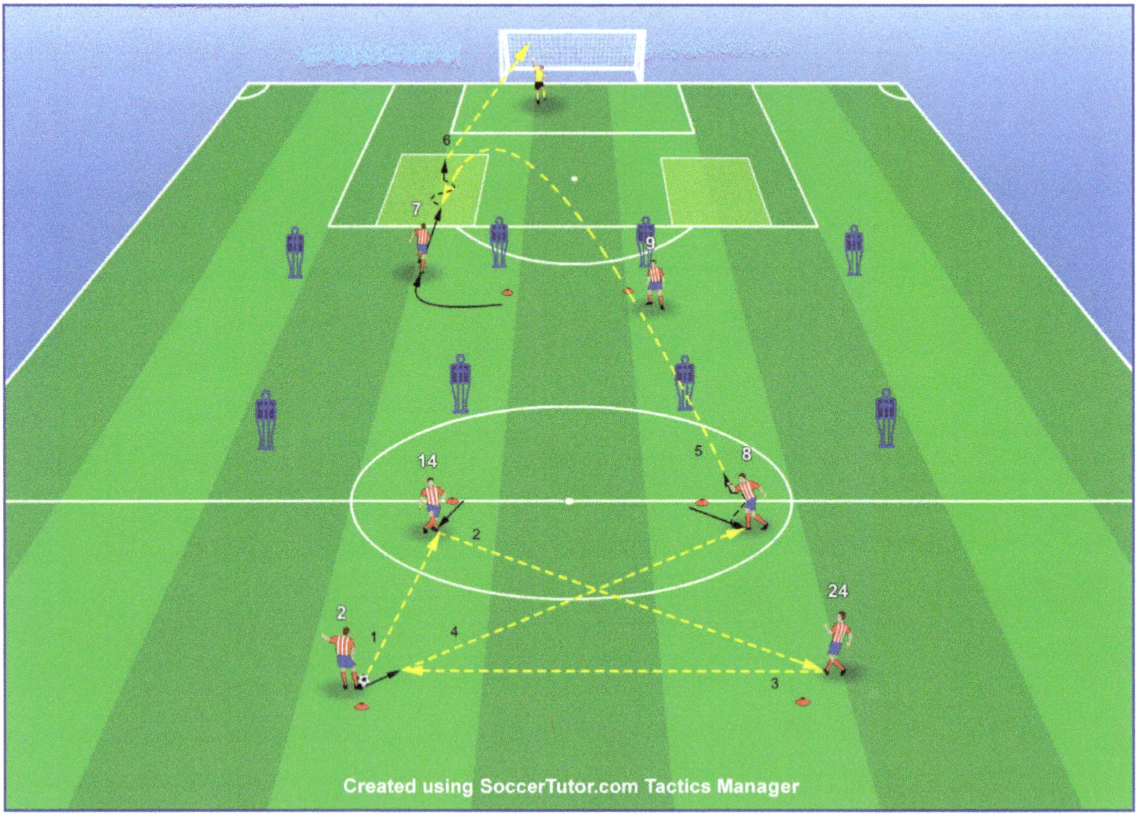

Description

- The practice starts with the centre backs and central midfielders passing to each other, as shown.
- As soon as the 4th pass is received by the central midfielder (**No.8** in diagram), the forward on the weak side **(7)** makes a run on the blind side of the mannequin (centre back).
- The central midfielder **(8)** looks up and plays an accurate long aerial pass into the path of the forward **(7)**, who receives and finishes using 2 touches.

Restriction: The ball must be received within the white areas.

Coaching Points

1. Well-timed run of the forwards on the blind side of the centre backs, so they are unable to see both the forward and the ball.
2. Accurate passing, receiving, and finishing.

©SOCCERTUTOR.COM

DIEGO SIMEONE'S ATTACKING TACTICS

Tactical Situation 9 - Making a Run on Blind Side of Defender to Receive a Long Pass in Behind

PROGRESSION

2. Making a Run on Blind Side of Defender to Receive a Long Pass in Behind in a Dynamic Zonal Practice

Description

- The practice starts in the marked-out low zone and the reds play 4v2. The aim is to move the ball to an unmarked central midfielder beyond the white forwards.

- As soon as this happens, the red forward on the weak side (**No.7** in diagram) makes a run on the blind side of the white centre back No.4 towards the 5 x 8 yard area in the box.

- The central midfielder (**8**) plays an accurate long pass into the forward's (**7**) path, who must receive within the small area and try to score past the GK.

- If the red forward does not successfully receive within the small area, the Coach throws a new ball to the white forwards and they try to score in the mini goals within 10 seconds.

Restrictions

1. The white centre backs can only defend within the red area.
2. The red forwards have to receive the long pass within the small white areas.
3. The forwards are allowed a maximum of 2 touches (receive and finish).

©SOCCERTUTOR.COM   DIEGO SIMEONE'S ATTACKING TACTICS

Tactical Situation 9 - Making a Run on Blind Side of Defender to Receive a Long Pass in Behind

PROGRESSION
3. Making a Run on Blind Side of Defender to Receive a Long Pass in Behind in a Conditioned Game

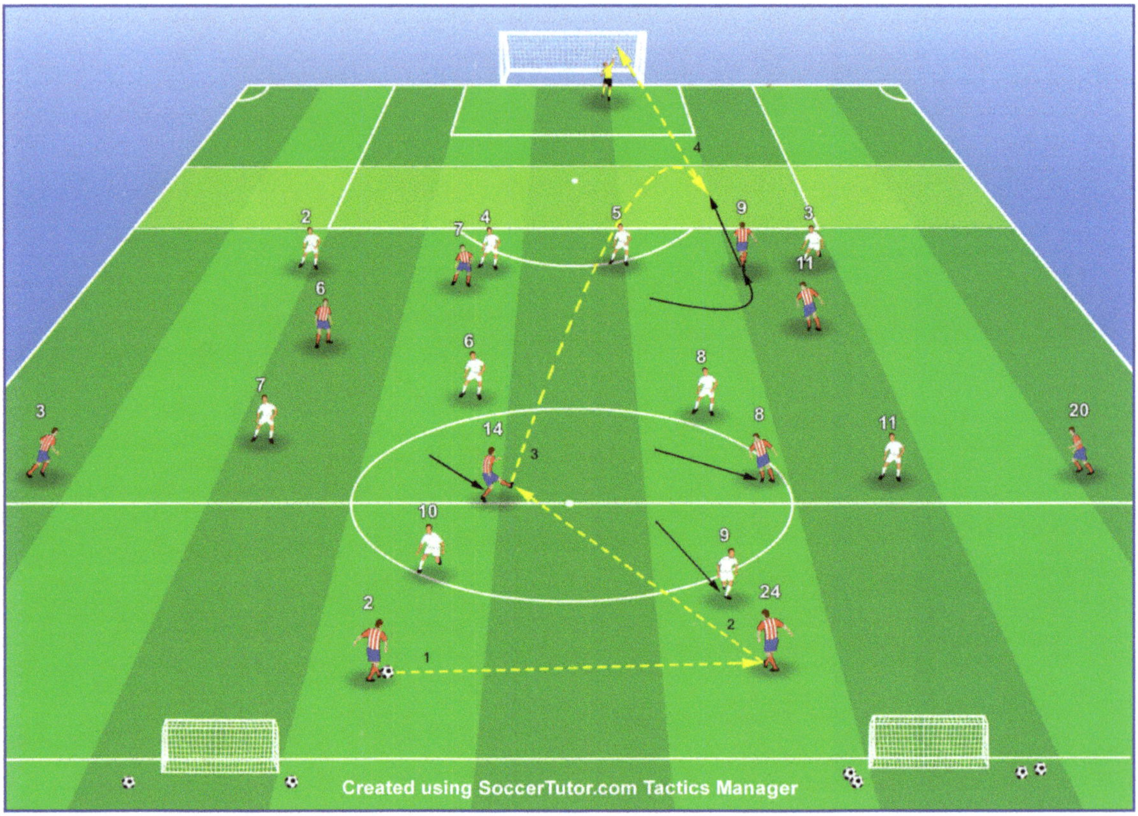

Description
- In the final practice of this session, the 2 teams play a 10 v 10 (+GK) game in 2/3 of the pitch. There is a 50 x 8 yard white zone for the forwards to receive in.
- The reds can score in any way, but if they score after a forward makes a run on the blind side of a defender, they score 3 goals.
- In the diagram example, the red central midfielder **(14)** plays a long pass to the forward on the weak side **(9)**, who has made a run on the blind side of white No.5. He then receives within the white zone and finishes.
- The white team try to win the ball and then score (counter attack) within 12-15 seconds.

Restrictions
1. The white players cannot enter the white zone until a red player receives inside it.
2. The white GK cannot enter the white zone.

Progression: The 2 teams play an 11 v 11 game in 2/3 of the pitch, with a large goal and GK added for the red team.

TACTICAL SITUATION 10

Forward Creates and Exploits Space to Receive in Behind

The content in this section is from analysis of Diego Simeone's Atlético Madrid teams during the 2017/2018 and 2018/2019 seasons.

The analysis is based on recurring patterns of play observed within the Atlético Madrid team. Once the same phase of play occurred several times (at least 10), the tactics would be seen as a pattern. The analysis on the following pages are examples of the team's tactics being used effectively.

Each action, pass, individual movement with or without the ball, and the positioning of each player on the pitch including their body shape, are presented.

Tactical Situation 10 - Forward Creates and Exploits Space to Receive in Behind

FORWARD CREATES AND EXPLOITS SPACE TO RECEIVE IN BEHIND

1. Forward Drops Back to Drag Marker Out of Position and Spins in Behind to Receive Central Midfielder's Long Aerial Pass

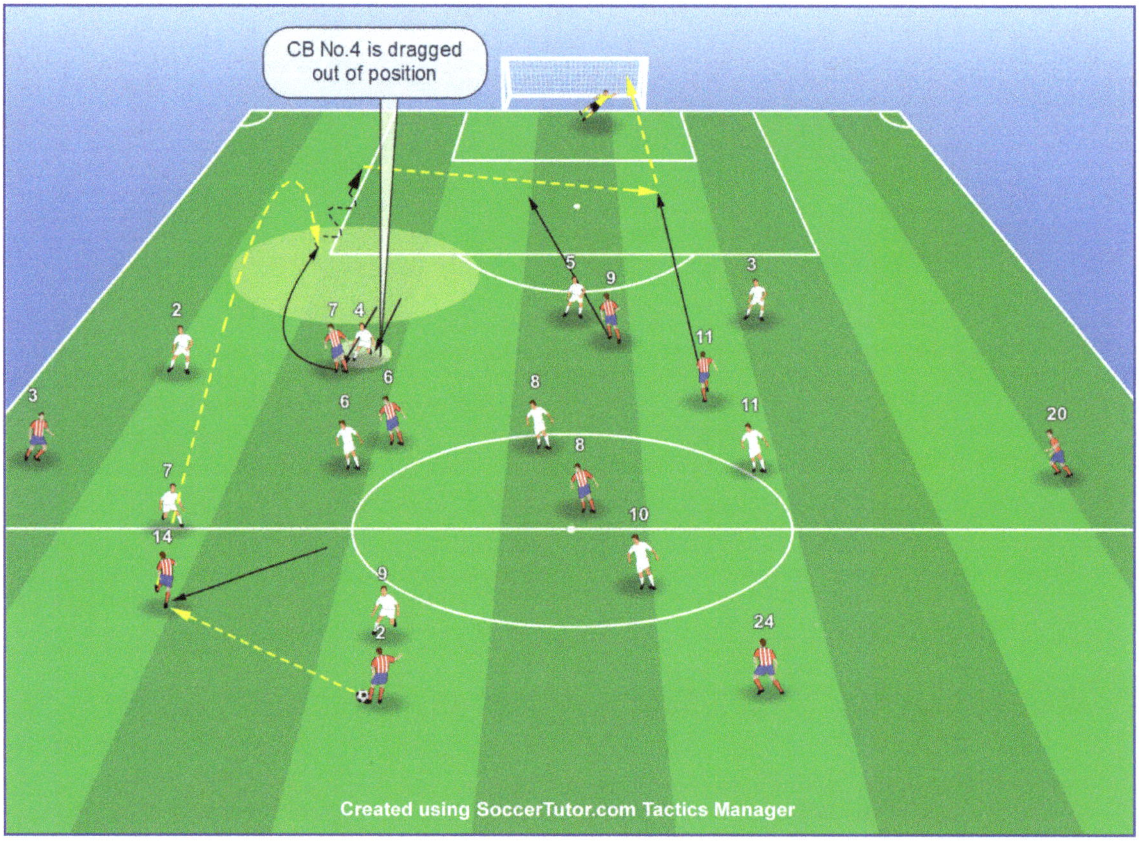

In addition to attacking actions which included teamwork and combination play, there were also individual actions from the forwards which helped Diego Simeone's Atlético Madrid team create scoring chances.

The Atlético forwards would often create space for themselves to exploit. To achieve this, good synchronisation and well-timed runs were needed.

The forward **Griezmann (7)** drops back as soon as the central midfielder **Gabi (14)** receives with time and space. As the white centre back No.4 follows the movement, space is created behind and **Griezmann (7)** makes a sudden and quick change of direction to attack the available space.

The central midfielder **(14)** plays a long aerial pass into the path of the forward **(7)**, who receives and crosses into the box.

©SOCCERTUTOR.COM   DIEGO SIMEONE'S ATTACKING TACTICS

Tactical Situation 10 - Forward Creates and Exploits Space to Receive in Behind

2. Forward Drops Back and Moves to Receive in a Wider Position from the Full Back's Ground Pass

The forward **Griezmann (7)** drops back to offer a passing option as soon as the ball is passed to the full back **F. Luis (3)**.

As the white centre back No.4 follows the movement, space is created behind and the forward **Griezmann (7)** makes a quick change of direction to attack the available space.

Griezmann (7) receives from **F. Luis (3)** and crosses into the box.

3. Forward Drops Back and Spins in Behind to Receive Behind the Opposing Centre Back from the Full Back's Ground Pass

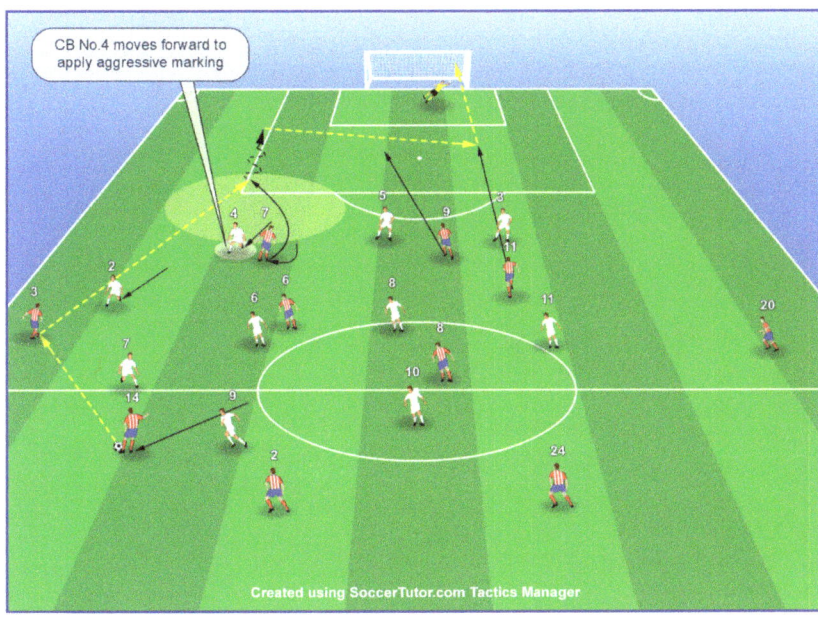

In this variation, the white centre back No.4 marks the forward **Griezmann (7)** in a way where he could reach the ball first if the ball is played to his feet.

Space is created and the forward **Griezmann (7)** makes a run in behind the back of white No.4 to receive.

Griezmann (7) receives a ground pass from **F. Luis (3)** and crosses into the box.

DIEGO SIMEONE'S ATTACKING TACTICS

Tactical Situation 10 - Forward Creates and Exploits Space to Receive in Behind

GETTING ONSIDE TO EXPLOIT THE SPACE BETWEEN THE OPPOSING DEFENDERS

1a. The Opposing Defenders Push Forward Collectively to Retain Cohesion Between the Lines

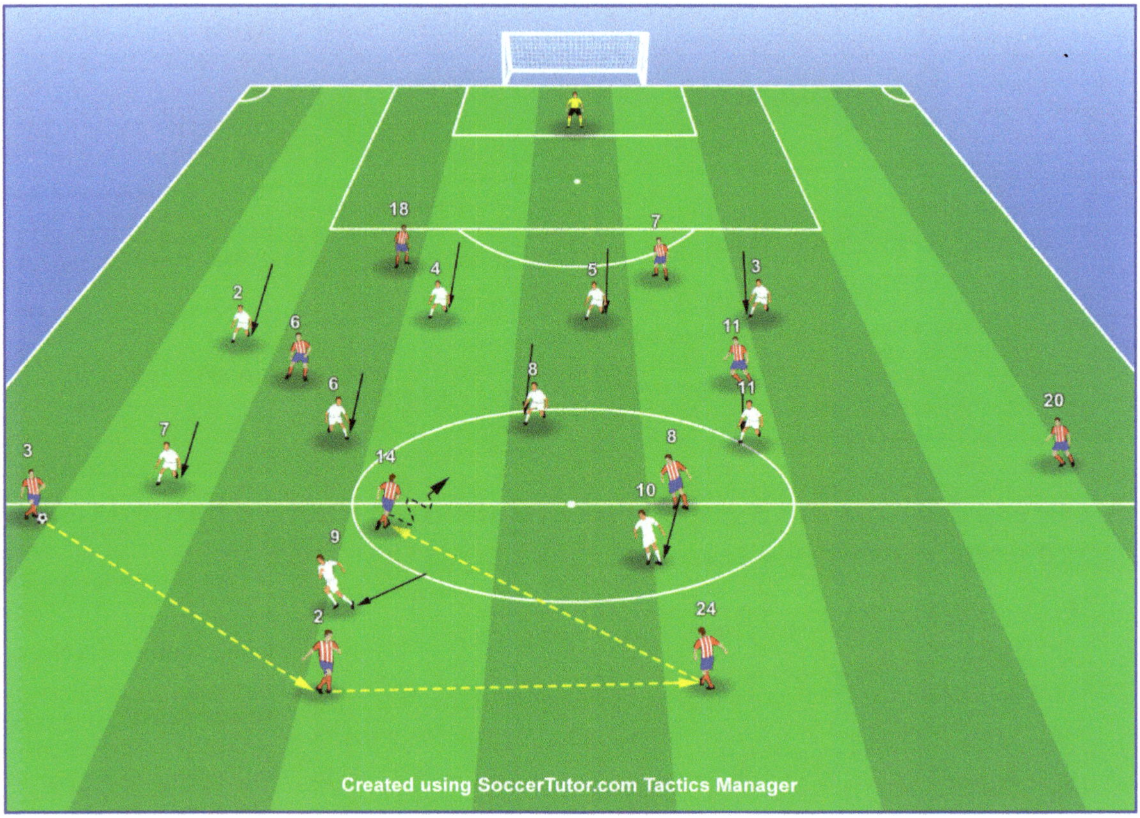

The Atlético forwards often tried to exploit the space between the defenders through intelligent positioning, and especially **Diego Costa (18)**.

This took place in situations when the opposition's defensive line moves forward a few yards to retain cohesion between the lines.

As soon as the pass from the left back **F. Luis (3)** is played back to the centre back **Godín (2)**, all the white players move forward collectively and leave the 2 Atlético forwards in offside positions.

However, the red defenders manage to direct the ball to the central midfielder **Gabi (14)**, who is able to receive unmarked and turn between the lines.

Tactical Situation 10 - Forward Creates and Exploits Space to Receive in Behind

1b. The Atlético Forwards Drop Back to Get Onside and then Move to Receive in Behind

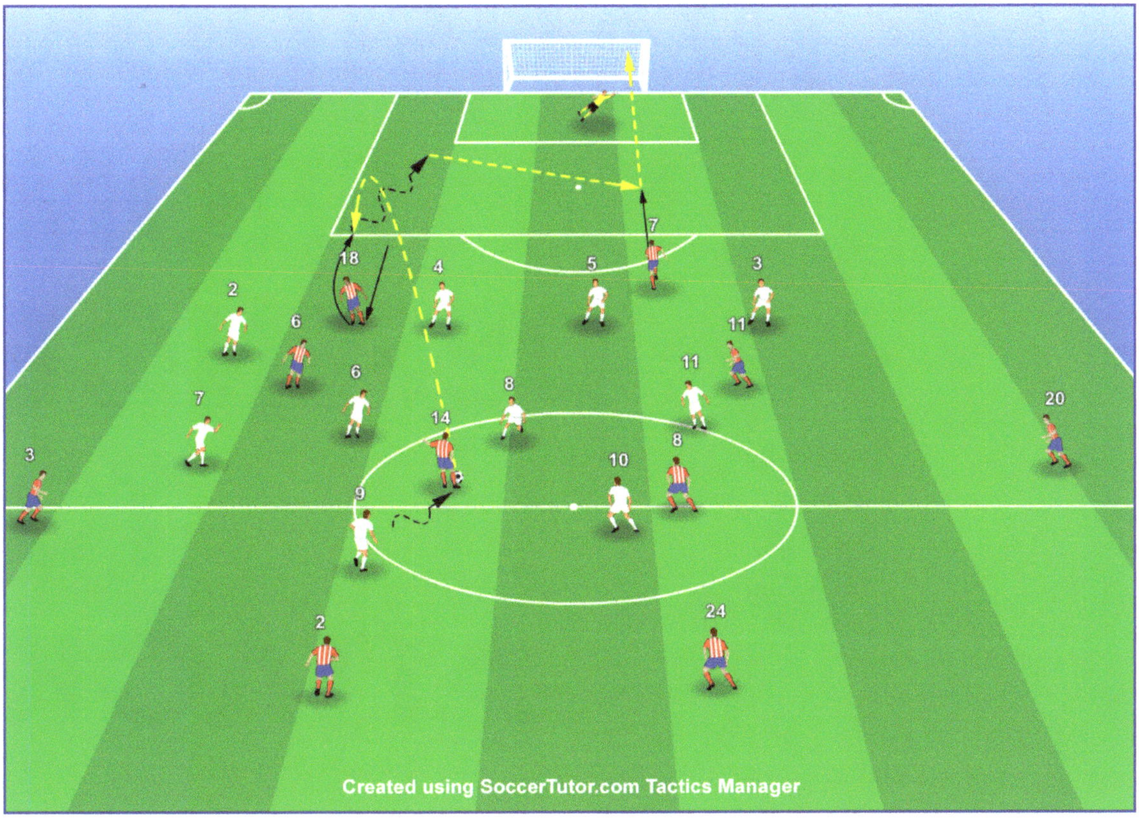

As soon as the ball is moved to the central midfielder **Gabi (14)**, the forward **D. Costa (18)** drops back into an onside position.

D. Costa (18) takes up a position in the gap between the white right back No.2 and the centre back No.4, so that he is free of marking.

D. Costa (18) synchronises his movement with the timing of the pass from the central midfielder **Gabi (14)**.

Gabi (14) plays an aerial pass in behind the defensive line for **D. Costa (18)**, who receives, dribbles forward and delivers a cross for the other forward **Griezmann (7)**, as shown.

DIEGO SIMEONE'S ATTACKING TACTICS

THE TRANSITION FROM DEFENCE TO ATTACK

The Transition from Defence to Attack

THE TRANSITION FROM DEFENCE TO ATTACK (POSITIVE TRANSITION)

DEFINITION

The transition from defence to attack (positive transition) is the phase which starts as soon as possession is won by the defending team and lasts until the opposing team successfully reorganise defensively.

DIEGO SIMEONE'S ATLÉTICO MADRID

Atlético Madrid is a club that owes much of its success in recent years on Diego Simeone's tactics during the transition from defence to attack (positive transition phase), where they have consistently been one of the best teams in Europe.

In the 2017-18 La Liga season, Diego Simeone's Atlético Madrid team had the second best record of goals scored from counter attacks (5). They were only just behind Villarreal CF (6).

THE STAGES OF THE POSITIVE TRANSITION PHASE

1. **Winning possession** (where).
2. **Securing the ball** (moving the ball to a player with available time and space to move forward or pass forward).
3. **Players in advanced positions move to receive** in available space.
4. **The man in possession plays a forward pass.**
5. **The target player receives and uses his skills to beat an opponent (1 v 1) and shoot** (direct threat) **or make a final pass/cross** (indirect threat).

FACTORS THAT AFFECT THE POSITIVE TRANSITION

FACTOR 1:
What area is the ball won in?

The first factor that affects the way the positive transition is carried out is the area where the ball is won, and possession is gained.

There are different ways of carrying out a positive transition if possession is won in the central area or wide areas.

FACTOR 2:
Defensive Positioning of Players

For a coach to prepare for the transition from defence to attack, he has to consider the defensive positions of his players (within the formation used) during the defensive phase.

The transition from defence to attack is strongly related to the defensive positions of the players at the moment the ball is won. This means that not only different formations provide different possibilities for carrying out this phase, but also small adjustments in the defensive positioning of the players within a formation.

In many occasions, the 2 Atlético forwards take up counter attack-minded positions within the 4-4-2 formation and this variation in positioning provides different possibilities for counter attacks.

FACTOR 3:
The Situation Around the Ball Area

Another factor that affects the transition from defence to attack is the situation which is created around the ball area at the moment the ball is won.

For example, the Atlético players (especially the forwards) react in a different way when there is an open ball situation compared to a closed ball situation.

In an **Open Ball Situation**, the ball carrier has time and space to pass forward immediately.

In a **Closed Ball Situation**, the ball carrier is pressed immediately and it is difficult to move forward or play a forward pass.

TACTICAL SITUATION 1

Counter Attack After Winning the Ball in a Wide Position

The content in this section is from analysis of Diego Simeone's Atlético Madrid teams during the 2017/2018 and 2018/2019 seasons.

The analysis is based on recurring patterns of play observed within the Atlético Madrid team. Once the same phase of play occurred several times (at least 10), the tactics would be seen as a pattern. The analysis on the following pages are examples of the team's tactics being used effectively.

Each action, pass, individual movement with or without the ball, and the positioning of each player on the pitch including their body shape, are presented.

The analysis is then used to create a session to coach this specific tactical situation.

Tactical Situation 1 - Counter Attack After Winning the Ball in a Wide Position

COUNTER ATTACK AFTER WINNING THE BALL IN A WIDE POSITION

1a. Full Back Wins the Ball in a Wide Area

FB F.Luis (3) intercepts and wins possession

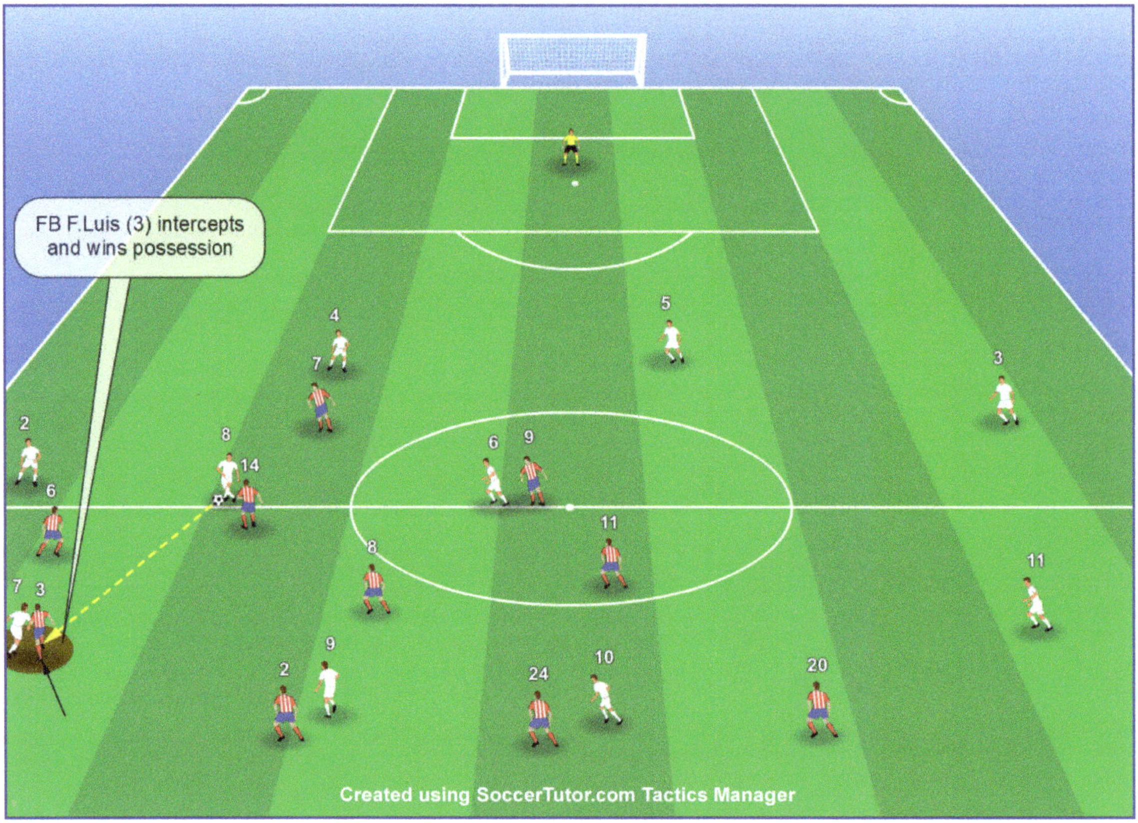

This tactical example shows what happens when Diego Simeone's Atlético Madrid team win the ball in a wide area.

The 2 forwards are in their usual defensive positions and the most advanced player is the forward on the strong side **Griezmann (7)**.

According to the positioning of the opposing defenders, the forward **Griezmann (7)** is most likely to receive in a wide position after Atlético win possession.

In this tactical example, the white central midfielder No.8 attempts to pass towards the right winger No.7.

The Atlético left back **F. Luis (3)** moves forward as soon as the pass is played, gets in front of white No.7, and wins the ball in a wide area.

DIEGO SIMEONE'S ATTACKING TACTICS

Tactical Situation 1 - Counter Attack After Winning the Ball in a Wide Position

1b. Available Forward Passing Options After Winning the Ball in a Wide Area

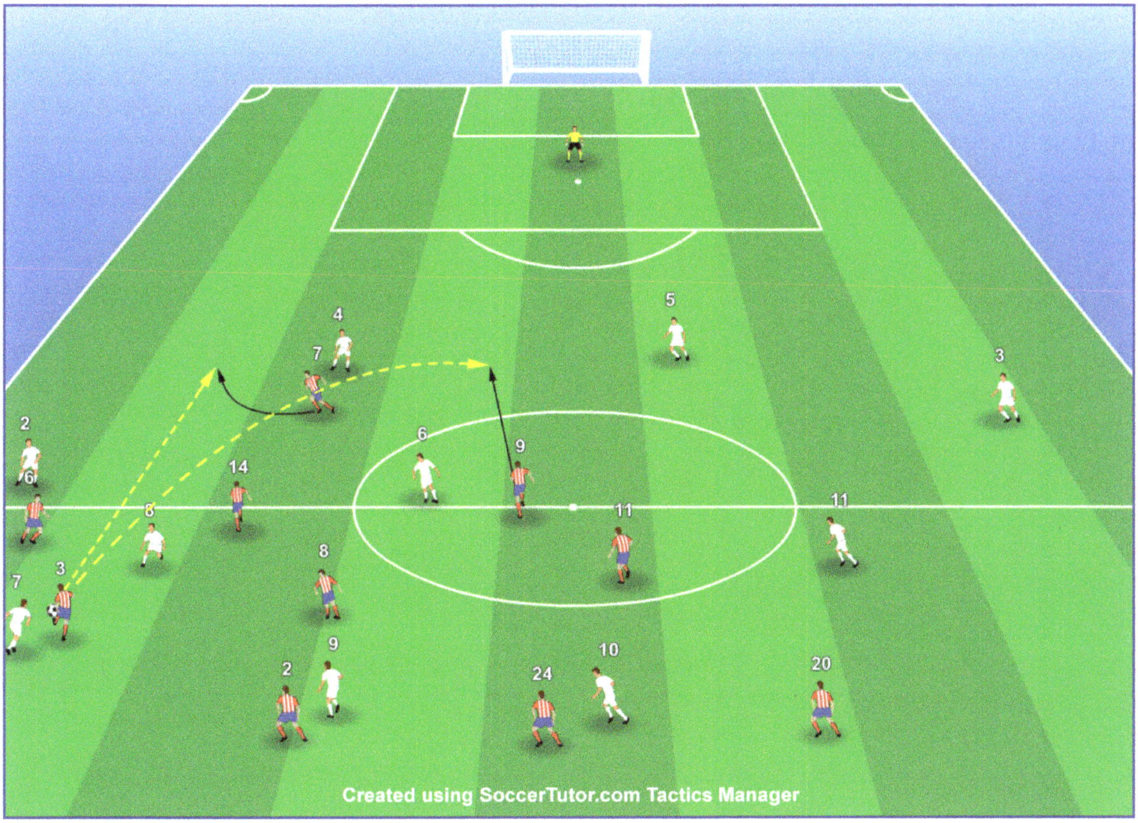

As soon as the Atlético left back **F. Luis (3)** wins the ball, the forward on that side **Griezmann (7)** moves towards the available space out wide and the other forward **Torres (9)** moves forward.

Winning the ball in a wide area provides limited forward passing options but the pass towards **Griezmann (7)** has the greatest chance of being successful.

The other option towards **Torres (9)** is much more difficult. This pass has little chance as it has to be at the exact right angle and weighted perfectly, white No.8 may be an obstacle, and the centre back No.5 can restrict the space by shifting towards the strong side.

In addition, **Torres (9)** is in a relatively deep position, so it would be difficult to exploit the space between the 2 white centre backs.

DIEGO SIMEONE'S ATTACKING TACTICS

Tactical Situation 1 - Counter Attack After Winning the Ball in a Wide Position

1c. Forward Moves Across to Receive in a Wide Position (Indirect Attacking Threat)

The forward on the strong side **Griezmann (7)** moves to receive from the left back **F. Luis (3)**, which is the easiest and best option.

This creates an indirect threat for the opposing team, as the new ball carrier normally can't score from this wide position and an extra pass is needed.

Griezmann (7) is most likely to dribble forward and deliver a cross for one of his team-mates.

2. Inside Pass to a Free Player in the Central Area with Forward Passing Options (Direct Attacking Threat)

If **F. Luis (3)** passes inside to central midfielder **Saúl (8)**, the forward passing options are increased.

By receiving in the central area, the conditions for making a successful forward pass are better and there is a strong possibility of creating a direct threat.

For example, a pass towards **Torres (9)**, who has moved into a more advanced position, can lead to a shot on goal.

SESSION (3 PRACTICES) FOR "COUNTER ATTACK AFTER WINNING THE BALL IN A WIDE POSITION"

Tactical Situation 1 - Counter Attack After Winning the Ball in a Wide Position

SESSION FOR THIS TACTICAL SITUATION (3 PRACTICES)
1. Counter Attack After Winning the Ball Wide in a Functional Practice (Passive Centre Backs)
Scenario A: Indirect Threat

Description (Scenario A)

- The wide midfielders, full backs and central midfielders are all positioned in the wide areas (15 yard squares), which can be adjusted depending on the level of the players.

- There is also a central yellow square (10 yards) for the white forward No.9.

- The practice starts with the Coach's pass to the white full back in a wide area (3v3). The whites try to move the ball to the forward No.9 inside the yellow square and score.

- The 3 red players within the wide white area try to win the ball. The reds then launch a counter attack and try to score within 8 seconds. The Coaches play as passive and stationary defenders, like mannequins.

- In this first example, a forward pass is played to **No.7** as soon as the ball is won. This creates an **Indirect Threat**, with **No.7** delivering a cross for a team-mate to try and score.

DIEGO SIMEONE'S ATTACKING TACTICS

Tactical Situation 1 - Counter Attack After Winning the Ball in a Wide Position

Scenario B: Direct Threat

Description (Scenario B)

- In this second scenario, the red full back **(3)** passes inside to the central midfielder **(8)**.

- By receiving in the central area, the conditions for making a successful forward pass are better and there is a strong possibility of creating a direct threat.

- The red central midfielder **(8)** passes in between the 2 Coaches (or mannequins) to the forward **(9)**, who has moved into a more advanced position, receives in behind (**Direct Threat**) and tries to score past the GK.

- The Coaches play as passive and stationary defenders, like mannequins.

Restriction: Any pass towards white No.9 should be played from within the wide area.

Coaching Points

1. Quick decision making is needed after winning the ball.
2. Synchronised movements by the forwards.

DIEGO SIMEONE'S ATTACKING TACTICS

Tactical Situation 1 - Counter Attack After Winning the Ball in a Wide Position

PROGRESSION
2. Counter Attack After Winning the Ball Wide in a Functional Practice (Active Centre Backs)

Description
- In this progression of the previous practice, we replace the Coaches (or mannequins) with 2 active white centre backs to make it more realistic and more difficult for the reds to score.
- The practice now starts with the GK's pass to the white centre back (No.4 in diagram) and then the centre back's pass into a wide area.
- From there, the practice works in the same way as the previous one.

Restriction: Any pass towards white No.9 should be played from within the wide area.

Coaching Points
1. Quick decision making is needed after winning the ball.
2. Synchronised movements by the forwards.

©SOCCERTUTOR.COM

DIEGO SIMEONE'S ATTACKING TACTICS

Tactical Situation 1 - Counter Attack After Winning the Ball in a Wide Position

PROGRESSION

3. Counter Attack After Winning the Ball Wide in a Conditioned Game

Description

- In the final practice of this session, the 2 teams play a 9v9 game in 2/3 of the pitch.
- The game starts with the white GK and the white team must move the ball into one of the wide white areas and then try to move the ball to the forward No.9 in the central yellow area to score against the GK.
- The reds try to win the ball in a 3v3 situation within the wide area and then launch a counter attack.

After winning the ball within the wide area, the reds can either:

1. Pass directly to the forward (**7**) in a wide position for a cross (**Indirect Threat**).
2. Pass inside to the central midfielder (**8**), who can then play a forward pass with more space, time and options. This has more potential to create a **Direct Threat**, with a pass to **No.9** who can score.

Restriction: Any pass towards white No.9 should be played from within the wide area.

DIEGO SIMEONE'S ATTACKING TACTICS

TACTICAL SITUATION 2

Counter Attack After Winning the Ball in the Centre (Direct Threat)

The content in this section is from analysis of Diego Simeone's Atlético Madrid teams during the 2017/2018 and 2018/2019 seasons.

The analysis is based on recurring patterns of play observed within the Atlético Madrid team. Once the same phase of play occurred several times (at least 10), the tactics would be seen as a pattern. The analysis on the following pages are examples of the team's tactics being used effectively.

Each action, pass, individual movement with or without the ball, and the positioning of each player on the pitch including their body shape, are presented.

The analysis is then used to create 2 practices to coach this specific tactical situation.

Tactical Situation 2 - Counter Attack After Winning the Ball in the Centre (Direct Threat)

COUNTER ATTACK AFTER WINNING THE BALL IN THE CENTRE (DIRECT THREAT)

1a. Central Midfielder Intercepts the Opposing Centre Back's Through Pass in a Central Area

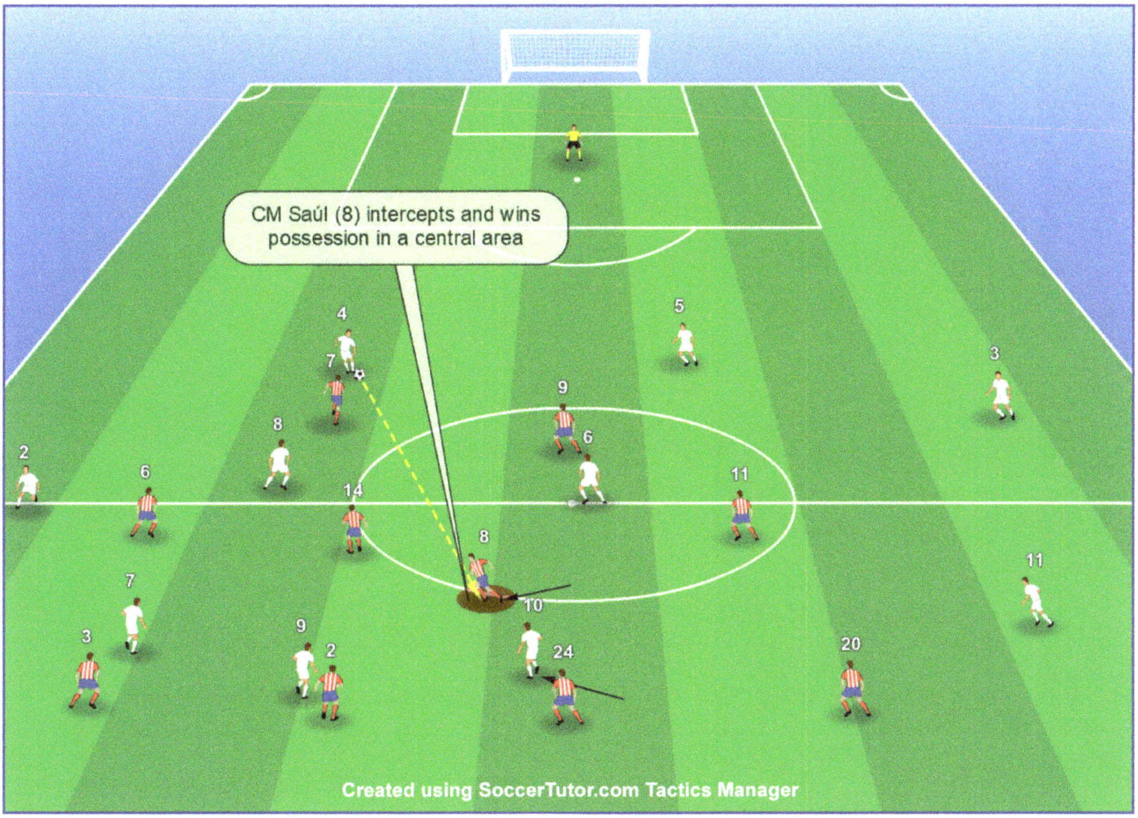

When the opposing team have a back 4, there is a strong possibility that they will always retain 3 players at the back to make sure they have a numerical advantage and safety against the 2 Atlético forwards.

The positioning of the opposing 3 man defence creates gaps which can be exploited by Diego Simeone's Atlético Madrid team as soon as they win the ball.

In this tactical example, the white centre back No.4 attempts to play a through pass but it is intercepted by the Atlético central midfielder **Saúl (8)** in a central area.

DIEGO SIMEONE'S ATTACKING TACTICS

Tactical Situation 2 - Counter Attack After Winning the Ball in the Centre (Direct Threat)

1b. Winning the Ball in a Central Area Increases the Available Forward Passing Options and Creates a Direct Threat

As soon as the ball is won in the central area, **Saúl (8)** has available time and space to pass forward, as white No.6 is relatively far away.

Depending on the positioning and reactions of the white defenders, some gaps may exist between them which should be exploited.

There are 3 available passing options:

1. **Torres (9)** - Direct threat
2. **Griezmann (7)** - Indirect threat
3. **Correa (11)** - Indirect threat

DIEGO SIMEONE'S ATTACKING TACTICS

Tactical Situation 2 - Counter Attack After Winning the Ball in the Centre (Direct Threat)

ASSESSMENT

1. It is obvious that winning the ball within the central area creates better possibilities for a successful counter attack than winning it out wide. If we recall the tactics of Diego Simeone during the defensive phase (**see other part of this 2 book set**), we realise that the defending team wants to force the ball towards the side-lines rather than towards the centre. This shows that Atlético's good defensive organisation is a higher priority for Diego Simeone than preparing for a potential successful counter attack.

2. When Atlético Madrid win the ball in wide areas, the available forward passing options are limited and it is more difficult to create a direct threat. However, if the ball is moved quickly from the wide areas to a free player in the central area, not only are there more available forward passing options but a direct threat could also be created.

2 PRACTICES FOR "COUNTER ATTACK AFTER WINNING THE BALL IN THE CENTRE (DIRECT THREAT)"

DIEGO SIMEONE'S ATTACKING TACTICS

Tactical Situation 2 - Counter Attack After Winning the Ball in the Centre (Direct Threat)

PRACTICES FOR THIS TACTICAL SITUATION (2 PRACTICES)
1. Counter Attack After Winning the Ball in the Centre in a Functional Practice

Description
- Within the 15 yard white central square (size depends on level of players), we have 2 white centre backs and 2 central midfielders versus 2 red forwards and 2 central midfielders. There is also a 10 yard yellow square area for the white forward No.9 and there are 2 red wingers in the positions shown, who only take part if there is a red counter attack.

- The practice starts with the Coach's pass to a white centre back and the whites try to move the ball to the forward No.9 inside the yellow square and score.

- The 4 red players within the white square try to win the ball. The reds then launch a counter attack (including the 2 wide midfielders) and try to score within 8 seconds. The red player that wins the ball should have 3 forward passing options for the counter.

Coaching Points
1. Quick decision making is needed after winning the ball.
2. Synchronised movements by the forwards.
3. Find the available space (gaps between white defenders) to exploit.

DIEGO SIMEONE'S ATTACKING TACTICS

Tactical Situation 2 - Counter Attack After Winning the Ball in the Centre (Direct Threat)

PROGRESSION
2. Counter Attack After Winning the Ball in the Centre in a Functional Game

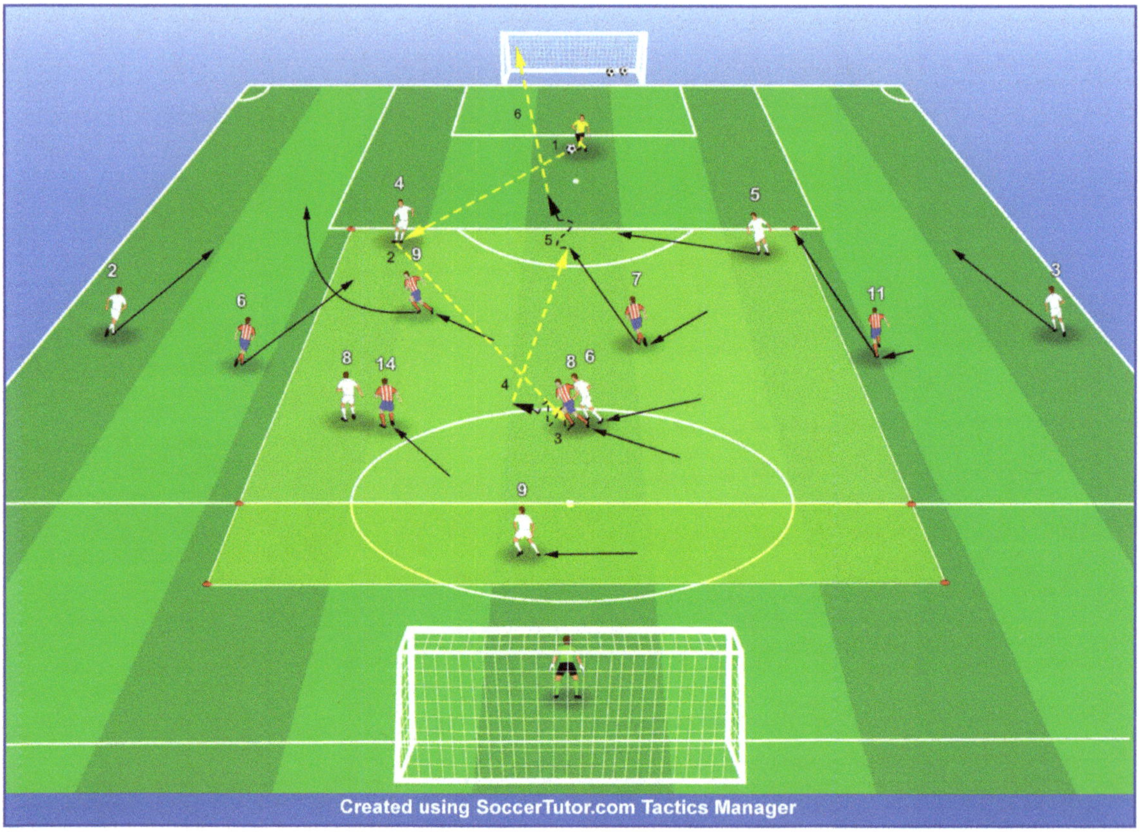

Description
- In the final practice of this session, the 2 teams play a 9v9 game in 2/3 of the pitch.
- The game starts with the white GK's pass to a centre back within the large white area.
- The whites aim to move the ball to the forward No.9 inside the yellow area, who tries to score past the GK.
- The 4 red players within the white area try to win the ball. The reds then launch a counter attack (including the 2 wide midfielders) and try to score as quickly as possible.

Restrictions
1. The red wide midfielders shift according to the position of the ball and they can also enter the white area. As soon as possession is won, they take part in the counter attack.
2. The white full backs take up attacking positions, pass the ball around (to centre backs) and take part in the defensive phase of the game (as soon as possession is lost).
3. Passes towards the white forward No.9 should be played from within the central area.

©SOCCERTUTOR.COM   DIEGO SIMEONE'S ATTACKING TACTICS

TACTICAL SITUATION 3

Defensive and Counter Attack-Minded Positioning of the Forwards

The content in this section is from analysis of Diego Simeone's Atlético Madrid teams during the 2017/2018 and 2018/2019 seasons.

The analysis is based on recurring patterns of play observed within the Atlético Madrid team. Once the same phase of play occurred several times (at least 10), the tactics would be seen as a pattern. The analysis on the following pages are examples of the team's tactics being used effectively.

Each action, pass, individual movement with or without the ball, and the positioning of each player on the pitch including their body shape, are presented.

The analysis is then used to create a session to coach this specific tactical situation.

Tactical Situation 3 - Defensive and Counter Attack-Minded Positioning of the Forwards

DEFENSIVE-MINDED POSITIONING OF THE FORWARDS

1a. Defensive-minded Positioning of Forwards with Ball in Centre

The way the positive transition is carried out is strongly related to the defensive positions of the players. Diego Simeone's Atlético Madrid team mainly use the 4-4-2 formation. In most of the matches, the 2 forwards took normal defensive positions.

The forwards tried to limit space between the lines. The closest forward to the ball is in an advanced position, with the other forward in a deeper position.

1b. Defensive-minded Positioning of Forwards with Ball Wide

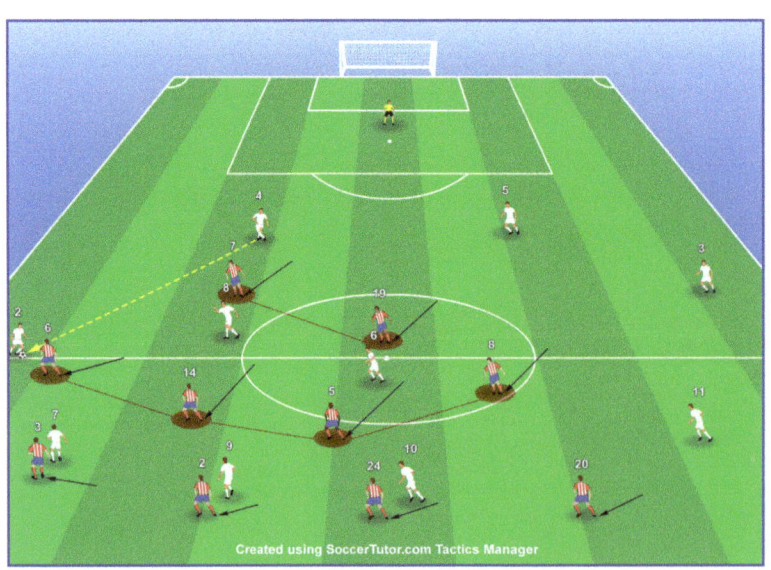

When the ball is moved from a central position to a wider and more advanced one, all the Atlético forwards and midfielders move back and across collectively.

All the same distances are maintained between the players and between the forward and midfield lines.

One forward is still in a deeper position than the other, as shown.

©SOCCERTUTOR.COM

DIEGO SIMEONE'S ATTACKING TACTICS

Tactical Situation 3 - Defensive and Counter Attack-Minded Positioning of the Forwards

2a. Available Space After Winning Possession in a Wide Area
(Defensive-minded Positioning of Forwards)

As soon as the ball is won, the forward on the strong side becomes the target player.

The available space to be exploited is out wide and behind the opposing full back No.2.

The left back **F. Luis (3)** wins the ball in a wide position and the target player **Griezmann (7)** moves across and forward into the available space.

2b. Forward Receives in Available Space Out Wide and Creates an INDIRECT THREAT

As soon as **Griezmann (7)** receives and is confronted by the white centre back No.4, he will most likely try to beat his opponent and deliver a cross for one of his team-mates, who make runs into the box.

This is an example of an indirect threat, which occurs due to the original defensive positioning of the forwards during the defensive phase.

DIEGO SIMEONE'S ATTACKING TACTICS

Tactical Situation 3 - Defensive and Counter Attack-Minded Positioning of the Forwards

3a. Available Space After Winning Possession in the Centre
(Defensive-minded Positioning of Forwards)

In this variation, the ball is won in the central area.

The target player **Griezmann (7)** again moves to exploit the available space out wide and behind the white full back No.2.

3b. Forward Receives in Available Space Out Wide and Creates an INDIRECT THREAT

As soon as **Griezmann (7)** receives and is confronted by the white centre back No.4, he will again try to beat his opponent and deliver a cross for one of his team-mates, who make runs into the box.

This variation (ball won in centre) shows a second example of an indirect threat being created due to the original defensive positioning of the forwards during the defensive phase.

DIEGO SIMEONE'S ATTACKING TACTICS

Tactical Situation 3 - Defensive and Counter Attack-Minded Positioning of the Forwards

COUNTER ATTACK-MINDED POSITIONING OF THE FORWARDS

1a. Counter Attack-minded Positioning of Forwards with Ball in Centre

Over Diego Simeone's time at Atlético Madrid, they have mainly used defensive-minded positioning of the forwards during the defensive phase. However, they have used counter attack-minded positioning of the forwards in many matches, especially when **D. Costa (19)** plays.

Atlético have 1 forward in a very advanced position and there is more space for the opposition to exploit between the forward and midfield lines.

1b. Counter Attack-minded Positioning of Forwards with Ball Wide

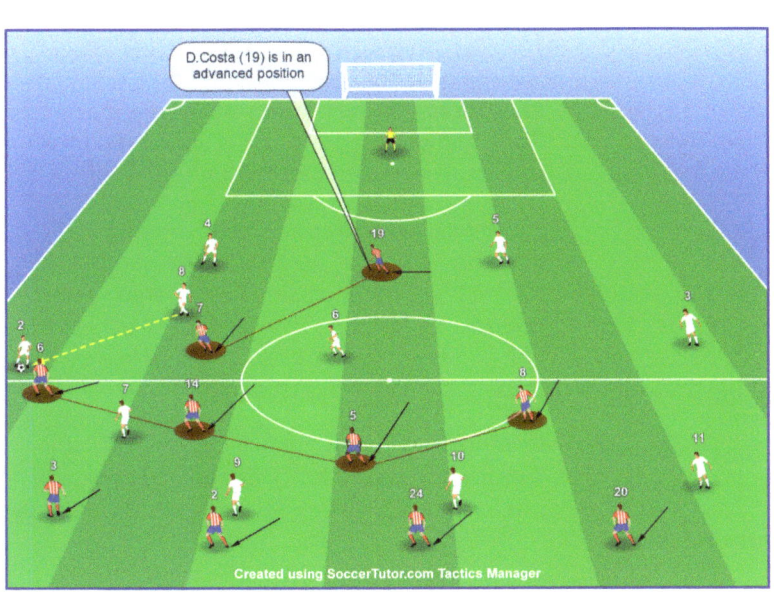

When using defensive-minded positioning of the forwards (**see last 3 pages**), both forwards are able to contribute in the defensive phase.

When using counter attack-minded positioning, only 1 forward contributes in the defensive phase, which is **Griezmann (7)**.

The other forward **D. Costa (19)** is in a dangerous position to exploit a potential direct counter attack if the ball is won.

DIEGO SIMEONE'S ATTACKING TACTICS

Tactical Situation 3 - Defensive and Counter Attack-Minded Positioning of the Forwards

2a. Available Spaces to Exploit After Winning Possession in a Wide Area (Counter Attack-minded Positioning of Forwards)

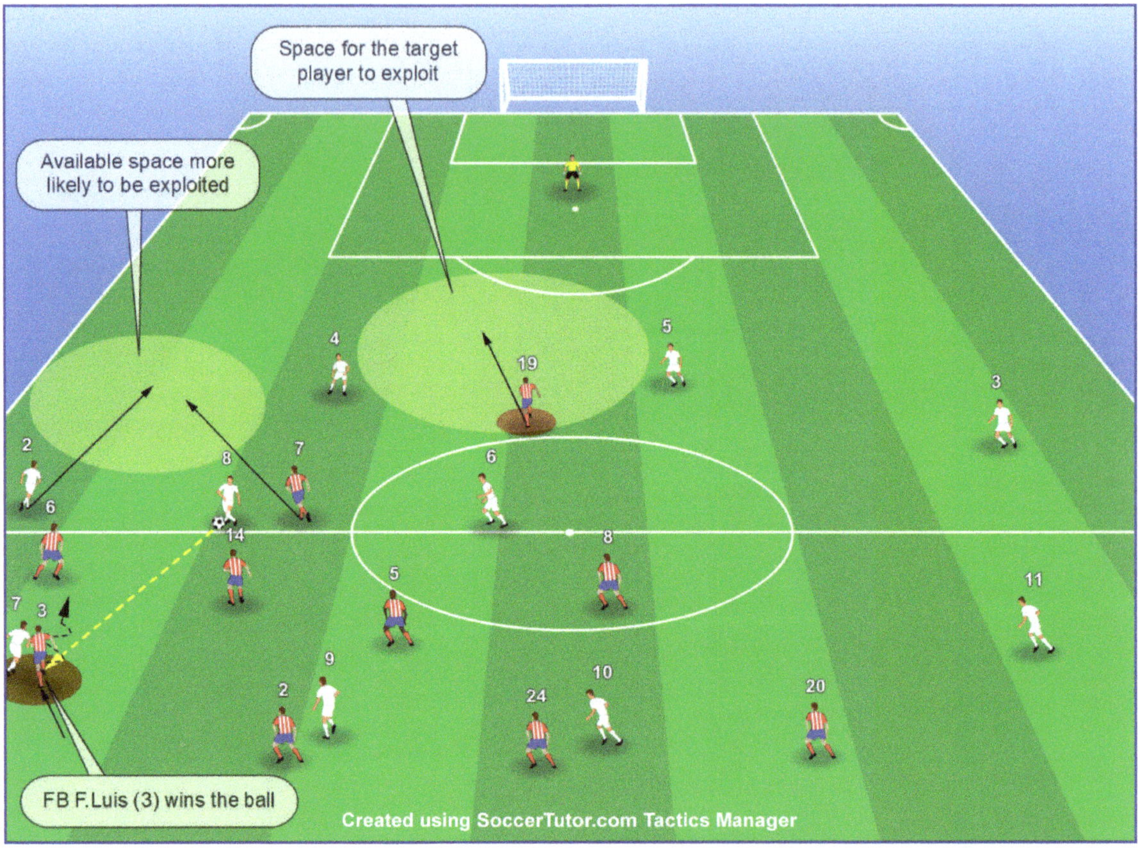

Despite the available space between the forward and midfield lines which can be exploited by the opposition, this positioning of the forwards provides benefits for the transition from defence to attack.

The main target player **D. Costa (19)** is close to the opponent's goal and the available space that can be exploited is in the central area. However, taking advantage of this after winning the ball in a wide area is not easy. It is far easier when the ball is won in the centre, which we show on **pages 162-164**.

In this example, the Atlético left back **F. Luis (3)** intercepts the pass to white No.7.

When winning the ball in a wide area, it is more likely that the space out wide and behind the opposing full back No.2 can be exploited.

However, with this counter attack-minded positioning of the forwards, **Griezmann (7)** is in a relatively deep position compared to the previous situation (normal defensive positioning of forwards) and the white full back No.2 can recover in time and fill the gap.

In addition, moving the ball into the available space in the centre for **D. Costa (19)** to exploit is not easy, as a perfectly accurate pass is needed.

DIEGO SIMEONE'S ATTACKING TACTICS

Tactical Situation 3 - Defensive and Counter Attack-Minded Positioning of the Forwards

2b. Forward Receives in Available Space Between the Centre Backs and Creates a DIRECT THREAT

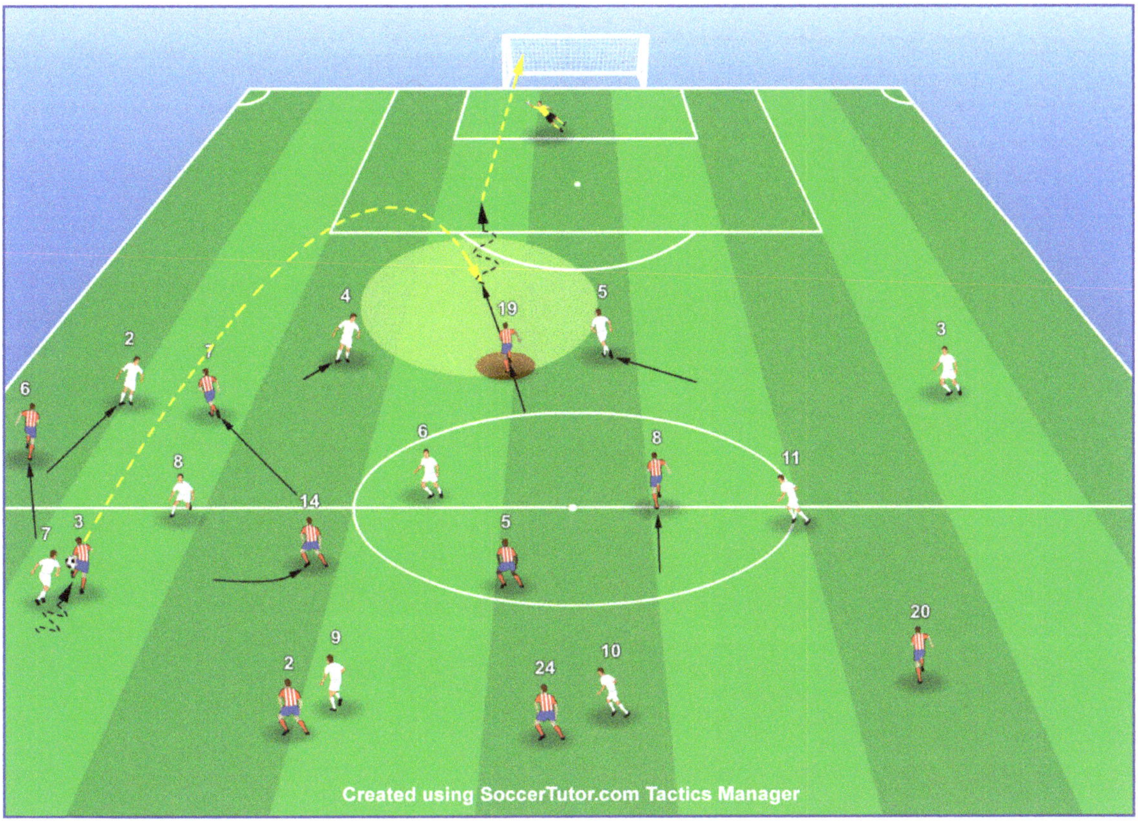

After winning the ball, the Atlético left back **F. Luis (3)** looks to play a forward pass.

The easiest forward passing option towards the forward on the strong side **Griezmann (7)** is covered by the white right back No.2.

Therefore, **F. Luis (3)** takes on the more difficult pass into the available space in the centre for the target player and other forward **D. Costa (19)**. If this pass is perfectly accurate, it can create a direct threat and shot on goal.

ASSESSMENT

The available space for the most advanced positioned forward **D. Costa (19)** depends on the positioning of the opposing centre backs (white No.4 and No.5).

If the white centre backs' positioning doesn't enable **D. Costa (19)** to take advantage of space in between them, then he should search to find space elsewhere (**see next page**).

Tactical Situation 3 - Defensive and Counter Attack-Minded Positioning of the Forwards

3a. Space on Blind Side of Centre Back After Winning Possession in a Wide Area (Counter Attack-minded Positioning of Forwards)

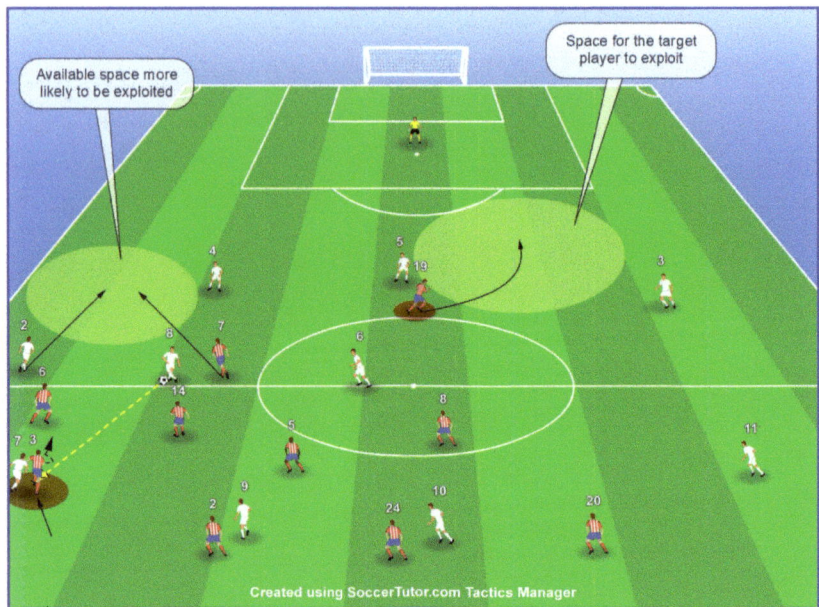

In this variation, the positioning of the white centre back No.5 prevents **D. Costa (19)** from exploiting the space between him and No.4.

In this situation, it was highly effective for the advanced Atlético forward to make a run into the available space on the blind side of the centre back, as he is unable to see both **D. Costa (19)** and the ball.

3b. Forward Receives in Available Space on Blind Side of Centre Back and Creates a DIRECT THREAT

However, it is difficult to achieve this kind of long aerial pass on the blind side of the white centre back No.5.

The Atlético left back **F. Luis (3)** needs quality, as well as enough time and space on the ball to play this accurate pass.

If he does it successfully and **D. Costa (19)** receives in behind, as shown in the diagram, Atlético create a direct threat to shoot on goal.

Tactical Situation 3 - Defensive and Counter Attack-Minded Positioning of the Forwards

4. Moving the ball Inside After Winning Possession in a Wide Area to Increase the Possibility of Playing an Effective Forward Pass

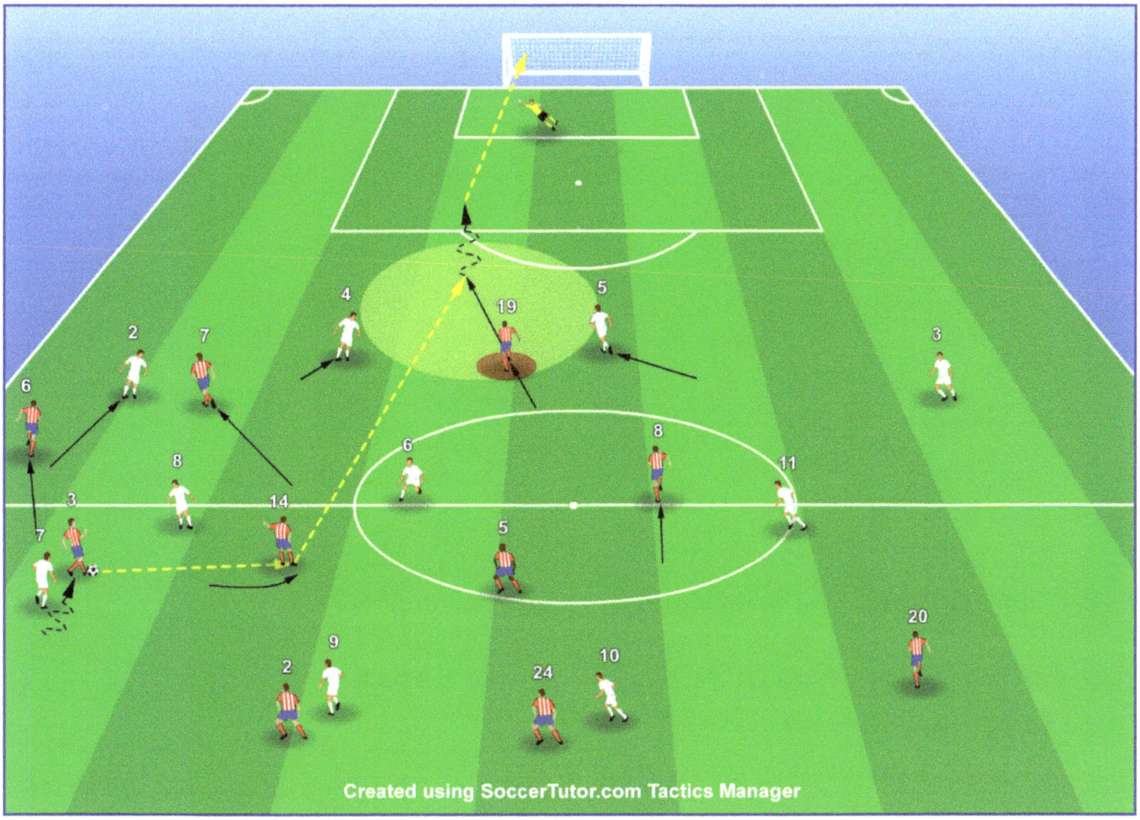

When Atlético win the ball in a central area, they are able to take advantage of the counter attack-minded positioning of the forwards and become extremely effective in the transition from defence to attack (**see next page**).

The best option to take advantage of the counter attack-minded positioning of the forwards if the ball is won in a wide area, is to move the ball quickly to a free player positioned within the central area.

With this inside pass, the pass towards the available space between the centre backs or on the blind side one of the centre backs can be played easier.

As soon as the Atlético left back **F. Luis (3)** intercepts the ball in this tactical example, he passes inside the central midfielder **Rodri (14)** in a central area, and he opens up to receive.

A pass from **Rodri (14)** towards the available space between the opposing centre backs is now easier to achieve.

A **Direct Threat** is created, as **D. Costa (19)** receives in an extremely dangerous position to shoot at goal.

Tactical Situation 3 - Defensive and Counter Attack-Minded Positioning of the Forwards

5a. Space in Between Centre Backs After Winning Possession in the Centre (Counter Attack-minded Positioning of Forwards)

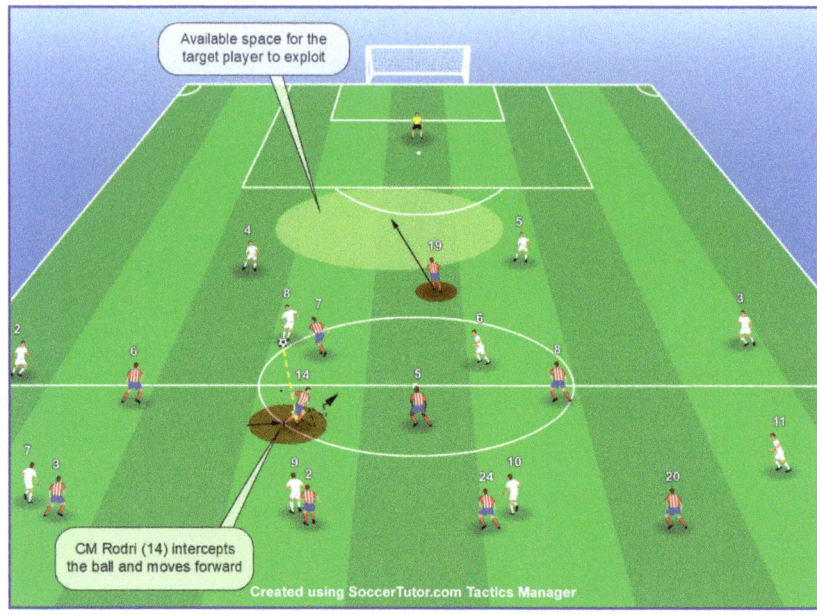

Exploiting the counter attack-minded positioning of the forwards when possession is won within the central area is much easier.

Atlético are able to move the ball to the target player (advanced forward) in the available space between the opposing centre backs.

In this example, central midfielder **Rodri (14)** intercepts the pass towards white No.9.

5b. Forward Receives in Available Space Between the Centre Backs and Creates a DIRECT THREAT

The forward closest to the opposition's goal **D. Costa (19)** is able to move immediately and exploit the available space between the 2 white centre backs.

The central midfielder **Rodri (14)** passes into the available space and a **Direct Threat** is created, as **D. Costa (19)** receives in an extremely dangerous position to shoot at goal.

DIEGO SIMEONE'S ATTACKING TACTICS

Tactical Situation 3 - Defensive and Counter Attack-Minded Positioning of the Forwards

6a. Space on Blind Side of Centre Back After Winning Possession in the Centre (Counter Attack-minded Positioning of Forwards)

Available space to exploit for the target player

CM Rodri (14) intercepts the ball and moves forward

In this variation, the positioning of the white centre back No.5 prevents the Atlético forward **D. Costa (19)** from exploiting the space between him and No.4.

In this situation, it was very effective for the advanced Atlético forward to make a run into the available space on the blind side of the centre back, as he is unable to see both **D. Costa (19)** and the ball.

As **Rodri (14)** moves forward with the ball, the available space is on the right side of the pitch, as shown by the highlighted area in the diagram.

DIEGO SIMEONE'S ATTACKING TACTICS

Tactical Situation 3 - Defensive and Counter Attack-Minded Positioning of the Forwards

6b. Forward Receives in Available Space on Blind Side of Centre Back and Creates a DIRECT THREAT

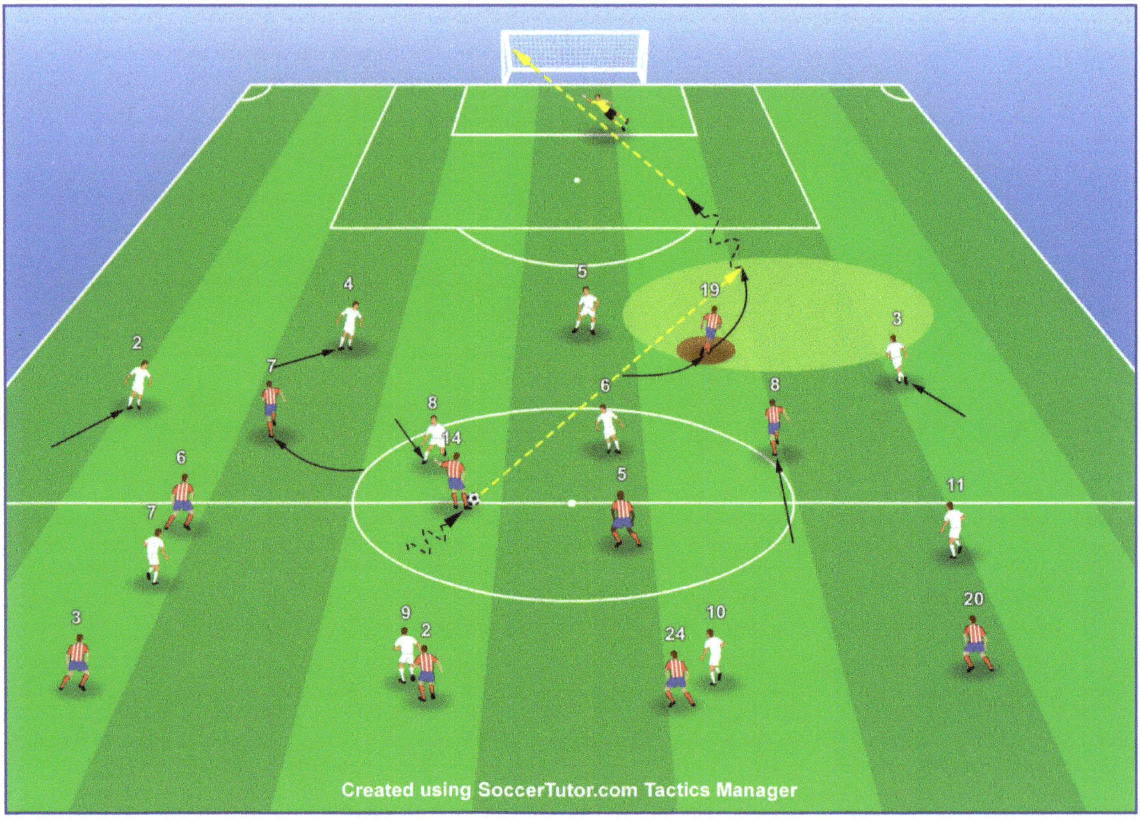

If the central midfielder **Rodri's (14)** pass into the available space is successful and **D. Costa (19)** receives in behind, as shown in the diagram, Atlético create a **Direct Threat** to shoot on goal.

In this example, **D. Costa (19)** dribbles into the box and scores past the goalkeeper.

ASSESSMENT

The counter attack-minded positioning of the forwards can be very effective in the transition from defence to attack, as long as the ball is won in the central area or is moved quickly inside to a free player if possession is won in a wide area.

DIEGO SIMEONE'S ATTACKING TACTICS

SESSION (4 PRACTICES) FOR "DEFENSIVE AND COUNTER ATTACK-MINDED POSITIONING OF THE FORWARDS"

Tactical Situation 3 - Defensive and Counter Attack-Minded Positioning of the Forwards

SESSION FOR THIS TACTICAL SITUATION (4 PRACTICES)
1. Positioning of the Forwards and Counter Attack After Winning the Ball Out Wide in a Functional Practice

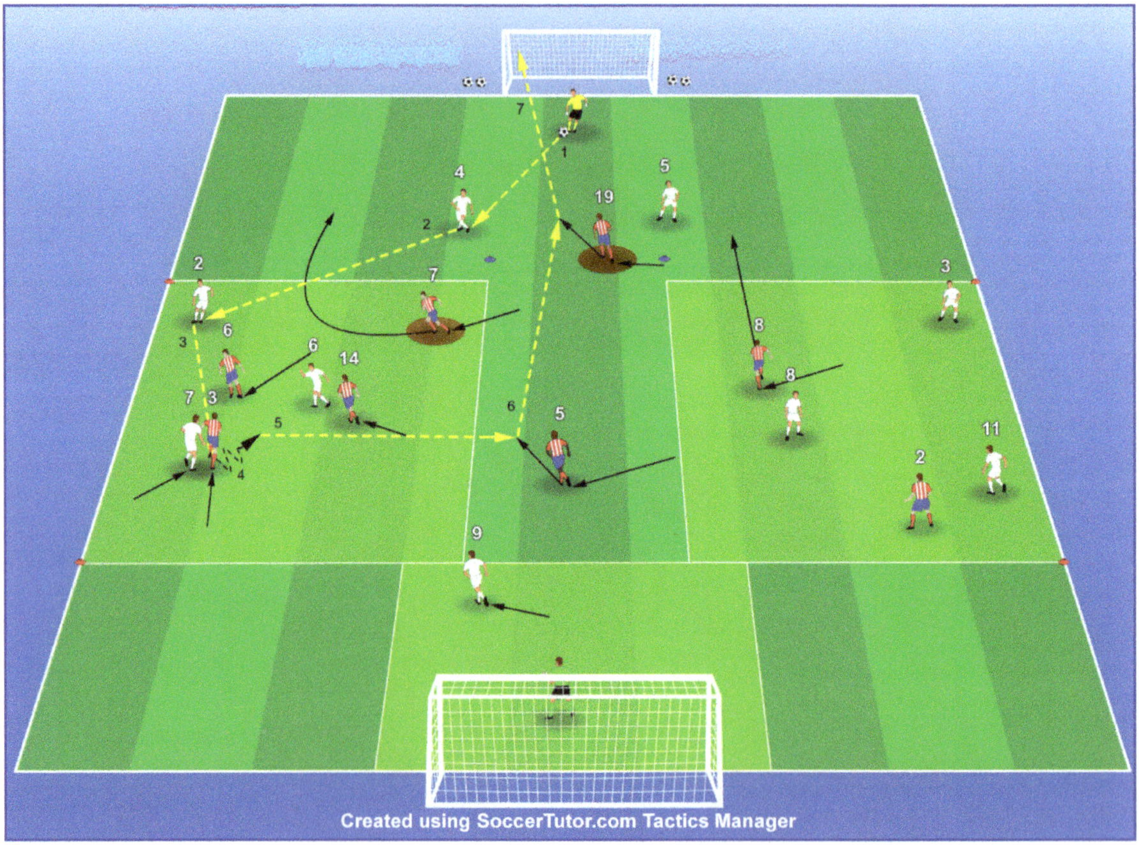

Description
- The wide midfielders, full backs and central midfielders are all positioned in the wide areas (15 yard squares). There is also a central yellow square (10 yards) for the white forward No.9.

- The practice starts with the GK and then the centre back passes to the full back in a wide area (3 v 3). The whites try to move the ball to the forward No.9 and score.

- The reds try to win the ball within the wide area and then score by exploiting the counter attack-minded positioning of the forwards.

Please **see the analysis pages** in this section for the correct decision making. As they are in a wide area, the player that wins the ball can:

1. Pass to the forward on the strong side **(7)** to create an **Indirect Threat**.
2. Pass directly to the advanced forward to create a **Direct Threat** (difficult pass).
3. Pass inside to the central midfielder **(5)**, who then passes to the advanced forward **(19)** to create a **Direct Threat**.

Restriction: Any pass towards white No.9 should be played from within the wide area.

DIEGO SIMEONE'S ATTACKING TACTICS

Tactical Situation 3 - Defensive and Counter Attack-Minded Positioning of the Forwards

VARIATION

2. Positioning of the Forwards and Counter Attack After Winning the Ball in the Centre in a Functional Practice

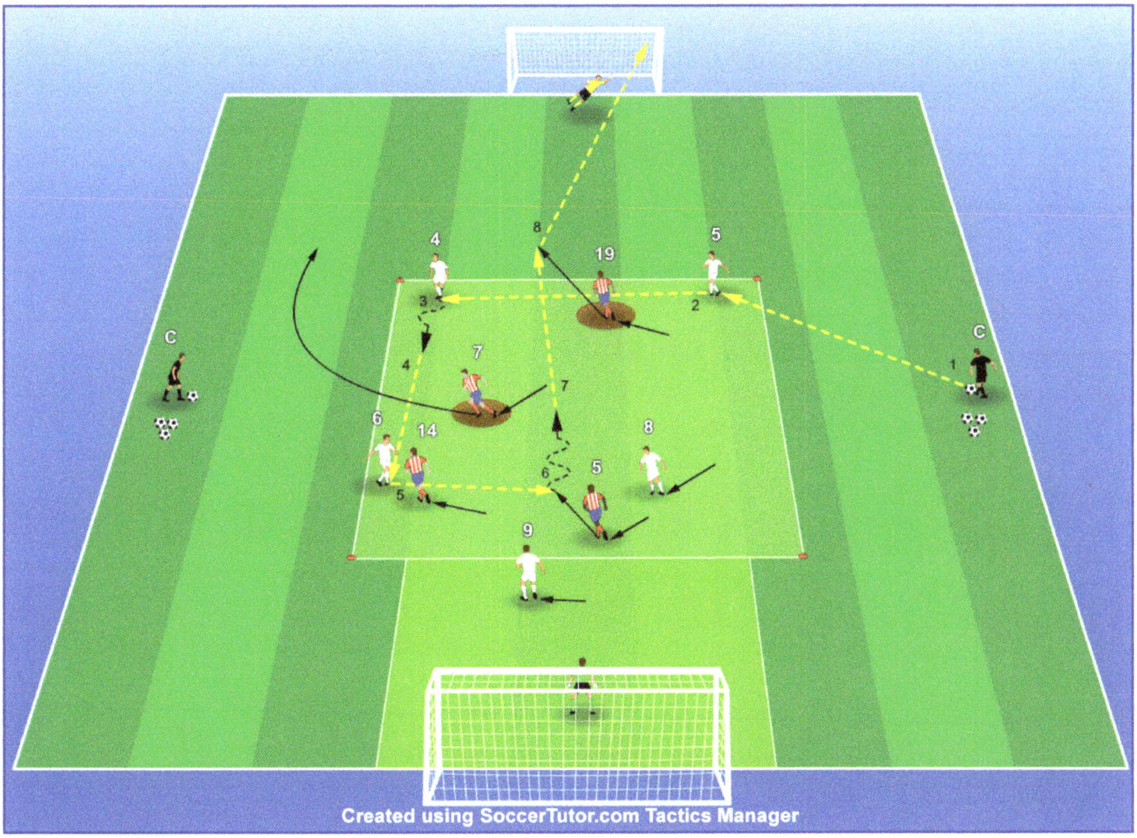

Description

- Within the 15 yard white central square (size depends on level of players), **we have 2 white centre backs and 2 central midfielders versus 2 red forwards and 2 central midfielders.**
- There is also a 10 yard yellow square area for the white forward No.9.
- The Coach passes to a white centre back and the whites try to move the ball to the forward No.9 inside the yellow square and score.
- Please **see the analysis pages** in this section for the correct decision making.

- As they are in a central area, the player that wins the ball should try to pass to the advanced forward **(19)** to create a **Direct Threat**. If this is not possible, a pass can be also played to the other forward (**Indirect Threat**).
- In this example, the central midfielder **(5)** wins the ball and immediately passes into the available space between the white centre backs to the advanced forward **(19)**.

Restriction: Any pass towards white No.9 should be played from within the central area.

DIEGO SIMEONE'S ATTACKING TACTICS

Tactical Situation 3 - Defensive and Counter Attack-Minded Positioning of the Forwards

PROGRESSION
3. Positioning of the Forwards and Counter Attack After Winning the Ball Out Wide in a Functional Game

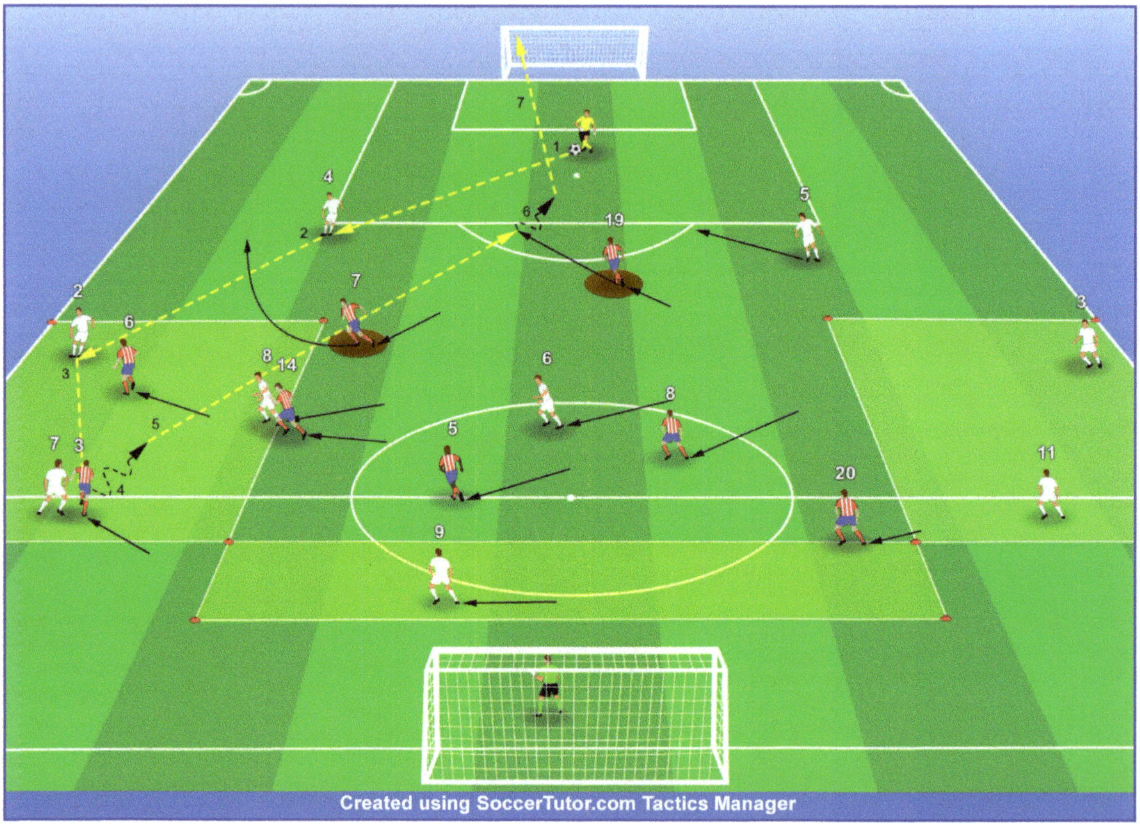

Description

- The 2 teams play a 9v10 game in 2/3 of the pitch.

- The game starts with the white GK and the white team must move the ball into one of the wide areas and then try to move the ball to the forward No.9 in the yellow central area to score against the GK.

- The reds try to win the ball in a 3v3 situation within the wide area and then launch a counter attack. Please **see the analysis pages** in this section for the correct decision making.

As they are in a wide area, the player that wins the ball can:

1. Pass to the forward on the strong side **(7)** to create an **Indirect Threat**.

2. Pass directly to the advanced forward **(19)** to create a **Direct Threat** (difficult pass).

3. Pass inside to the central midfielder **(5)**, who then passes to the advanced forward **(19)** to create a **Direct Threat**.

Restriction: Any pass towards white No.9 should be played from within the wide area.

DIEGO SIMEONE'S ATTACKING TACTICS

Tactical Situation 3 - Defensive and Counter Attack-Minded Positioning of the Forwards

VARIATION

4. Positioning of the Forwards and Counter Attack After Winning the Ball in the Centre in a Functional Game

Description

- In this variation of the previous practice, we now practice exploiting the counter attack-minded positioning of the forwards after winning the ball in the centre.

- Within the central area, we have 2 white centre backs and 2 central midfielders versus 2 red forwards and 2 central midfielders. There is also a yellow area for the white forward (9).

- The white full backs take up attacking positions, pass the ball around (to centre backs) and take part in the defensive part of the game (as soon as possession is lost).

- The 2 red wide midfielders shift defensively according to the position of the ball and can enter the white area. As soon as possession is won, they take part in the counter attack. Please **see the analysis pages** in this section for the correct decision making.

- As they are in a central area, the player that wins the ball **(5)** immediately passes into the available space between the centre backs to the forward **(19)** to create a **Direct Threat**.

Restriction: Any pass towards white No.9 should be played from within the central area.

DIEGO SIMEONE'S ATTACKING TACTICS

TACTICAL SITUATION 4

Counter Attack with an Open Ball Situation

The content in this section is from analysis of Diego Simeone's Atlético Madrid teams during the 2017/2018 and 2018/2019 seasons.

The analysis is based on recurring patterns of play observed within the Atlético Madrid team. Once the same phase of play occurred several times (at least 10), the tactics would be seen as a pattern. The analysis on the following pages are examples of the team's tactics being used effectively.

Each action, pass, individual movement with or without the ball, and the positioning of each player on the pitch including their body shape, are presented.

The analysis is then used to create 2 practices to coach this specific tactical situation.

Tactical Situation 4 - Counter Attack with an Open Ball Situation

POSSESSION IS WON IN THE CENTRAL AREA AND AN OPEN BALL SITUATION IS CREATED

a. Winning the Ball in the Central Area

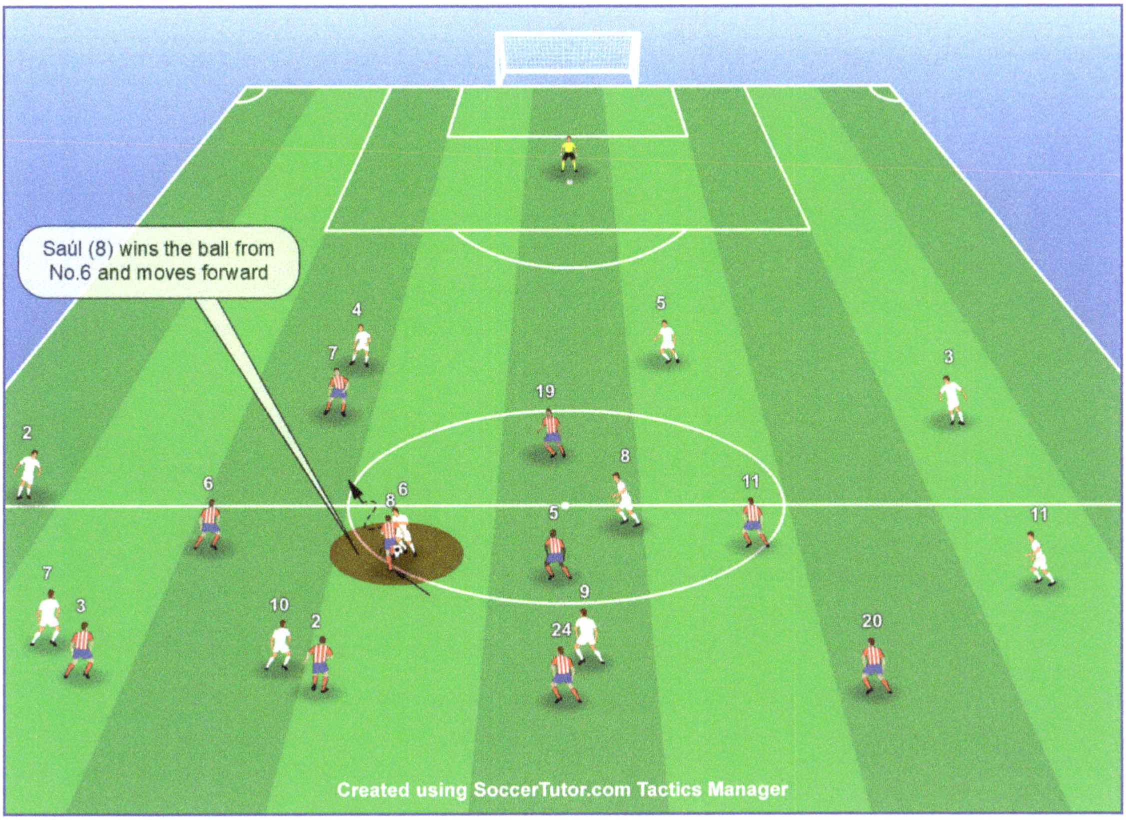

The situation around the ball area at the moment possession is won is an important factor that influences the way the transition from defence to attack is carried out.

If the player who wins the ball is put under pressure (closed ball situation), the Atlético forwards move towards the available passing lanes to receive a potential pass to either turn (if they are free of marking) or move the ball to another player who has available time and space on the ball. As soon as an open ball situation is created, the forwards move forward.

The closed ball situation is full analysed in the next section.

When the player who wins the ball has available time and space on the ball to make a forward pass (**Open Ball Situation**), the reaction of the Atlético forwards is to make forward movements to exploit the potential available spaces.

In this example, the white No.6 tries to dribble past the Atlético central midfielder, but he fails and **Saúl (8)** is able to win possession.

DIEGO SIMEONE'S ATTACKING TACTICS

Tactical Situation 4 - Counter Attack with an Open Ball Situation

b. Ball Carrier Has Time and Space (Open Ball Situation)

As soon as the central midfielder **Saúl (8)** wins possession, there is an open ball situation for Atlético Madrid.

This means **Saúl (8)** can make an accurate forward pass.

Tactical Situation 4 - Counter Attack with an Open Ball Situation

c. Forwards Make Runs into the Available Spaces in Behind

[Figure: Tactical diagram showing "Available spaces" with players positioned on the pitch]

This open situation around the ball area triggers the forward movements of both Atlético forwards into the available spaces. **Griezmann (7)** exploits the space near the side-line and if he receives, he is likely to deliver a cross, thus providing an **Indirect Threat**.

D. Costa (19) moves into the available space between the 2 white centre backs. If he receives, a **Direct Threat** is created because he can shoot at goal.

ASSESSMENT

1. The positioning of the opposing defenders is crucial in these kinds of situations, as the available spaces depend upon it. For example, if the white centre back No.5 was more centrally positioned, then **D. Costa (19)** would probably move into the gap between No.5 and No.3 and exploit the space on the blind side of No.5 instead.

2. The good organisation during the attacking phase is also very important. A well organised and balanced team during the attacking phase can better control the available spaces and eliminate the possibility of a successful counter attack from their opponents if possession is lost.

©SOCCERTUTOR.COM — DIEGO SIMEONE'S ATTACKING TACTICS

Tactical Situation 4 - Counter Attack with an Open Ball Situation

ROLE OF THE MIDFIELDERS DURING A COUNTER ATTACK WITH AN OPEN BALL SITUATION

When Diego Simeone's Atlético Madrid have a counter attack with an open ball situation, the midfielders play a crucial role in them being successful.

As explained in the defending part of this book set, the Atlético midfielders retain short distances between each other during the defensive phase, which makes them very compact. Most often, it is the central midfielders who are involved in winning possession and making the first forward pass.

However, there are several situations when the wide midfielders take over this role too. As they are positioned within a compact formation, they are in or close to the central area. They therefore attack the central areas rather than the wide ones during counter attacks.

If the forward pass is played towards a wide area for a forward, the wide midfielder on the weak side runs into the box to finish a potential cross, while the other wide midfielder moves into a supporting position to the forward in possession.

a. Central Midfielder Wins the Ball in the Centre and Both Wide Midfielders Move Forward to Join Attack

In this example, central midfielder **Saúl (8)** has won the ball and there is an open ball situation. As the Atlético forwards move towards the available spaces, a pass is played to **Griezmann (7)** in a wide position.

The wide midfielder on the weak side **Correa (11)** moves forward to provide an option for a potential cross.

The wide midfielder on the strong side **Koke (6)** moves into a supporting position to provide a passing option for **Griezmann (7)** if he can't move forward with the ball.

Tactical Situation 4 - Counter Attack with an Open Ball Situation

b. Both Wide Midfielders Provide Attacking Options to Finish the Attack

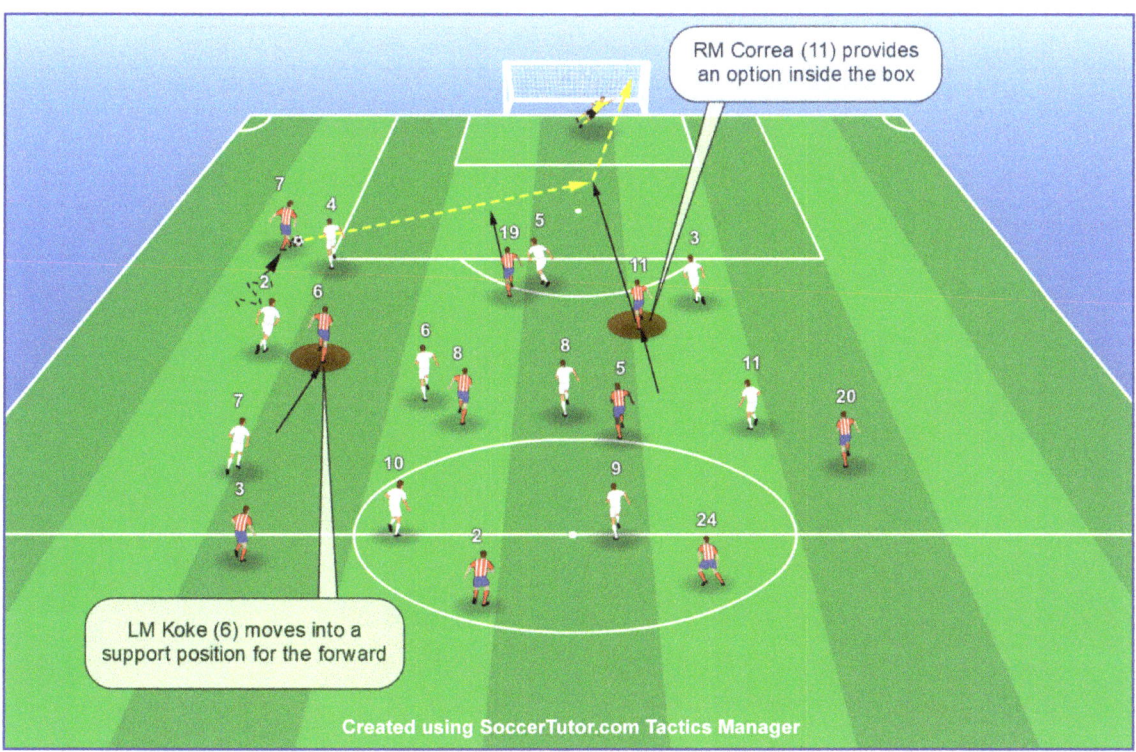

When **Griezmann (7)** delivers the cross, the other forward **D. Costa (19)** and the wide midfielder **Correa (11)** are inside the box, ready to receive and score. The other wide midfielder **Koke (6)** offers an option for a back pass.

The central midfielders and defenders have all moved forward to keep the team compact and are ready to defend a potential clearance.

ASSESSMENT

As the Atlético wide midfielders are centrally positioned during the defensive phase, they are also often the players to win possession and then make the first pass towards the forwards in a counter attack.

This together with the fact that the wide midfielders don't move into wide areas during the attacking phase or the transition from defence to attack, explain why Diego Simeone prefers wide midfielders with the characteristics of central midfielders, rather than with the characteristics of wingers.

The wide areas are usually attacked by the full backs, which will be shown later in the "**Tactical Situation 6: Exploiting Width During a Counter Attack**" section.

2 PRACTICES FOR "COUNTER ATTACK WITH AN OPEN BALL SITUATION"

Tactical Situation 4 - Counter Attack with an Open Ball Situation

PRACTICES FOR THIS TACTICAL SITUATION (2 PRACTICES)

1. Counter Attack with an Open Ball Situation in a 6v6 (+GK) Functional Practice

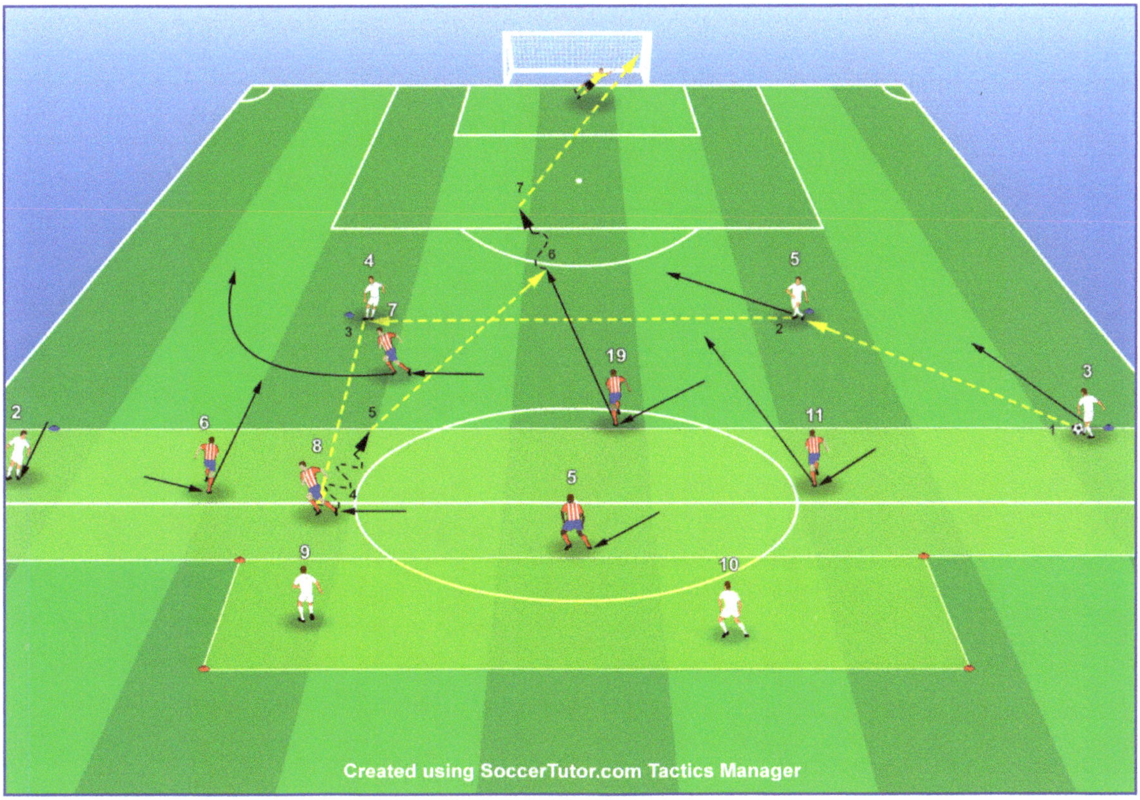

Description

- The practice starts with the 4 white defenders passing the ball around, trying to find a way to play a through pass to one of the forwards inside the yellow area.

- The red players keep compact and try to intercept any attempted through passes.

- As soon as the reds win the ball, the forwards can exploit the open ball situation, as there are no white midfielders to put pressure on the ball.

- The red forwards move towards the available spaces to receive and score within 8 seconds.

- In this example, the forward on the left **(7)** moves into the available space out wide and the forward on the right **(19)** makes a run into the available space in between the 2 white centre backs.

- **No.19** receives (**Direct Threat**) and tries to score.

Coaching Points

1. Quick decision making is needed immediately after winning the ball.
2. Synchronised movements by the forwards.
3. Fast movements into available spaces.

DIEGO SIMEONE'S ATTACKING TACTICS

Tactical Situation 4 - Counter Attack with an Open Ball Situation

PROGRESSION

2. Counter Attack with an Open Ball Situation in a 6 v 8 (+GK) Functional Practice

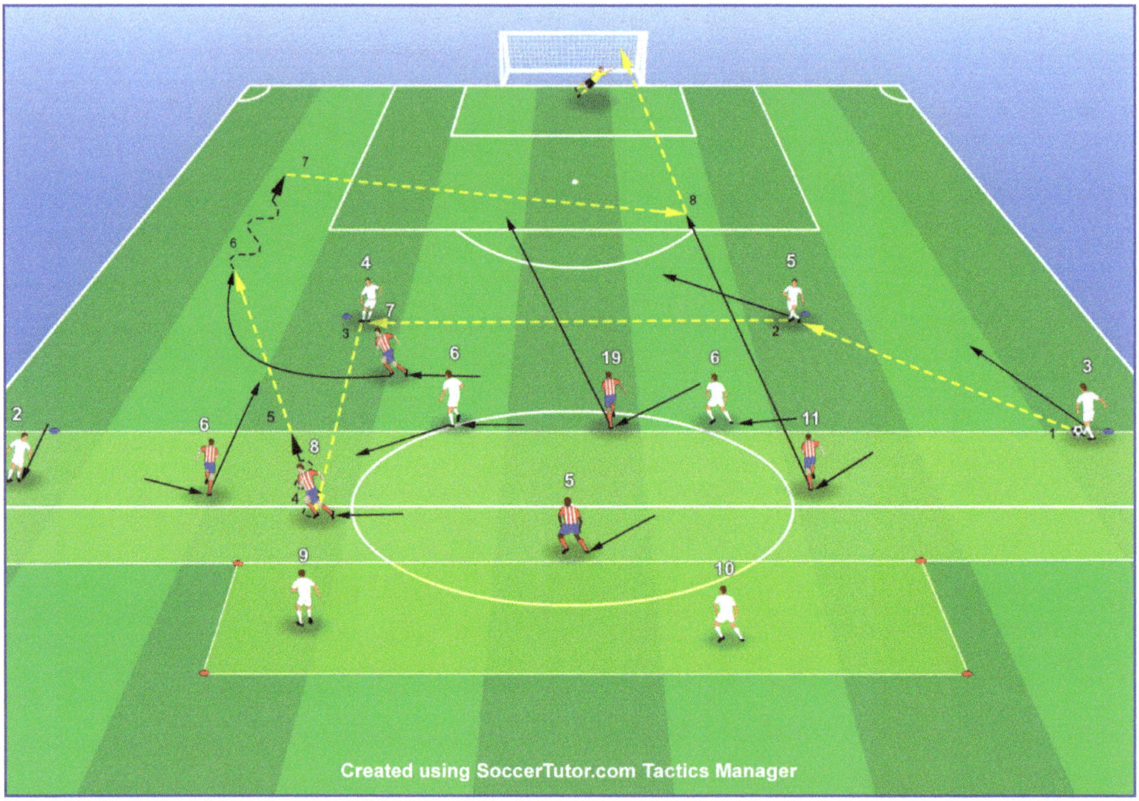

Description

- In this progression of the previous practice, we add 2 white central midfielders (No.6 and No.8), but they are not allowed to enter the large white zone unless the reds win the ball.

- As the 2 white central midfielders stay outside the white zone initially, the red midfielders have time and space available after intercepting attempted through passes.

- Before the white midfielders are able to apply pressure, the reds try to exploit the open ball situation, with the aim to play to the forwards in the available spaces.

- The reds try to score within 8 seconds and the white players try to defend the counter attack.

Restriction: The white central midfielders can enter the white zone only after possession has been lost.

Coaching Points: Same as previous practice.

TACTICAL SITUATION 5

Counter Attack with a Closed Ball Situation

The content in this section is from analysis of Diego Simeone's Atlético Madrid teams during the 2017/2018 and 2018/2019 seasons.

The analysis is based on recurring patterns of play observed within the Atlético Madrid team. Once the same phase of play occurred several times (at least 10), the tactics would be seen as a pattern. The analysis on the following pages are examples of the team's tactics being used effectively.

Each action, pass, individual movement with or without the ball, and the positioning of each player on the pitch including their body shape, are presented.

The analysis is then used to create 2 practices to coach this specific tactical situation.

COUNTER ATTACK WITH A CLOSED BALL SITUATION

If there is pressure applied to an Atlético player immediately after he wins the ball, time and space are restricted and the chances of a successful forward pass are extremely limited.

This situation is called a **Closed Ball Situation** and the reactions of the forwards are totally different compared to when Atlético have an open ball situation.

The forwards do not move forward into available spaces to receive, as there is no time and space for the ball carrier to play this kind of pass, so instead move into available passing lanes to receive short passes.

The aim for the Atlético forwards is to create an open ball situation for themselves or for a team-mate.

An **Open Ball Situation** can be created in 2 ways:

1. A forward manages to receive a pass and turn unmarked.
2. If pressed and turning is impossible, then a forward's lay-off to an unmarked team-mate on the move can create an open ball situation.

As soon as an open ball situation is created, the players in advanced positions move into the available spaces to receive a forward pass and provide a **Indirect Threat** (receive wide and deliver a cross) or an **Direct Threat** (receive centrally and shoot at goal).

Tactical Situation 5 - Counter Attack with a Closed Ball Situation

TACTICAL SOLUTIONS AFTER WINNING THE BALL IN A CLOSED BALL SITUATION

1a. Winning the Ball in a Wide Area

In this example, the Atlético central midfielder **Saúl (8)** intercepts the pass towards white No.10.

1b. Closed Ball Situation is Created Around the Ball Area and Options are Blocked

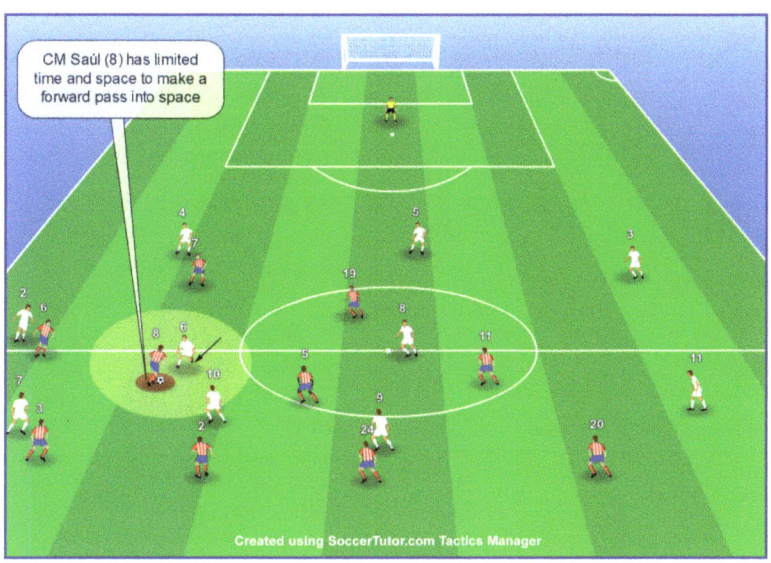

As soon as central midfielder **Saúl (8)** wins the ball, the white central midfielder No.6 presses him. This limits his available time and space on the ball.

This creates a closed ball situation around the ball area and forward passing options are blocked.

Tactical Situation 5 - Counter Attack with a Closed Ball Situation

1c. Team-mates Move Towards the Ball Area to Create Available Passing Lanes

The reaction of the forwards is to move into available passing lanes to provide short passing options. The other players close to the ball area do the same.

The next step is for **Saúl (8)** to make the best possible decision about where to direct the ball. The main focus is on passing the ball forward and to leave as many opposing players as far away from effective defensive positions as possible.

1d. First Pass Breaks Through Pressure and Creates an Open Ball Situation for the Counter Attack

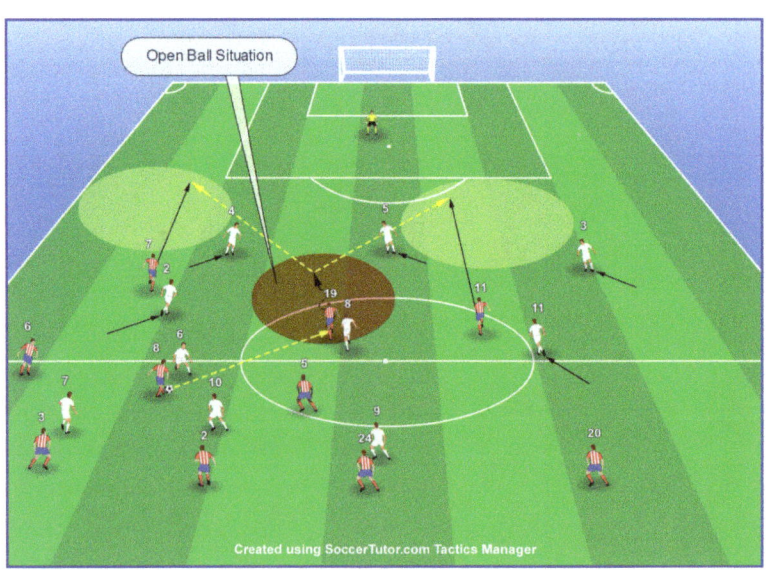

The central midfielder **Saúl (8)** chooses to pass to the deepest forward **D. Costa (19)**.

D. Costa (19) is unmarked, so is able to receive and turn. An **Open Ball Situation** has now been created.

As soon as a forward pass can be played, the players in advanced positions move into the available spaces to receive in behind. In this example, these are **Griezmann (7)** and **Correa (11)**.

Tactical Situation 5 - Counter Attack with a Closed Ball Situation

2a. Closed Ball Situation is Created After the New Ball Carrier's First Pass of the Counter Attack

In this variation of the example on the previous page, we show what happens if the Atlético Madrid forward **D. Costa (19)** is put under pressure by the white centre back No.5 when receiving and therefore unable to turn.

The second aim is to move the ball to a player with available time and space to create an open ball situation.

2b. Providing Passing Options to the Marked Forward with Back to Goal to Create an Open Ball Situation

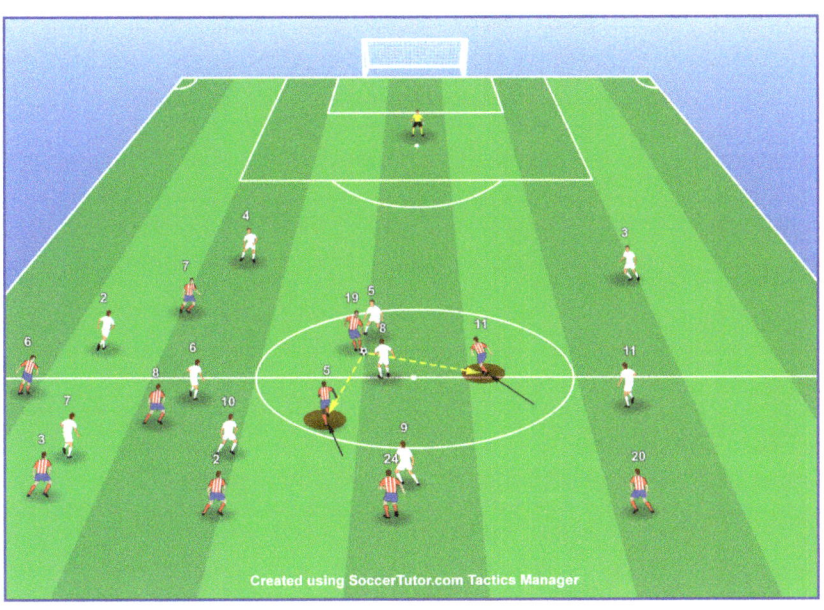

As **D. Costa (19)** is unable to turn, in order for Atlético to find time and space on the ball (open ball situation), the players closest to the ball should move into available passing lanes.

In this example, central midfielder **Thomas (5)** and right midfielder **Correa (11)** move into supporting positions and **D. Costa (19)** has 2 available passing options.

©SOCCERTUTOR.COM

DIEGO SIMEONE'S ATTACKING TACTICS

Tactical Situation 5 - Counter Attack with a Closed Ball Situation

2c. Creating an Open Ball Situation with a Back Pass and Exploiting it with Forward Runners and a Fast Counter Attack

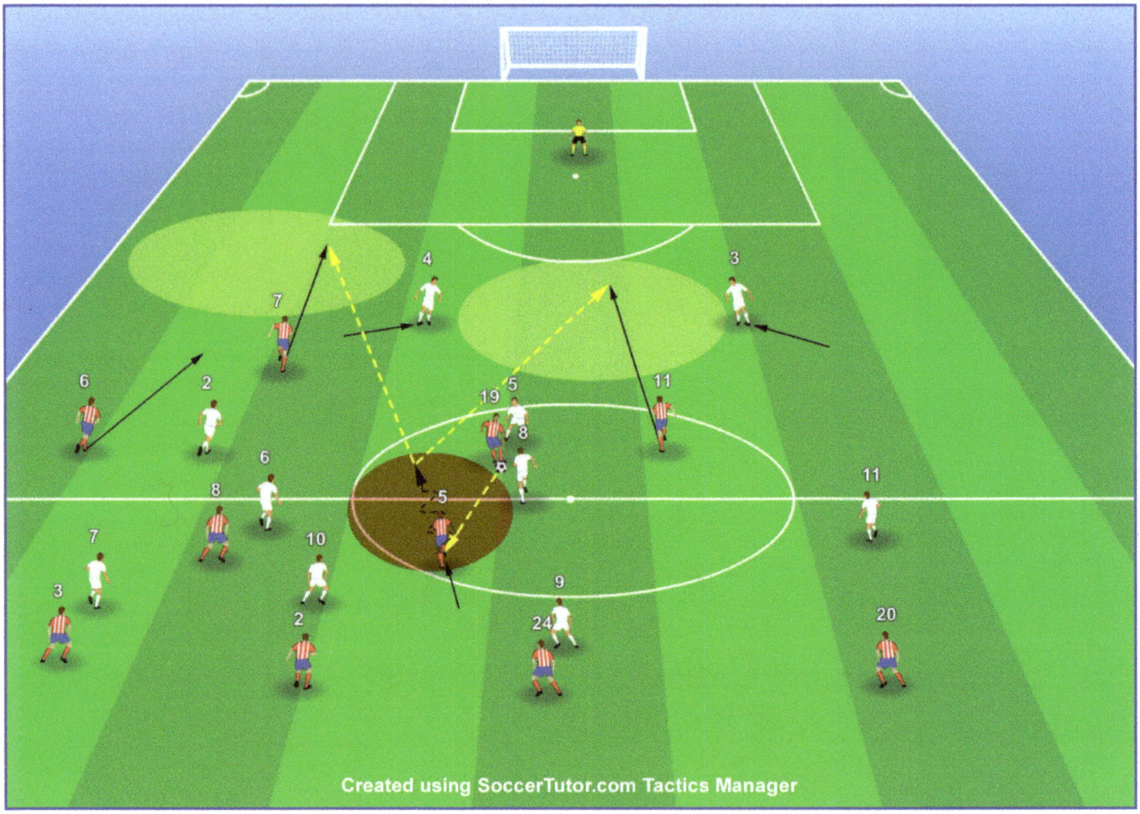

In this example, the forward **D. Costa (19)** passes back to the central midfielder **Thomas (5)**, who receives unmarked with time and space on the ball. Diego Simeone's Atlético Madrid team have therefore created an **Open Ball Situation**.

As soon as **Thomas (5)** receives and a forward pass can be played, the players in advanced positions run forward into the available spaces to receive in behind.

In this example, the other forward **Griezmann (7)** can receive in a wide position, dribble forward and deliver a cross to create an **Indirect Threat**. The right midfielder **Correa (11)** can receive in between the 2 white centre backs and shoot at goal to create a **Direct Threat**.

ASSESSMENT

The inside pass from **Saúl (8)** to the deeper forward **D. Costa (19)** is the best option in this situation. Due to his central position, he has many available passing options if he receives free of marking. If he is pressed, his direct marker will leave available space behind him, which can be exploited for a **Direct Threat** to be created.

2 PRACTICES FOR "COUNTER ATTACK WITH A CLOSED BALL SITUATION"

Tactical Situation 5 - Counter Attack with a Closed Ball Situation

PRACTICES FOR THIS TACTICAL SITUATION (2 PRACTICES)
1. Forwards Read the Situation (Open or Closed Ball) & Apply Correct Decision Making in a Functional Practice

Scenario A: Open Ball Situation

Description (Scenario A)
- The full backs, central midfielders and wide midfielders of both teams are positioned within the main 25 x 15 yard area. The white forward No.9 is in a 15 x 10 yard yellow area.
- The practice starts with the Coach's pass and we have a 6v6 situation within the main area.
- The whites try to move the ball to No.9 inside the yellow area and score.
- The reds try to win the ball and counter attack. The forwards must recognise the situation at the moment possession is won and react accordingly.
- In Scenario A, **No.8** wins the ball with an open ball situation (unmarked(. The forwards move to receive in the available spaces in behind.
- The central midfielder **(8)** plays a straight pass to the forward **(7)** to create a **Direct Threat**.

©SOCCERTUTOR.COM   DIEGO SIMEONE'S ATTACKING TACTICS

Tactical Situation 5 - Counter Attack with a Closed Ball Situation

Scenario B: Closed Ball Situation

Description (Scenario B)

- In this second scenario, the central midfielder **(8)** wins the ball again but there is a closed ball situation this time, as the opposing central midfielder (white No.6) moves to press the ball.

- As there is a closed ball situation, both forwards No.9 and No.7 move into available passing lanes to provide options for **No.8** and create an open ball situation.

- As soon as an open ball situation is created (when left midfielder **No.6** receives lay-off from the forward **No.19** in diagram example), both forwards then move to receive in the available space in behind.

Coaching Points

1. The forwards need to be able to read the tactical situation and have the right reaction to it.

2. They also need well-timed and fast movements into the available spaces in behind to avoid being offside.

DIEGO SIMEONE'S ATTACKING TACTICS

Tactical Situation 5 - Counter Attack with a Closed Ball Situation

PROGRESSION
2. Counter Attack with a Closed Ball Situation in a Dynamic Conditioned Game

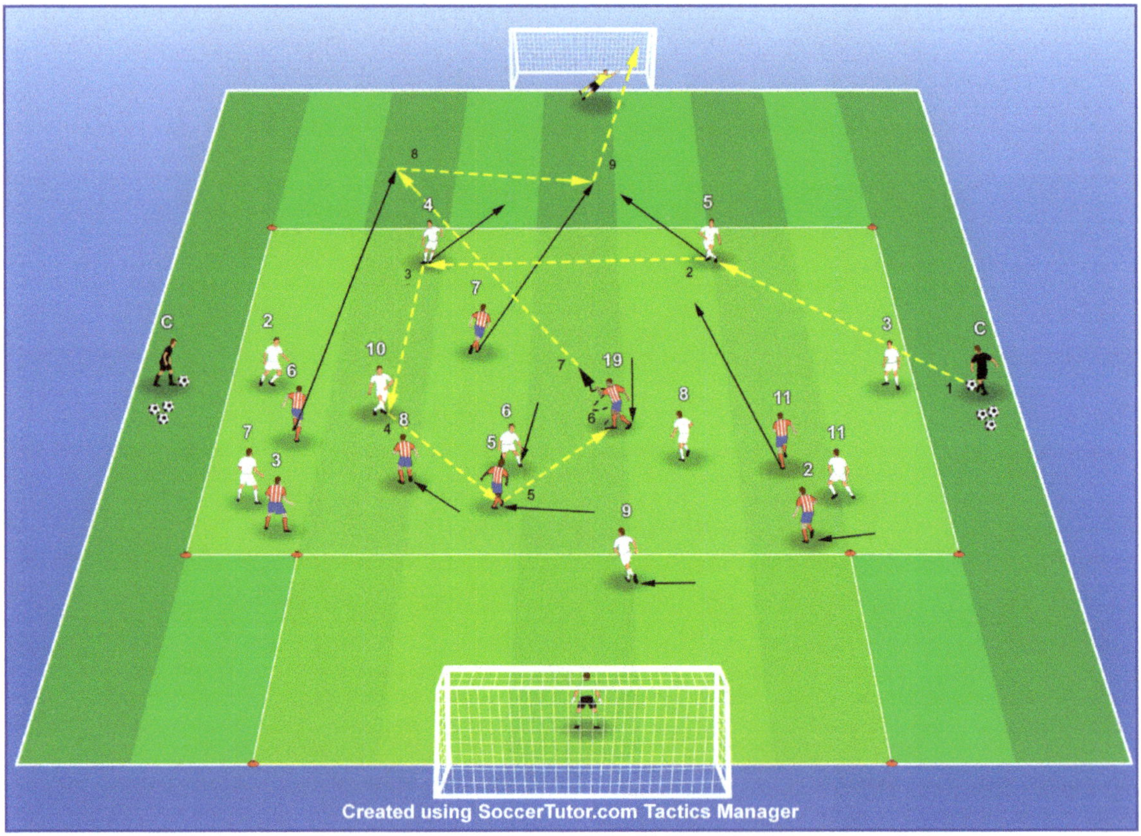

Description

- The central white zone is 40 x 30 yards and the yellow zone for the white No.9 is 25 x 15 yards. The 2 teams play an 9 v 11 game with the reds in a 2-4-2 shape and the whites in a 4-3-3.

- The practice starts with the Coach and the white team try to move the ball to the forward No.9 inside the yellow zone and score.

- The reds try to win the ball and then score with a counter attack within 10-15 seconds.

- As the whites have an extra player in midfield, they can immediately press the new ball carrier if they lose possession and create a closed ball situation for the reds.

- The red players around the ball area have to read the situation and react accordingly by providing short passing options in order to move the ball to a free player, create an open ball situation and score.

Note: If it is difficult for the reds to create counter attack situations against 3 midfielders, then one of the white midfielders can be removed.

DIEGO SIMEONE'S ATTACKING TACTICS

TACTICAL SITUATION 6

Exploiting Width During a Counter Attack

The content in this section is from analysis of Diego Simeone's Atlético Madrid teams during the 2017/2018 and 2018/2019 seasons.

The analysis is based on recurring patterns of play observed within the Atlético Madrid team. Once the same phase of play occurred several times (at least 10), the tactics would be seen as a pattern. The analysis on the following pages are examples of the team's tactics being used effectively.

Each action, pass, individual movement with or without the ball, and the positioning of each player on the pitch including their body shape, are presented.

The analysis is then used to create a practice to coach this specific tactical situation.

Tactical Situation 6 - Exploiting Width During a Counter Attack

EXPLOITING WIDTH DURING A COUNTER ATTACK

1a. Opposing Midfielders are Compact to Create a Closed Ball Situation

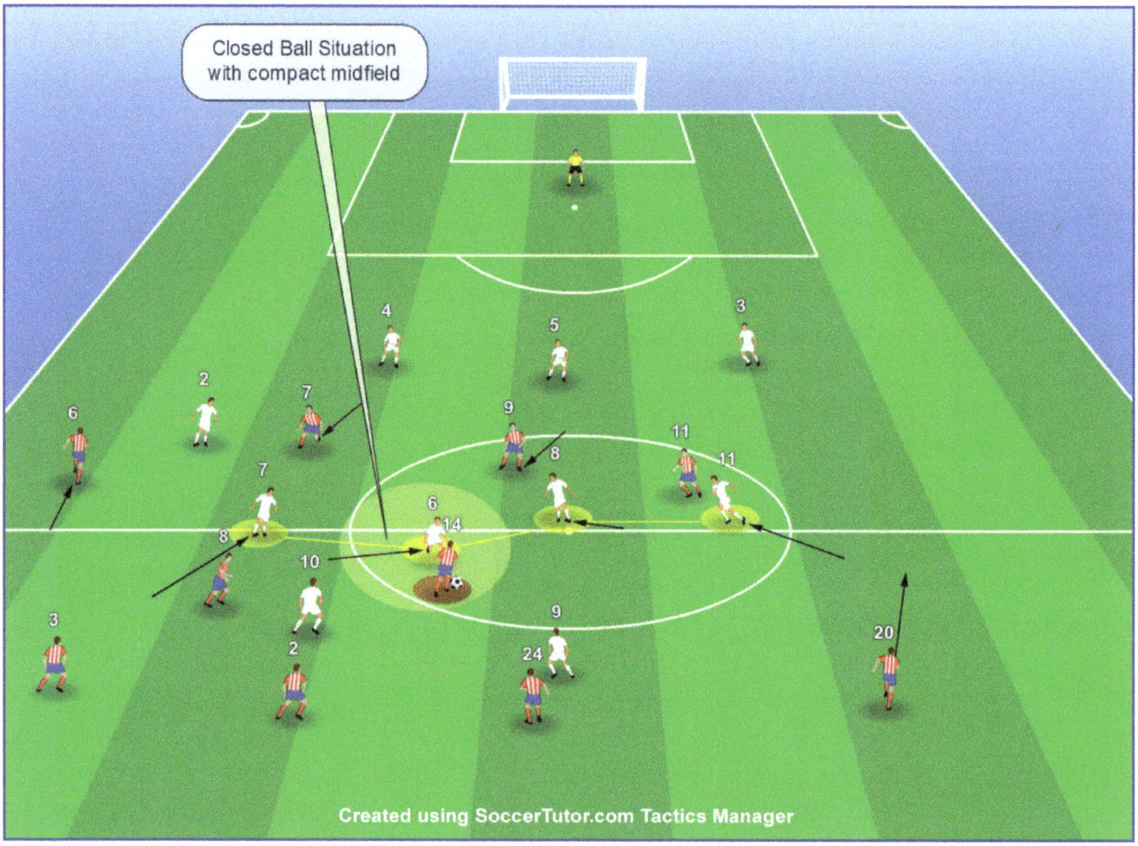

If the opposing midfielders put pressure on the ball immediately after losing possession (closed ball situation) and the opposing wide midfielders converge inside to achieve good compactness to block through passes towards the Atlético forwards, Diego Simeone's team used alternative options to produce successful counter attacks.

This is done by exploiting the available spaces near the side lines.

As Atlético Madrid's wide midfielders are usually positioned close to the centre and therefore can't occupy the wide areas immediately, the role of exploiting the space near the side-lines is given to the full backs.

In this example, the central midfielder **Gabi (14)** has won the ball in the centre and there is a closed ball situation with no possibility to play a forward pass.

©SOCCERTUTOR.COM DIEGO SIMEONE'S ATTACKING TACTICS

Tactical Situation 6 - Exploiting Width During a Counter Attack

1b. Full Back Runs Forward to Provide Forward Passing Option and Exploit the Available Space Out Wide

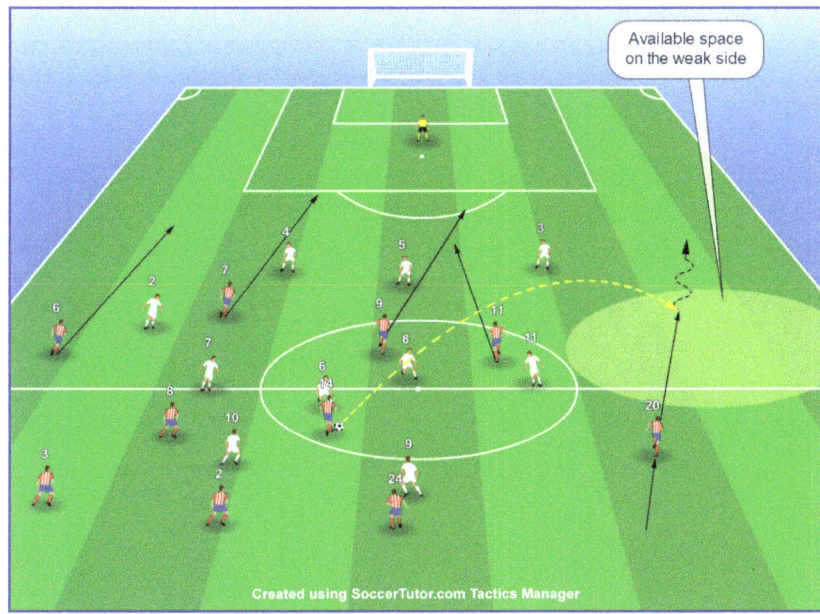

The available space for Atlético can be found near the side-lines.

The right back **Juanfran (20)** moves quickly forward and receives a pass from **Gabi (14)** on the run.

1c. Full Back Receives in an Advanced Position to Deliver a Cross or Pass into the Box

The right back **Juanfran (20)** moves forward with the ball and delivers a cross from a deep position into the space between the defenders and the GK.

This means that the cross can be finished on the run by one of the forwards.

In this example, it is **Griezmann (7)** who finishes.

DIEGO SIMEONE'S ATTACKING TACTICS

Tactical Situation 6 - Exploiting Width During a Counter Attack

Variation: Pass Forward to the Wide Midfielder and Drag the Opposing Centre Back Out of Position

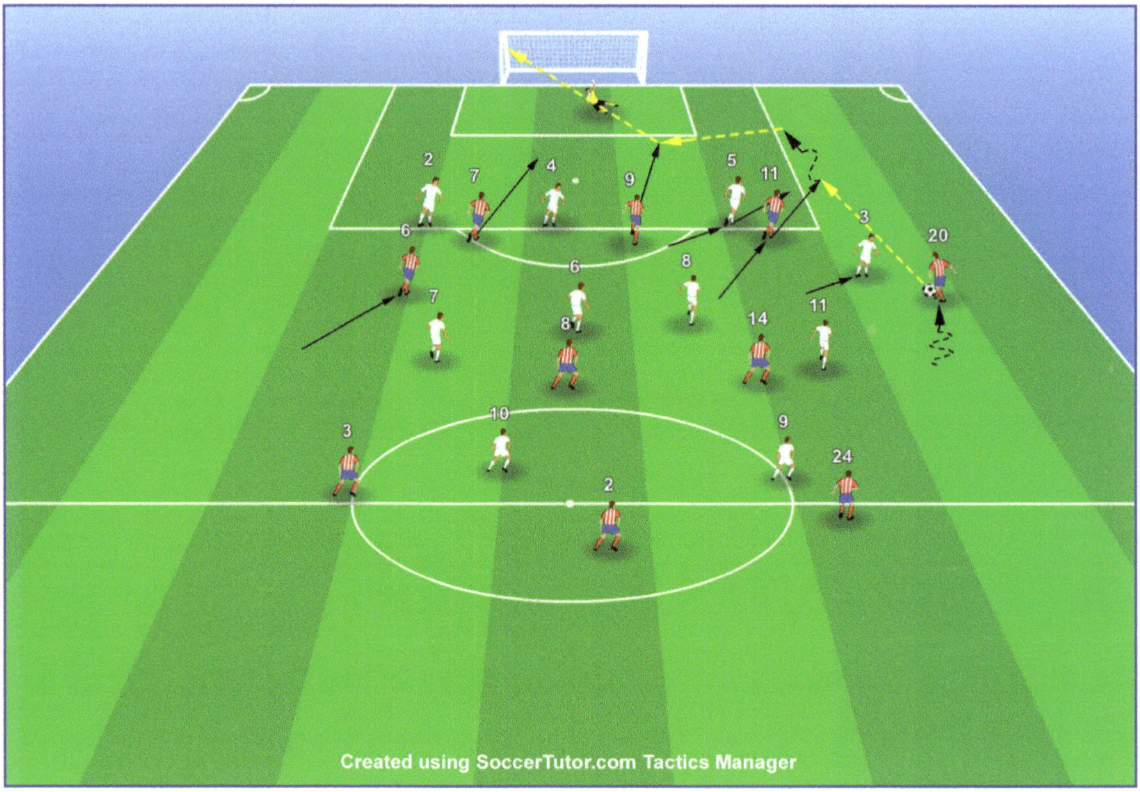

This variation shows another option for Atlético Madrid in this situation.

The right back **Juanfran (20)** does not deliver a cross and passes into the path of the right midfielder **Correa (11)** instead.

Correa (11) makes a run in behind the opposing left back No.3, which drags the centre back No.5 out of position.

More space is created inside the box for the Atlético forwards to exploit and **Torres (9)** meets the cross at the near post to finish.

DIEGO SIMEONE'S ATTACKING TACTICS

PRACTICE FOR "EXPLOITING WIDTH DURING A COUNTER ATTACK"

Tactical Situation 6 - Exploiting Width During a Counter Attack

PRACTICE FOR THIS TACTICAL SITUATION
Exploiting Width During a Counter Attack in a Dynamic Conditioned Game

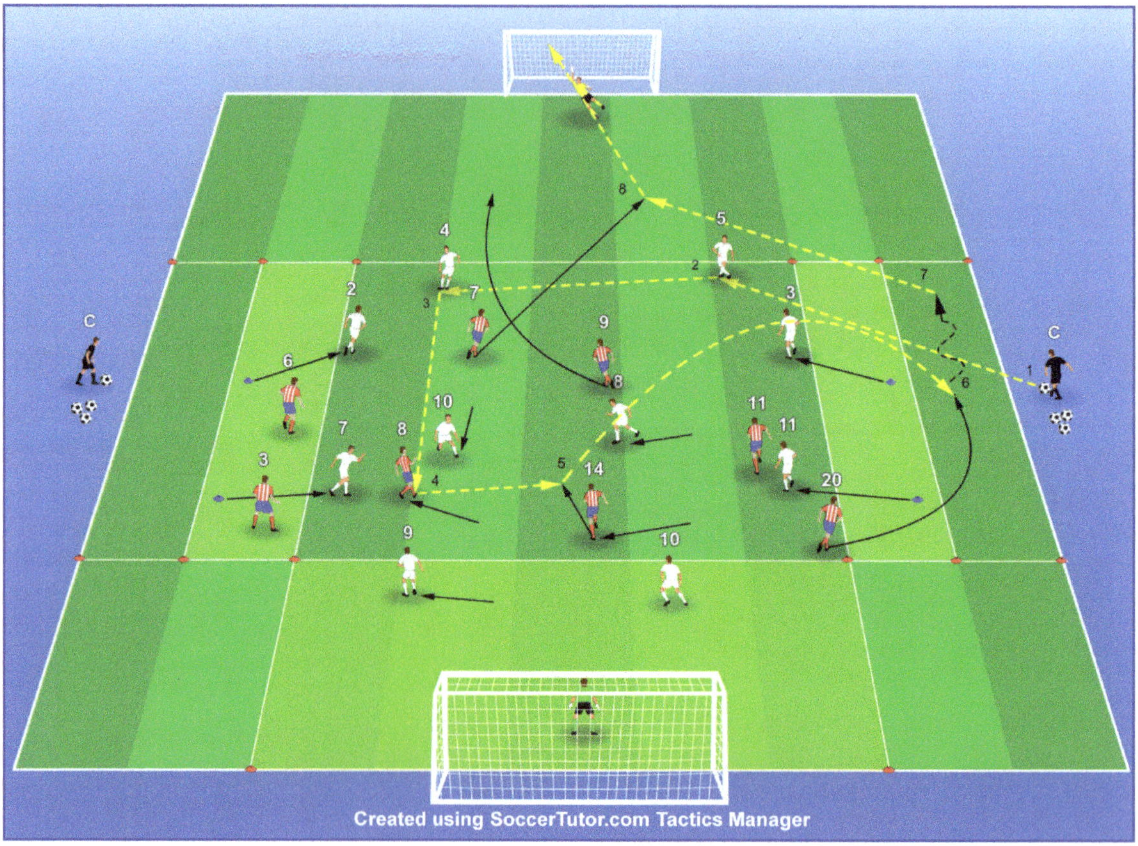

Description

- Within a 45 x 65 yard area, mark out the zones as shown. The central square is 25 x 25 yards. We play a 9 v 11 game with the reds in a 2-4-2 shape and the whites in a 4-4-2.

- The practice starts with the Coach and the white team try to move the ball to the forwards inside the yellow zone and score. The reds try to win the ball and then score with a counter attack within 10-15 seconds.

- If the reds score by counter attacking through the central square, they score 3 goals.

- To prevent this, the white wide players (full backs and wide midfielders) must enter the central square as soon as they lose possession to block forward passes.

- If this happens, the reds must utilise the wide areas, as shown in the diagram, with the red full back **(20)** receiving on the run and then passing in behind for the forward **(7)** to score.

Restriction: During the white team's attacking phase, the space stays limited (35 yard width without widest zones). When the reds win the ball, they can utilise the full width (45 yards).

DIEGO SIMEONE'S ATTACKING TACTICS

FREE TRIAL

TACTICS MANAGER
Create your own Practices, Tactics & Plan Sessions!

www.SoccerTutor.com/TacticsManager
info@soccertutor.com

PC Mac iPad Tablet Web

www.ingramcontent.com/pod-product-compliance
Lightning Source LLC
Chambersburg PA
CBHW040932240426
43673CB00051B/1955